Facts, Not Fear

Teaching Children about the Environment
(Canadian Edition)

Michael Sanera and *Jane S. Shaw*

Adapted for Canadian readers by
Liv Fredricksen and *Laura Jones*

Foreword by
Patrick Moore

THE FRASER INSTITUTE

The Fraser Institute

Vancouver, Canada

1974·1999   1999

Published in Canada by The Fraser Institute,
4th Floor, 1770 Burrard Street,
Vancouver, British Columbia, Canada, V6J 3G7.

The authors of this book have worked independently and opinions expressed by
them are, therefore, their own, and do not necessarily reflect the opinions of the
members or the trustees of The Fraser Institute.

Designed and typeset by Lindsey Thomas Martin.

Cover designed by Ted Staunton.

Printed in Canada.

Canadian Cataloguing in Publication Data

Sanera, Michael.
    Facts, not fear

    Includes bibliographical references.
    ISBN 0-88975-194-3

    1. Environmental education.   2. Environmental sciences--Study and teaching.
I. Shaw, Jane S., 1944-.   II. Fredricksen, Liv.   III. Jones, Laura 1970-   IV. Fraser
Institute (Vancouver, B.C.)   V. Title.

GE70.S26 1999   363.7   C99-910189-7

Contents

The original edition of *Facts, Not Fear* was the product of many people's efforts. Our special thanks go to Gary Palmer of the Alabama Family Alliance for the inspiration for this book. Gary's steadfast efforts and patience in helping bring it to fruition are deeply appreciated. We thank Fred Smith of the Competitive Enterprise Institute for helping us launch the project, and we appreciate the contributions of many CEI staff members, especially Jonathan Adler and Helen Hewitt, in completing it.

We are grateful to Marcia Sielaff and Bob Dean for their research assistance, and to Michael's students at Northern Arizona University, who provided a welcome "reality check."

We also thank the staff and associates of the Political Economy Research Center (PERC) in Montana. Terry Anderson, Donald Leal, and Richard Stroup helped us look afresh at many environmental issues. The staff, under the direction of Monica Lane Guenther, worked carefully without complaint under great pressure. We especially thank Dianna Rienhart, Michelle Johnson, and Pamela Malyurek for their contributions to the administration and word processing of the project.

The Earhart Foundation, the Jacquelin Hume Foundation, and several individuals provided support at critical times and we thank those scientists and other specialists who took the time to read our chapters and correct our errors. Additional thanks go to Margaret Conditt and Daniel K. Benjamin. Any errors that remain are ours.

Our special thanks go also to the Donner Foundation, which provided the funding for the collection of the Canadian data and for the writing of the Canadian edition of *Facts, Not Fear*.

Michael Sanera   Jane S. Shaw

Liv Fredricksen is a researcher at The Fraser Institute. While at the Institute, she has been the co-author of "The Green Team" and "The Greening of Education" for *Fraser Forum* and of "'Green Team' Pollutes the Classroom" for the *Financial Post*. She also assisted in the research and development for *Waiting Your Turn: Hospital Waiting Lists in Canada (7th edition), Federal Regulatory Reform: Rhetoric or Reality?* as well as several upcoming publications including *Environmental Indicators 1999* and an inquiry into endangered species legislation in Canada. Ms Fredricksen received her B.A. in English Literature from the University of British Columbia in 1995 and also holds a Diploma from the Dubrulle French Culinary School. Before coming to the Institute, she worked in public relations and television production.

Laura Jones is the Director of Environmental Studies at The Fraser Institute. She joined The Fraser Institute in 1996 to develop the Institute's policy on the environment. During 1997, she edited *Fish or Cut Bait! The Case for Individual Transferable Quotas in the Salmon Fishery of British Columbia* and *Global Warming: The Science and the Politics*. Ms Jones has also published articles in *Fraser Forum, The Vancouver Sun,* the *Ottawa Citizen*, and the *Financial Post*, and was co-author of the Fraser Institute Critical Issues Bulletins *Environmental Indicators for Canada and the United States* (1997, 1998) and

Environmental Indicators for North American and the United Kingdom (1999). She received her B.A. in Economics from Mount Holyoke College in Massachusetts, and her M.A. in Economics from Simon Fraser University in British Columbia. Prior to joining the Institute, she taught economics at Coquitlam College and is currently teaching *Economic Issues* at the British Columbia Institute of Technology.

MICHAEL SANERA earned his Ph.D. in political science from the University of Colorado at Boulder in 1979. He currently serves as the Director of, and Research Fellow at, the Center for Environmental Education Research, a division of the Claremont Institute. For the past 17 years, he has been a professor teaching political science and public administration at Northern Arizona University in Flagstaff. He has been the coauthor and coeditor of two books. During the 1980s, he held several positions in Washington, DC, including Assistant Director at the Office of Personnel Management and consultant at the United States Department of Education.

JANE S. SHAW is a Senior Associate of the Political Economy Research Center (PERC) in Bozeman, Montana. PERC is a nonprofit institute that applies market approaches to environmental problems. Shaw directs PERC's editorial outreach program, which prepares and distributes articles on economics for the popular and non-academic press. Before joining PERC in 1984, Shaw was an Associate Economics Editor of *Business Week* and, before that, was a correspondent for McGraw-Hill Publications in Washington, D.C., and Chicago. Shaw received her B.A. degree from Wellesley College.

PATRICK MOORE

The environmental movement has given a whole new meaning to the idea of teaching our children about the birds and the bees. Not only has the subject matter expanded to include everything under the sun, we are now faced with the challenge of helping our children separate fact from fiction in a highly charged political debate.

As a father and an environmentalist, I am often discouraged by the amount of misinformation conveyed to our young people through the school system and the media. I am particularly dismayed by the degree of pessimism for the future that is generated by predictions of an environmental apocalypse. It's as if the lessons of Chicken Little and not crying wolf have been completely forgotten.

How can we help our children reach informed and balanced opinions on the multitude of issues and ideas that are collectively called "environmentalism"? This book is a good starting point as it calls into question many of the assumptions that have seeped into popular culture through constant repetition. From endangered species to forests to climate change there is often a feeling that all the trends are negative and that nothing can be done about them. Both these attitudes are entirely incorrect.

The environmental movement came by its association with fear for the future honestly. In the late 1960s when the movement was born, the threat of toxic waste and pollution loomed large. In her landmark book *Silent Spring*, Rachel Carson predicted that pesticide use would eliminate songbirds from the land. She was partially correct in that DDT was responsible for major population declines in birds of prey such as hawks and eagles. But DDT was successfully banned and the populations of birds of prey have recovered. Songbird populations have actually remained quite stable; despite considerable changes to their habitats and the continued use of pesticides in agriculture. In short, we fixed the specific problem and the world did not come to an end.

There are a number of important lessons and ideas that should be given to the generation now growing up in order to help them see the world in a more positive light. First, they should be told of the many success stories; that commercial whaling has been virtually ended, toxic waste cleaned up, air quality improved, forest practices reformed, and endangered species protected. This should be balanced against an awareness of ongoing concerns over poverty and the loss of tropical forests. Environmentalism should be at least as much about celebrating life and our ability to maintain it as it is about fear of future loss and change.

Second, we must teach our children to think critically and to learn more then we ever knew about science, geography, and the use of language. They should be able to tell fact from opinion, to question assertions of truth, and to spot inconsistencies in logic and argument. And, whether it is viewed as a struggle between left and right, yin and yang, or green and brown, they will benefit from a desire to seek a balanced view that takes all factors into account.

Third, we should give young people the ability to see the connections between the environment, the economy, and our communities. "Learning for sustainability" means both recognizing the real needs of six billion fellow humans, while at the same time understanding that those needs affect the environment, sometimes negatively. The emphasis should be on practical solutions to the problems rather than on looking for someone to blame. Field trips should include visits to rural work-sites and communities as well as parks and wilderness.

Fourth—and this is a good lesson for life in general—our children must learn how to set priorities. The environmental movement tends to portray every issue as if it were a dire threat to the survival of the planet. It is often difficult to determine what the real risks are from a particular activity. This requires an understanding of "risk management" and often involves judgments and sometimes best guesses about which issues are most important. Making informed judgments and not being afraid to change opinions in the face of new evidence are key to maintaining a sense of priority.

There can be no doubt that the future will hold many challenges for the new generation. They need the tools to meet those challenges. *Facts, Not Fear* can help parents provide these tools and give their children a positive attitude towards the environment. Both parents and children can benefit by working together towards a better understanding of this wonderful world and all its natural beauty.

Chapter 1

A Letter to Parents

Like you, the authors of this book are parents. We—Michael and Jane—are worried about what our children are learning.

❋ Jane was sitting with her husband and seven-year-old son David at a pizza place near her home. David looked at the plastic cup that held his Dad's soft drink.

"Do you know what you could do that would really help, Mom?" he said.

"No," Jane replied. "What?"

"You could stop using Styrofoam."

She looked into his blue eyes and saw his bright, hopeful look. He was sure that his mother would agree that plastic is bad. Together, they would help the Earth by getting rid of it. Jane's heart sank. She knew that using plastic does not harm the Earth any more than using paper or glass. But how could she explain that to a seven-year-old? And what else had David learned that was mistaken? And how could she dare undermine his trust in his teachers, who were, after all, her friends? She didn't know what to say.

"Maybe plastic isn't all that bad," she mumbled.

❋   Several years ago, Michael was driving his son Andy and a friend to a movie. As Michael listened to the boys talking, he noticed that they weren't discussing last Sunday's Denver Broncos game or the latest Sylvester Stallone film. They were figuring out the exact date on which the world would run out of oil. When Michael asked them about it, the boys explained that their science textbook said that proven reserves of oil could only last seventy years. Michael knew that "proven reserves" simply means the amount of a resource that can be taken out economically. They have little to do with the actual amount of oil in the Earth. But his son didn't know. Michael began to realize why Andy was forming a gloomy view of the future.

We are far from alone.

❋   One early spring night, as Jane's friend Linda put her son to bed, she glimpsed the full moon shining on the snow outside the window.
"Let's look at the moon," she said to five-year-old Henry.
She turned off the light and they gazed at the brilliant circle of light emerging from shifting wisps of cloud. But Henry pointed to the clouds.
"Look at the pollution!" he said.

❋   Merrilee, the mother of four boys, was looking forward to her second-grader's Christmas program. The children had been given an assignment to write on "What I would give to the world," and Merrilee expected a message of peace and joy. Instead, one by one, the children discussed "the need for a new Earth because we had destroyed ours through pollution, disappearing rain forests, and the elimination of the ozone layer."[1]

❧ Another mother tells how sad her six-year-old daughter seemed one night as she settled into her new bed. When asked why by her mother, the girl replied: "They killed trees to make my bed."[2]

Plastic is bad. Pollution is everywhere. Trees are being killed.

If you have children between kindergarten and the twelfth grade, chances are good that they have learned all this and more. The Earth is badly polluted, the rainforest is about to disappear, global warming will flood the earth—to name a few of the imminent calamities.

And who do they learn is responsible for this careening toward ecological disaster? We are. Parents, the current generation, have brought the Earth to the edge of doom.

The good news is that these claims are not true.

The goal of this book is twofold: to alert you to what your children are learning, and to offer you a more balanced view of the many environmental issues they encounter. With the help of many people, we have gathered the facts about environmental issues. We believe we have the background to help you correct the misinformation your children have been taught. Our research has been aided by people familiar with each environmental issue we write about. Before we can help, though, you need to understand how severe the problem is.

Apocalypse Tomorrow

"Our Earth is getting hotter every minute and the only way we can stop it is to stop burning styrofoam," wrote Catherine, an elementary school student. "I'm also too young to die, might I add, so *stop burning the Earth!*"[3] Catherine was worried about dying because her elementary-school textbooks taught her that global warming and a thinning ozone layer threaten her life. Never mind that the greenhouse effect and the so-called "hole" in the ozone layer have little to do with each other, or that burning Styrofoam has little to do with either one. Catherine's information may be scientifically weak but it's emotionally potent. Although environmental education differs from school to school and from region to region, our children are learning that the world is in danger and it is their job to save it.

Consider the following.

* *The Canadian Junior Green Guide*, a children's book, outlines an experiment in which kids try to get seeds to sprout. Some of the seeds are in pure vinegar and some in water. The results "tell you about the effect of acid (and acid rain) on plants,"[4] the book says. Yet the largest scientific study of acid rain ever conducted (at a cost of more than $500 million) couldn't find convincing evidence that acid rain is destroying forests.

* Global warming will cause ocean temperatures to rise, says one text. That could cause an ice mass in Antarctica to "slip off its rock and float into open water," which could "push the sea level up several metres and cause coastal flooding such as we've never even dreamed."[5] But most scientists believe that if the world gets warmer, the sea level might increase by between six and 40 *inches,* and over a sufficiently long time period for us to adapt to the change.[6]

* *Rainforest*, a story book for small children, tells how a man on a bulldozer destroys the rainforest and its animal life. Justice is done when the rains come and wash the bulldozer over a cliff, killing the man. (A drawing shows the man falling to his death.) "The Machine was washed away!" the book concludes. "But the creatures of the rain forest were safe."[7]

* An environmental supplement to the *Weekly Reader* states that CFCs (chlorofluorocarbons) "break down and go directly to the

ozone layer and destroy it." These CFCs "are found in the plastic foam from which cups, plates, and some fast food containers are made."[8] But by 1992, when this issue appeared, plastic foam products had been CFC-free for two years.[9]

In some cases, the textbooks have rewritten history to make their point. For example:

✤ "Did you know?" asks the text *Science Probe 9*. "Over 2000 years ago, the golden age of Greek civilization ended not because of conquest or war but because of damage to the country's most precious resource—soil. Trees were cut from every hillside to build cities and ships, as well as for fuel. Without trees to prevent erosion and enrich the soil, the land was not able to support farming. The famine that followed killed many people."[10] Classical scholars whom we consulted were at a loss as to what the source of this information was. One classicist, upon hearing this, responded: "What famine?"

These are just some of the many examples found during a review of more than 160 textbooks and 130 environmental books for children available throughout Canada and the United States. Numerous examples of curriculum materials from environmental and business groups were also reviewed. Unbiased materials are a rare exception, as most materials either present only one side of an issue, select worst-case examples, or omit important information.

Armageddon in the Press

Finding these lessons in our children's school-books shouldn't surprise us, since they merely echo the sort of messages conveyed by the mass media.

❉ "The world's leaders meet in Rio next week for the first Earth Summit," reported *Newsweek* magazine in its coverage of the event. "Their mission: to save the ship from its passengers. Their efforts will be judged not by us, but by our children." It goes on to stress the importance of the issue "because no matter what your cause ... it won't matter if the environment collapses, taking the world's economy with it."[11]

❉ "Let there be no illusions," wrote *Time* magazine in its "Planet of the Year" special issue. "Taking effective action to halt the massive injury to the earth's environment will require a mobilization of political will, international cooperation and sacrifice unknown except in wartime." Sprinkled through the issue were statements such as: "Nearly every habitat is at risk," "Greenhouse gases could create a climatic calamity," and "Swarms of people are running out of food and space."[12]

❉ Actress Meryl Streep appeared on the Phil Donahue Show to warn mothers about a substance called *Alar*, a growth regulator used on apples. CBS's "60 Minutes" presented the charges, too. Both were part of a public relations campaign conducted in 1989 for the Natural Resources Defense Council (NRDC). The group claimed that one out of every five thousand preschoolers exposed to *Alar* residues was likely to get cancer. Parents were terrified. Schools stopped selling apples in their vending machines. (NRDC's claims were never substantiated.)[13]

❉ Captain Planet, a cartoon on the Turner cable network, begins a typical episode with this narration: "Our world is in peril. Gaia, the spirit of the Earth, can no longer stand the terrible destruction plaguing our planet." One of the shows features "Hoggish Greedly" and "Dr. Blight," who are trying to destroy the rainforest and make it into a golf course.[14]

Reinforcing the Message

Some scientists and other prominent citizens reinforce the messages conveyed by the media. In fact, they often speak through the media. While scientists must be objective and careful when they publish articles in scientific journals, they can speak dramatically for popular consumption.

* Philip Austin, an atmospheric scientist at the University of British Columbia in Vancouver, told *Maclean's* readers: "If you look at current CO_2 levels compared with historical levels in the planet's history, it's clear we're headed right off the chart."[15] As we will explore in chapter 13, the carbon dioxide "problem" is still a matter of debate within the scientific community.

* Stephen Schneider, a scientist at Stanford University and the National Center for Atmospheric Research in Boulder, Colorado, told *Good Housekeeping* readers that "world global warming would mean that food and water supplies would be threatened (temporarily, at least), that certain diseases might go haywire, that numerous species of animals or plants—even whole ecosystems—would be endangered, and that both the temperature and the level of the oceans would rise, leading to more likelihood of severe storms and flooding of the coastlines."[16] Each of these statements is questioned by equally reputable scientists.

* James E. Hansen, who directs the Goddard Institute for Space Studies, told *Newsweek* that even the deep snow blanketing the East in the winter of 1996 was caused by global warming. "As you get more global warming, you should see an increase in the extremes of the hydrologic cycle—droughts and floods and heavy precipitation," he explained.[17]

Since so much scientific research is funded by government grants, scientists often can improve their access to funds if they can convince politicians that their work may "save the planet."

On the other hand, scientists who down play crises may find themselves in hot water because they are threatening the budgets of their colleagues.

❋ Melvyn Shapiro, the chief of research at a laboratory of the National Oceanic and Atmospheric Administration, told *Insight* magazine that much of the reason for alarm about ozone depletion was budgetary. "If there were no dollars attached to this game, you'd see it played on intellect and integrity," he said. "When you say the ozone threat is a scam, you're not only attacking people's scientific integrity, you're going after their pocketbook as well. It's money, purely money." But shortly after the article appeared, Shapiro stopped accepting calls from the press and word circulated that his superiors had told him to quit talking.[18]

But perhaps the most accomplished promoters of crisis are environmental groups. Many environmental groups were born out of genuine alarm about air and water pollution or other issues, but advocacy has transformed them into multi-million-dollar businesses housed in skyscrapers and managed by well-paid executives who spend much of their time as lobbyists. If these organizations are to continue to exist in their comfortable style and maintain their political power, they need to maintain the income received from donations. As a result, their fund-raising letters are calculated to grip the reader's attention.

❋ "It is entirely possible that we may be the last generation of humans to know this wondrous earth as it was meant to be," warns the Sierra Club Legal Defense Fund.[19]

✤ "In the time it takes you to read this letter, nine hundred acres of rainforest will have been destroyed forever," says the Rainforest Action Network.[20]

✤ "Without firing a shot, we may kill one-fifth of all species of life on this planet in the next 20 years," proclaims the World Wildlife Fund.[21]

However, these fears are overstated. The environment is *not* significantly worse than it used to be. As this book will show, by most measures the environment in North America has *improved* substantially.

✤ Air quality has improved dramatically in the last few decades. For example, according to Environment Canada the level of carbon monoxide in the air declined by 73 percent between 1974 and 1994, and the level of sulfur dioxide declined 62 percent between 1975 and 1994. These declines occurred in spite of substantial economic growth.[22]

✤ Water quality has also improved across the country. In 1994, Alberta and Saskatchewan met their water-quality goals over 90 percent of the time; British Columbia and New Brunswick met their goals over 85 percent of the time; Manitoba met its goals over 70 percent of the time.[23]

✤ Concentrations of the pesticide dichloro-diphenyl-dichloro-ethylene (commonly called DDE) fell almost 85 percent in both Lake Ontario and Lake Superior from peak levels in 1975.[24]

✤ Forests in Canada are increasing as growth exceeds harvest.[25]

✤ The amount of land set aside for parks, wilderness, and wildlife is increasing in Canada.[26]

✤   Many wildlife populations are greater than they were 80 or 100 years ago.[27]

So, just as the texts are often irresponsible in predicting the future, they are often negligent in describing the past and present.

Saving the Planet without Scaring Kids

How can you give your children a more balanced view of environmental problems? One way is gently to supply the information that is missing in their classrooms. This book will give you the facts and insight into the scientific controversies that are not covered in the textbooks.

Simply learning that reputable scientists often disagree with the claims of imminent catastrophe will keep your children from blindly fearing the future. Such information will also help your children see that environmental science is a discipline that reflects scientific uncertainty and is open to continual discovery. Your children can learn about environmental issues and develop their critical thinking skills at the same time. As scientists do, they can collect the facts and see whether the theories that have been advanced actually fit the facts.

With this greater objectivity, students can also begin to think critically about the causes of environmental problems, and develop their understanding of human nature. They won't be so quick to accept the simplistic claims of catastrophic global destruction. Your children will probably stop pestering you to take up the cause of the day, or at least they will be willing to consider that their crusade may not be for everyone.

Each chapter concludes with a few questions and answers that will help you summarize the information for your children. Each also has activities that you and your children may like to read and perhaps try out. The activities offer concrete evidence that supports the information in the chapter. However, the activities are merely suggestions that can make a richer experience out of a trip to the lumberyard, say, or the supermarket. We recognize that you are a busy parent, with many goals other than teaching your children environmental science.

Unlike the authors of some environmental books for kids, we don't expect you or your children to picket a fast-food restaurant or write a protest letter to your local politician. We think your children should have a chance to learn about the environment rather than be mobilized into trendy campaigns. This book can help them.

Notes

1 Merrilee A. Boyack, "The End of the Innocence: Schoolchildren Are Saddled with Too Many Worries," *San Diego Union-Tribune*, August 18, 1994, B13.

2 Nancy Bray Cardozo, "Reading, Writing & Ruin," *Audubon*, January/February 1994, 112.

3 Illustrated newsletter of Kids FACE, Nashville, TN: Kids FACE, March/April 1991, 3.

4 Teri Degler and Pollution Probe, *The Canadian Junior Green Guide* (Toronto: McClelland & Stewart, 1990), 23.

5 Fagan, Margaret, *Challenge for Change* (Toronto: McGraw-Hill Ryerson, 2nd ed., 1991), 246.

6 J. J. Houghton, et al., eds., *Climate Change 1995: The Science of Climate Change.* Contribution of Working Group I to the Second Assessment Report of the Intergovernmental Panel on Climate Change. (New York: Cambridge University Press, 1996), passim.

7 Helen Cowcher, *Rainforest* (New York: Farrar, Straus and Giroux, 1988), no page numbers.

8 Bonnie Ferraro and Karen Brumley, *Saving Our Planet* (Columbus, OH: American Education Publishing, Weekly Reader, 1992), 5

9 W. A. Dart, "Viewpoint: Pitching in the Foam Cup to Save the Planet," *Miami Herald*, April 22, 1990, and letter from David Jolly, Environmental Affairs Representative, Dart Container Corporation, September 11, 1992, p. 5.

10 Peter Beckett, et al., *Science Probe 9* (Scarborough, ON: Thomson Canada, Nelson Edition, 1995), 499.

11 "The Future is Here," *Newsweek*, June 1, 1992, 18–43.

12 "What on Earth Are We Doing?" *Time*, January 2, 1989, 26–71.

13 Eliot Marshall, "A Is for Apple, *Alar*, and ... Alarmist?" *Science*, Vol. 254 (October 4, 1991), 22.

14 Reported in S. Robert Lichter, Linda S. Richter, and Daniel R. Amundson, "Doomsday Kids: Environmental Messages on Children's Television" (Washington, DC: Center for Media and Public Affairs, April 1995).

15 Mark Nichols, "Feeling the Heat," *Maclean's*, April 24, 1995, 52.

16 Stephen H. Schneider, "Dealing With the Greenhouse Effect," *Good Housekeeping*, April 1991, 78–79.

17 Sharon Begley, "He's Not Full of Hot Air," *Newsweek*, January 22, 1996, 24.

18 Ronald Bailey, *Eco-Scam: The False Prophets of Ecological Apocalypse* (New York: St. Martin's Press, 1993), 120.

19 Letter from Vawter "Buck" Parker, Acting President, Sierra Club Legal Defense Fund, 180 Montgomery Street, Suite 1400, San Francisco CA 94104, n.d.

20 Letter from Randall L. Hayes, Executive Director, Rainforest Action Network, 301 Broadway, San Francisco CA 94133, n.d.

21 Letter from Russell E. Train, Chairman of the Board, World Wildlife Fund & The Conservation Foundation, 1250 Twenty-fourth St. NW, Washington, DC 20037 (1991 or 1992).

22 Steven Hayward and Laura Jones, Environmental Indicators for North America and the United Kingdom. *Fraser Institute Critical Issues Bulletin* (April 1999), 8–15.

23 DeWiel, et al., 9.

24 DeWiel, et al., 9.

25 DeWiel, et al., 9.

26 DeWiel, et al., 9.

27 Winston Harrington, "Severe Decline and Partial Recovery," in *America's Renewable Resources: Historical Trends and Current Challenges*, Kenneth D. Frederick and Roger A. Sedjo, eds. (Washington DC: Resources for the Future, 1991), 237–8.

Chapter 2

Trendy Schools

Childhood was once supposed to be idyllic and carefree. Children were allowed to be children. But today many schools are plunging our children into serious environmental activism.

"Kids have a *lot* of power," writes John Javna, the author of *50 Simple Things Kids Can Do to Save the Earth,* a best-selling book found in many classrooms. "Whenever you say something, grown-ups *have* to listen ... So if saving the Earth is important to you, then grown-ups will have to follow along."[1]

We want our children to learn good citizenship. We don't want them to be polluters when they grow up. But often, instead of being taught information that will lead to intelligent choices in the future, they are being enlisted in trendy causes and sent out to bring their parents "on board."

Environmental activism is the latest in a series of social reforms championed in our schools. Schools are fighting the war on drugs, encouraging physical fitness, fostering self-esteem, teaching about sex—you name it. And now our children are supposed to save the Earth. The way these issues are taught shapes the way our children think.

The *Vancouver Sun* recently published a piece in which children spoke out about environmental concerns. This poem by an 8-year-old, was typical:

> Pollution is killing us, what should we do?
> Recycle and reuse, that's what to do.
> Don't drive cars, you know what to do.
> Walk, ride your bike, hiking is good, too.
> If you put garbage in the right place,
> it will make earth a better place.
> So remember now what I said today.
> It will make earth a better place to stay.[2]

While many forces affect children's ideas, schools are among the most important. "The public schools have been described as the best sucker list in America," said U.S. Commissioner of Education Francis Keppel in 1976. "Because of the delivery powers of the attendance officer, educational policy is highly vulnerable to use by special interests to forward their personal or public causes. Sooner or later, many social reformers get around to trying to influence what is taught and how."[3]

However valuable these goals may be, they are driving out basic education in Canada and the United States. Science instruction is particularly weak. In 1995, the Third International Mathematics and Science Study (TIMSS) tested 500,000 seventh- and eighth-grade students from 45 countries. Canadian math students ranked eighteenth, seventh-grade science students ranked nineteenth, and eighth-grade students ranked sixteenth. The United States did not do significantly better.

The US National Commission on Excellence in Education concluded in 1983 that American schools had "lost sight of the basic purposes of schooling."[4] It pointed out that test scores had been declining almost steadily since the 1960s in the United States.[5] Unfortunately, instead of strengthening our science programs, environmental education has made them worse.

Straying from Science, and Then Some

In the past, most environmental education was called ecology and it was taught as a part of science. The eighth-grade text *General Science*, for example, still does this.[6] Its chapter on the environment describes the biomes (deserts, forests, rain forests, etc.) and discusses the interdependence of plant and animal communities. Children learn about the carbon, nitrogen, and water cycles. This text exemplifies the way science books used to cover ecological issues.

Starting in the 1970s, however, as interest in the environment exploded throughout the country, "environmental science" began to crowd out traditional science. Environmental education spread from junior high and high school to the primary grades, while invading other subjects in an oversimplified way. Texts on health, geography, and history now typically contain one or more environmental chapters.

Unfortunately, the textbook authors often know little about the environment. Environmental groups fill the information gap, peppering schools with their materials.

* The National Wildlife Federation published an eighteen-book series dealing with topics from endangered species to wetlands. Each "Nature Scope" book contains everything the teacher needs to present a series of lessons on the topic. In the early 1990s, teachers were buying close to 60,000 of these books a year.

* Zero Population Growth publishes readings and activities featuring the harms of overpopulation. "At the heart of these ecological crises is the unprecedented rise of human numbers," reads ZPG publicity. A typical exercise asks junior high students to discuss the appropriate distribution of food throughout the world in order "to demonstrate the unevenness in the distribution of population and resources and the resulting social problems."[7]

✤ World Resources Institute has a *Teacher's Guide* to accompany its annual report on the world's natural resources. To combat global warming, it recommends that national governments impose fuel efficiency measures, encourage solar energy, and increase reforestation. To preserve biodiversity, it recommends slowing population growth and creating protected areas.[8]

Textbooks endorse such groups as sources of information. *Your Health*, for example, recommends that students contact Greenpeace, Zero Population Growth, Planned Parenthood, and Earth First![9] among others. Certainly, many environmental organizations have useful material, but it is often unscientific and unbalanced. And consider:

✤ Earth First! is an activist organization best known for spiking trees with metal, so that when the tree is cut, either in the forest or a sawmill, it can break up the machinery. (Spiking has seriously injured at least one logger.)

✤ Greenpeace is an international organization that originated in Vancouver, British Columbia. It opposes nuclear testing and commercial whaling, and has called for a total ban on chlorine, which is used to keep drinking water safe.

Some businesses produce materials, too, but these often echo the same themes. The Shell Environment Fund promotes "innovative, action-oriented projects that improve and protect the Canadian environment."[10] *Earth Action*, a department in *Owl* magazine sponsored by Shell, says: "Air pollution is a big problem for our planet. Air pollution can make allergies and breathing problems worse, harm plants, and it can even make farmers' harvests much smaller."[11] As we will see later, the air pollution "problem" is not bad in this country, and is improving every day.

Efforts at environmental indoctrination in Canadian schools have not yet reached the level of those in the United States. However, the textbooks being used in Canadian schools contain environmental fallacies, and the government is bowing to pressure groups who want more environmental advocacy in the schools. For example, the British Columbia Ministry of Environment funds a group called the *Green Team* to go into classrooms and discuss environmental issues such as the ecological devastation caused by hydroelectric dams, the supposed garbage crisis in this country, and the wasteful use of non-renewable resources.[12] One of the stated goals of the program is to motivate students "to take personal and collective action to protect the environment."[13]

Meanwhile, in the United States, the federal government is expanding the environmental education effort. In 1990, Congress authorized $65 million over five years to support environmental education. The Environmental Protection Agency (EPA) now has an Office of Environmental Education. Marcia Wiley, who coordinated an EPA-funded pilot program in Washington State, explained that the goal was "to catalyze systemic change," and said one sign of success was that "youth environmental stewardship behaviors" increased 35 percent.[14] Thirty states have passed laws mandating environmental education.[15] The model law recommended by the Council of State Governments says that students should have a "commitment to act for a healthy environment . . . [and] . . . contribute to decision-making processes."[16] Is this the path that the Canadian government will follow?

Behaviour Modification

Turning children into environmental crusaders is often an explicit goal. In practice, this can mean doing what the teacher says. One student came home from school after a lesson on recycling and told his parents he wanted his lunch packed in reusable plastic containers, not plastic bags and disposable juice boxes. His father discussed the pros and cons of these alternatives with his son. He pointed out that plastic bags take up little space in a landfill. Because juice boxes are rectangular, many can be packed into a single truck, reducing fuel use. And unlike bottles, they don't spill before lunch time.

The boy decided to keep using the plastic bags and juice boxes. At school the next day, when asked by the teacher why he was still using a plastic sandwich bag, the boy recounted his conversation with his father. When the father picked the boy up after school, the teacher asked him not to interfere with her lessons, stating, "We're trying to make the children more environmentally sensitive." The father replied that he felt the lesson was one-sided, to which the teacher exclaimed, "It's what we are teaching them and I wish you wouldn't interfere."[17]

Closely allied to behavioural modification are public and political activism. Some Grade 5 students in Milton, Ontario were lauded for writing a newsletter containing articles entitled: "Acid Rain Eating Away Our Buildings," "Chemicals in the Niagara Mist," and "The Endangered Eagle."[18] *Kid Heroes of the Environment* praises children for picketing businesses, conducting petition drives, and organizing letter-writing campaigns to political leaders.[19]

Children are advised to write their political representatives about policies they disagree with. However, because "letter writing often doesn't get satisfying results," Anne Love and Jane Drake, in the World Wildlife Fund's child-directed book *Take Action*, advise that: "Kids' letters get action if ... they aren't overly polite— passion helps."[20] Politicians frequently receive letters from school children alarmed by the loss of species or by some other environmental "crisis."

The "Green Team"

Since education in Canada falls under provincial jurisdiction, teaching about the environment differs around the country. One provincial government that has taken an active role in environmental education is British Columbia, the birthplace of Greenpeace. The British Columbia Ministry of Environment sponsors an "Eco Education Program," which includes a "Green Team" that travels throughout the province to educate students about environmental issues. Although it is not a required part of the provincial curriculum, the program is heavily promoted and publicly funded.

If the "Green Team" focused on teaching environmental science, it could be very useful. However, in addition to learning about the water cycle and the effects of pollution, students learn attitudes. They learn about the wasteful "throw-away society" in which they live. They learn about the environmental damage caused by hydroelectric dams, which "just sit there; they don't do anything."[1] Teachers are informed that "the Eco Education Program examines people's behaviors and the threats they pose to environmental health."[2]

Once in the classroom, the "Green Team" introduces the "ecological footprint." This is defined as "the sum of the natural resources consumed, the land base and the energy required to support current life-styles."[3] The larger the footprint, the larger the amount of energy and resources being "wasted." The footprint of the average person living in Canada is 4.3 hectares, or more than four football fields. This is compared to the 5.1 hectares taken up by someone living in the United States, the .04 hectares of someone living in India, and the 1.8 hectares of the average person in the world.[4] The implication is that North America is consuming more than its fair share.

Students are encouraged to recycle, to travel by foot, bicycle, and bus instead of by car (thereby reducing carbon dioxide emissions and the greenhouse effect), and to avoid wasteful consumption of unnecessary and unenvironmental products. These may not be bad lessons, but do we want Canadian children to feel guilty each time they ride in a car?

Notes

(1) Observation of the "Green Team" at William Van Horne Elementary School, Vancouver, BC, June 1997.

(2) The Green Team, *Green Team Teachers' Guide "Eco Education Program"* (Victoria: BC Environment, March 1996), 3.

(3) The Green Team, 15.

(4) The Green Team, 15.

Environmental Education: A Morality Play

The ideas underlying environmental materials are often overly simplistic, casting humans as villains and nature as their victim. There
are a number of popular themes.

People Are Bad—Nature Is Good

A book for first graders about Antarctica shows a helicopter flying
near the nests of penguins. As the penguins flee in fear, birds of prey
called skuas swoop in on their eggs. The book explains: "The penguins and the seals have always shared their world with ancient en-
emies, the skuas and the leopard seals. But these new arrivals
[humans] are more dangerous."[21]

A book about acid rain shows a photograph of a "tombstone" in
Hawaii, reading: "IN MEMORY OF MAN 2,000,000 BC – AD 2030—HE WHO
ONCE DOMINATED THE EARTH DESTROYED IT WITH HIS WASTES, HIS POISONS, AND
HIS OWN NUMBERS.[22] Describing tropical deforestation, *Journeys in Sci-
ence* states that "the rain forests of South America and Asia are fall-
ing under the axe and are not being replanted."[23]

The book that tops the list for its depiction of humans as the enemy is *Gaia: An Atlas of Planet Management*, used as a geography
text book in some high schools. Claiming that "humanity is becoming
a super-malignancy on the face of the planet," it uses a "cancer cell"
as a metaphor for our population.[24]

Nature Is Pure and Only People Pollute

In fact, nature is far from benign. The struggle for survival is often
brutal and pollution existed long before human beings began to add
to the problem. Earthquakes and volcanoes are natural and a natural haze hangs over the Smoky Mountains of North Carolina and
Tennessee. Many animal species became extinct without human intervention. Climate changes naturally, from Ice Ages to warm peri-
ods of lush vegetation and back.

What we think of as "natural" is often the result of centuries of human intervention. Science writer Stephen Budiansky points out that red cedars take over abandoned cow pastures these days, but only because centuries of grazing have suppressed hardwoods such as oaks.[25]

And people don't just cause problems; they also solve them. They create wildlife refuges, prevent forest fires, and restock streams. They restore land that has been mined or damaged by drought, turning it into productive farmland, forests, or parks. They work with nature to create beautiful gardens and arboreta. (Chapters 10 and 11 will discuss what people are doing to protect animals, plants, and natural beauty.) Facts such as these are omitted from most texts that discuss the environment.

Consumption Is Bad

Although overpopulation is viewed as the earth's biggest problem, overconsumption in nations like the United States and Canada is seen as being almost as bad. A constant theme is that these countries are too rich and consume too much of the world's energy and resources. "Rich western countries, with only 20% of the world's population, use 70% of the world's energy," says one book of science experiments.[26] Another book accuses: "If we in Canada use more than our share of energy and resources, it means somebody in the world gets less."[27]

Science Probe 9, a science text, also emphasizes Canada's unequal share of the world's resources. It asks you to "keep in mind the following fact: Canadians use more energy per person than people in any other country in the world."[28] It then goes on to suggest: "If both the energy used by each person and the world population continue to increase, the energy resources we use will be in danger of being used up."[29] Such comparisons are designed to make children feel guilty and to promote the governmental redistribution of existing wealth to poorer countries.

This stress on cutting consumption and redistributing wealth omits the fact that the Western world produces a disproportionate amount of goods. These goods are used around the world, benefiting poor countries as well as rich ones. It also omits the fact that wealth must be created; it is not a "given." Unless the poorer countries create wealth, redistribution will accomplish nothing. (These issues will be discussed more fully in Chapters 5, 6, and 7.)

Technology Is Bad

Most environmental education condemns technology. Children learn that factories and cars pollute the air, air conditioners and refrigerators contain CFCs that destroy the ozone layer, and burning fossil fuels increases the CO_2 in the atmosphere, causing global warming. In contrast, primitive life-styles are exalted.

* A geography text, *Towards Tomorrow: Canada in a Changing World*, suggests that "the Industrial Revolution created a great deal of human suffering as the price to be paid for progress."[30]

* *The Greenhouse Effect,* a book found in an elementary school library, goes further. It has a picture of Chinese farmers using their feet to operate an irrigation device. "Their lives would be easier if a machine could do the same job," the caption says, "but if the machine ran on fossil fuels, its use would increase the amount of carbon dioxide in the atmosphere."[31]

* *A Great Round Wonder,* a book found in a university's education library, recalls with nostalgia the pre-industrial age. Illustrated with an idyllic farm scene, it romanticizes: "Back in the old days, when your great-great-grandparents were growing up ... there were no electric lights, televisions, telephones, or refrigerators ... Life was hard work, but the air and water and soil were clean and healthy."[32]

❧   Betty Miles' book *Save the Earth* has a picture of thirty or forty bicycle riders with the caption: "Bicycles are inexpensive, convenient and non-polluting."[33] She does not mention that bikes are not very useful for other than short distances and are not convenient in rain or snow.

These books ignore the fact that if the people on the Earth are to become healthier and live longer, they will do so through technology, not ideology.

Business Is Evil

Children learn that greedy lumber companies cut down forests. Gluttonous fast food companies clear the rain forests to raise cattle for hamburgers. Profit-seeking hunters extinguished the passenger pigeon. But in the 1970s, things began to change. Environmentalists began to warn that natural resources were being abused and destroyed by the reluctance of the government to curb industrial growth, and the greed of businesses who cared only for profit at the expense of environmental responsibility.[34]

It is true that business and industry are sometimes guilty of damaging the environment. But halting economic growth is probably not the proper solution.

Things Are Getting Worse

"For most of the time that human beings have lived on Earth ... [w]e could just take what we needed from nature and feel pretty sure there would always be more." The children's book *Looking at the Environment* continues:

Now, about 160 years later ... [t]here are huge numbers of human beings ... But that's not the only problem. Modern people have invented machines such as chain-saws that let us cut down trees with frightening speed. We have bulldozers that level land

and fill in ponds and marshes. We have huge factories that spew poisons into the air and water. We spread deadly chemicals on farmland. These chemicals end up in our food and water. Our cars pollute the air. We are ruining the habitats of other animals, and poisoning the air, water, and soil that all living things need.[35]

Although the book admits that human inventions have "helped us eat better, stay healthier, and live longer," most young readers would conclude that the nation remains in desperate straits.

Yet, the environment is better than it used to be. Problems remain, but air quality in most places has improved significantly since 1975.[36] Cities that suffer from air pollution are still far cleaner than cities in the less-developed world such as Mexico City.

The impression given our children is that the past was pristine, but it was not. Streets were mired in animal excrement, the air was choked with coal dust, and children died from contagious diseases carried by unsanitary water. For a baby born early in the century, life expectancy in Canada was 59 years.[37] Today it is 78 years.[38] The enormous improvements in health and environment are not reflected in most of our children's textbooks.

Government Is the Answer

From slowing the use of fossil fuels to requiring recycling, the solutions proposed are always government solutions. While government involvement is sometimes necessary—in the case of urban air pollution, for example—the textbooks are wrong always to assume that governments can correct a problem.

In fact, the worst pollution problems have occurred in nations in which governments have had the most power. The collapse of the former Soviet Union led to shocking revelations of poisoned streams and unhealthy air throughout that country. And even in our own democracy, the government is not always a good steward of its own properties.

Real Education: Unraveling Scientific Mysteries

Real environmental education would be far different. It would teach children critical thinking skills. It would inform students of science as it really is: an ongoing search for truth.

Acid rain, for example, remains a scientific mystery story. We still don't know what caused the acidic lakes in Nova Scotia or the Adirondack mountains. Acid rain does fall on these lakes and their surrounding area, but there is evidence that the water in some of these lakes was historically acidic. One theory is that the water temporarily lost its acidity in the late nineteenth or early twentieth century when nearby forests were burned. The wood ash was washed into the lakes, making the water alkaline.[39] In other words, according to this theory, the acidity is more "natural" than the alkalinity. Exploring this question could be fascinating.

Students would also learn that protecting the environment is more complicated than "good guys" battling "bad guys." Controlling pollution can be costly and can slow economic growth. Slower growth can reduce people's interest in further environmental protection and their ability to bring it about. Children would also learn that regulations often have unintended consequences. For example, tough fuel economy standards to save fuel have led car manufacturers to build lighter cars, and lighter cars mean more deaths when accidents occur.[40]

In sum, environmental education could be a valuable part of science instruction. Instead, it often merely repeats the nostrums of the environmental movement, and molds children into smug crusaders whose foundation of knowledge is shaky at best.

Notes

1 John Javna, ed., *50 Simple Things Kids Can Do to Save the Earth* (Kansas City, MO: Andrews and McMeel, 1990), 7.

2 "Kids Corner," *The Vancouver Sun*, May 6, 1995.

3 Aspen Institute, *Educational Policy in the Next Decade* (Aspen, CO: Program on Education for a Changing Society, Aspen Institute, 1976), 1.

4 National Commission on Excellence in Education, *A Nation At Risk* (Washington, DC: U.S. Department of Education, 1983), 6.

5 National Commission on Excellence in Education, 8.

6 Peter Alexander, et al., *General Science: Book Two* (Morristown, NJ: Silver Burdett & Ginn, 1989), 144–75. (In the chapters that follow, textbooks will be identified in most cases by their publishers rather than authors. A list of major texts is presented in Appendix A.)

7 "Food for Thought" (Washington, DC: Zero Population Growth, 1984), 1.

8 Mary Paden, ed., *Teacher's Guide to World Resources 1990-91* (Washington, DC: World Resources Institute, 1990), 15, 36.

9 Joan Luckmann, *Your Health* (Englewood Cliffs, NJ: Prentice Hall, 1990), 542.

10 *Owl* Magazine, May 1997, 31.

11 *Owl* Magazine, May 1997, 31.

12 Observation of the Green Team at Sir William Van Horne Elementary in Vancouver, British Columbia, June 18, 1997.

13 BC Environment, *Green Team Teachers' Guide, "Eco Education Program"* (Victoria, March 1996), 4.

14 Marcia Wiley, "Washington's Environmental Education Model Schools Program," *Environmental Communicator* (North American Association for Environmental Education, Troy, OH, December 1995), 10–11.

15 Environmental Education Associates, *State-by-State Overview of Environmental Education Standards* (Washington, DC, 1992).

16 Council of State Governments, Environmental Education Subcommittee, National Environmental Task Force, *Model Environmental Education Act* (Lexington, KY, 1992), 2.

17 Thomas Harvey Holt, "Growing Up Green," *Reason* magazine, October 1991, 36.

18 Anne Love and Jane Drake, *Take Action* (Toronto: Kids Can Press, 1992), 89.

19 Catherine Dee, ed., *Kid Heroes of the Environment* (Berkeley, CA: Earth Works, 1991).

20 Love and Drake, 89.

21 Helen Cowcher, *Antarctica* (New York: Scholastic, 1990), no page numbers.

22 Mary Turck, *Acid Rain* (Don Mills, ON: Collier Macmillan Canada, 1990), 38.

23 Peter Beugger and Larry Yore, *Journeys in Science* (Toronto: Collier Macmillan Canada, Canadian ed., 1990), 226.

24 Norman Myers, *Gaia: An Atlas of Planet Management* (London, UK: Anchor Books, 1993), 20.

25 Stephen Budiansky, "Unpristine Nature," *The American Enterprise*, September/ October 1995, 64.

26 Susan V. Bosak, *Science Is ...* (Richmond Hill/Markham, ON: Scholastic Canada/ Communication Project, 2nd ed., 1991), 354.

27 Teri Degler and Pollution Probe, *The Canadian Junior Green Guide* (Toronto: McClelland and Stewart, 1990), 58.

28 Peter Beckett et al, *Science Probe 9, Nelson Edition* (Scarborough, ON: Thomson Canada, 1995), 362.

29 Beckett et al, 367.

30 Stewart Dunlop, *Towards Tomorrow: Canada in a Changing World–Geography* (Toronto: Harcourt Brace Jovanovich Canada, 1987), 158.

31 Rebecca L. Johnson, *The Greenhouse Effect: Life on a Warmer Planet* (Minneapolis: Lerner, 1990), 101.

32 Shelley Tanaka, *A Great Round Wonder: My Book of the World* (Toronto: Douglas and McIntyre, 1993), 40.

33 Betty Miles, *Save the Earth: An Action Handbook for Kids* (New York: Alfred A. Knopf, 1991), 78.

34 For example see Gary B. Nash, *The American Odyssey: The United States in the Twentieth Century* (Lake Forest, IL: Glencoe, 1991), 757.

35 David Suzuki and Barbara Hehner, *Looking at the Environment* (Toronto: Stoddart, 1989), 79–80.

36 Boris DeWiel, Steve Hayward, Laura Jones, and M. Danielle Smith, *Environmental Indicators for Canada and the United States.* Critical Issues Bulletin (Vancouver: The Fraser Institute, March 1997), 10–21.

37 Jonina Wood, Editor-in-Chief, *The 1997 Canada Year Book* (Ottawa: Statistics Canada, 1996), 116.

38 The World Bank, *World Development Report 1992: Development and the Environment* (New York: Oxford University Press, 1992), 218, Table 1.

39 Edward Krug, "Fish Story," *Policy Review,* Spring 1990, 44–48.

40 Robert W. Crandall and John D. Graham, "The Effect of Fuel Economy Standards on Automobile Safety," *The Journal of Law and Economics,* April 1989, 97–118.

Chapter 3

Last Chance to Save the Planet

For years before we started writing this book, we considered ourselves pretty knowledgeable about environmental issues. And we thought we were immune to hysteria.

Even so, Jane "lost her cool" in 1989 when Meryl Streep appeared on the Phil Donahue Show warning parents about Alar, a chemical used on apples. After seeing the show, Jane remembers driving in her car, listening to the "news" about Alar on the radio. She told herself that this was probably just another hyped-up "scare of the month." But she was also calculating how much apple juice her fourteen-month-old son drank each day, and trying to figure out if his chances of getting cancer had gone up.

It isn't just our children who are afraid. We are, too. Where do these fears come from?

During the past three decades, a few emotionally powerful ideas—technology is harmful, we are running out of resources, the population is out of control—have taken hold. Although these ideas are misguided and therefore not likely to stand the test of time, they have not been allowed to die a natural death. Influential groups, especially environmental organizations, continue to hawk these ideas.

Today's environmental movement has roots in the conservation movement that started at the turn of the century. Its goals were to protect natural resources as industry grew, but not to halt growth. The Commons, Footpaths, and Open Spaces Preservation Society, for example, was founded in Britain in 1865. The world's first private environmental group, its goal was, in part, to preserve the urban commons for the enjoyment of the increasing numbers of urban workers.[1]

The modern push to protect the environment, which started in the 1960s, is different. It encompasses many more issues, has broader public support, and is built on a foundation of alarm.

Three Landmark Books

Three landmark books shaped the modern environmental movement. These books were based on limited and, in some cases, even sloppy science and economics, but their impact has been incalculable.

Silent Spring

Before the 1960s, the term "ecology" didn't mean much to anyone except scientists. But in 1962, a single book made ecology—the "web of life"—a household word. Rachel Carson's *Silent Spring*[2] changed the emotional landscape. Consider the opening of the book, "A Fable for Tomorrow."

> There was once a town in the heart of America where all life seemed to live in harmony with its surroundings. The town lay in the midst of a checkerboard of prosperous farms, with fields of grain and hillsides of orchards where, in the spring, white clouds of bloom drifted above the green fields . . .
> Then a strange blight crept over the area and everything began to change. Some evil spell had settled on the community:

mysterious maladies swept the flocks of chickens; the cattle and the sheep sickened and died. Everywhere was a shadow of death ...

There was a strange stillness. The birds, for example— where had they gone? Many people spoke of them, puzzled and disturbed. The feeding stations in the backyards were deserted. The few birds seen anywhere were moribund; they trembled violently and could not fly. There was a spring without voices ...

No witchcraft, no enemy action had silenced the rebirth of new life in this stricken world. The people had done it themselves.[3]

The idea that chemicals—pesticides—could cause a "silent spring" hit like a bombshell. Human beings had turned the "web of life" into a web of death.[4] DDT, the chief target of the book, had protected millions of people by killing insects that carried malaria. But now it was viewed as a killer of birds. Indeed, all chemicals were suspect.

Silent Spring began a campaign against DDT. In 1967, residents of Long Island, New York, formed the Environmental Defense Fund (EDF), with the goal of outlawing DDT. The movement was joined by concerned citizens in Canada. In 1969, the Canadian government began the phase-out process which led to a discontinuation of production and importation of DDT in 1985, although existing stocks were permitted to be in use until 1990. (The U.S. EPA banned the pesticide in 1972.) The success of this campaign made the EDF the model for the new environmental movement. From now on, litigation and lobbying would be the focus of environmentalism.

Because *Silent Spring* changed the environmental movement, its impact was greater than its effect on DDT or even on pesticides generally. *Silent Spring* shook up a culture that had been comfortable with technology, and sowed seeds of doubts about its benefits for humankind. For her clarion call to arms, Rachel Carson is a revered heroine in today's environmental education programs. Textbooks in many fields, from science to geography, highlight her career and her fight against pesticides.

The Limits to Growth

In 1972, *The Limits to Growth*[5] caused another sensation. Published by an international group of business executives and academics calling themselves the Club of Rome, this book predicted economic collapse by the end of the twenty-first century.

The authors based their claims on a computer model of the world economy. "If the present growth trends in world population, industrialization, pollution, food production, and resource depletion continue unchanged," they wrote, "the limits to growth on this planet will be reached sometime within the next one hundred years. The most probable result will be a rather sudden and uncontrollable decline in both population and industrial capacity."[6] The authors urged massive international governmental intervention.

When the price of oil skyrocketed in 1973 as a result of the embargo by OPEC nations, the predictions of *The Limits to Growth* were confirmed, or so it seemed. It appeared that we were running out of our most important natural resources. *The Limits to Growth* became an international best seller, with more than ten million copies sold.

In the nearly twenty-five years since the publication of the *The Limits to Growth*, however, the fears have proved groundless. Oil is plentiful and cheap. The world did not run out of gold by 1981, or zinc by 1990, or petroleum by 1992, as the book predicted.[7] Food supplies have not diminished. Instead, they have grown faster than world population has.[8] Air pollution levels in Canada and the United States have decreased.[9] Water pollution has also dropped significantly. Population growth is not out of control. Instead, the rate of growth has been decreasing since the mid-1960s, and world population is expected to level off by the end of the next century.[10] (See chapters 6, 7, 12, and 16.)

Nor has economic growth severely harmed the environment. Rather, it has provided the wealth to correct the problems that accompany growth. With higher living standards, people want to protect the environment and are more willing and more able to pay the costs.[11] But despite the spectacular inaccuracy of the doomsday predictions in *The Limits to Growth,* the notion that the world is poised on the edge of disaster is still being taught in our schools.

Global 2000

The message of *The Limits to Growth* resurfaced in 1980 with the US federal government's stamp of approval. *Global 2000,* a 760-page book, was compiled by the departments of State, Interior, Energy, and Agriculture and nine other government agencies in the Carter administration.[12] Over one million copies were distributed. In its opening paragraphs, *Global 2000* echoed the conclusions of the Club of Rome:

> If present trends continue, the world in 2000 will be more crowded, more polluted, less stable ecologically, and more vulnerable to disruption than the world we live in now. Serious stresses involving population, resources, and the environment are clearly visible ahead. Despite greater material output, the world's people will be poorer in many ways than they are today.
>
> For hundreds of millions of the desperately poor, the outlook for food and other necessities of life will be no better. For many it will be worse. Barring revolutionary advances in technology, life for most people on earth will be more precarious in 2000 than it is now—unless the nations of the world act decisively to alter current trends.[13]

The news media covered the report uncritically. *Time's* story was headlined "Toward a Troubled 21st Century: A Presidential Panel Finds the Global Outlook Extremely Bleak."[14] *Newsweek's* article was titled "A Grim Year 2000."[15]

Four years later, 24 respected scholars challenged the report. *The Resourceful Earth: A Response to Global 2000*[16] was written by experts such as D. Gale Johnson, a prominent agricultural economist at the University of Chicago, Marion Clawson, a longtime natural resource scholar at Resources for the Future, and H. E. Landsberg, professor emeritus at the Institute for Fluid Dynamics and Applied Mathematics at the University of Maryland. Some of their conclusions were:

* life expectancy has been rising rapidly throughout the world, a sign of demographic, scientific, and economic success;

* the birth rate in less developed countries has been falling substantially during the past two decades, from 2.2 percent yearly in 1964 to 1.75 percent in 1982-3;

* many people are still hungry, but the food supply has been improving since at least World War II;

* trends in world forests are not worrying, though in some places deforestation is troubling;

* there is no statistical evidence for rapid loss of species in the last two decades;

* the climate does not show signs of unusual and threatening changes; and

* mineral resources are becoming less, rather than more, scarce.[17]

These rebuttals received little media coverage. The authors of *The Resourceful Earth*, though eminent, were out of step with the times, and the optimistic message was not considered newsworthy.

Scaring the Rest of Us

The pattern of exaggeration that took form in the 1970s and 1980s is still with us today. Let us look more carefully at the groups that promote these claims.

* Environmental groups are often portrayed as good guys who are battling evil big business. But environmental organizations have become big businesses themselves.

* The Canadian Wildlife Federation, the largest conservation organization in the country, had 500,000 members and supporters and a budget of $7 million in 1996.[18]

* Greenpeace Canada, the best-known environmental group in the nation, had 187,000 members in 1997[19] and a budget of $5.57 million in 1995.[20]

* The World Wildlife Fund Canada, with over 55,000 members, had a budget of $10.7 million in 1996. The WWF is the largest international conservation organization in the world, with over five million members and offices in seventy countries worldwide.[21]

The budgets of the twelve most prominent environmental organizations in the United States added up to $569.6 million, according to the editors of *Outside Magazine*. There are more than 1800 environmental organizations at the national, provincial, and local level throughout Canada,[22] and even more in the United States.

However, these organizations are not as healthy as these numbers suggest. By the early 1990s, membership and revenues for several big environmental groups were stagnant or falling. In the United States, the Wilderness Society's members fell by 3 percent in 1993 and by 17.8 percent in 1994, for example, while membership numbers leveled off for Audubon and the Natural Resources Defense Council.[23] In 1997, partially in response to a decline in membership from one million to 400,000 in a matter of years, Greenpeace USA reduced its infrastructure from 11 nationwide offices employing over 400 people, to one permanent office staffed by 65.[24] To stay strong, these organizations must keep up the drumbeat of impending disaster.

* "In 1998, the <u>relentless assault</u> on Canada's wild animals and wild places continues ..." opens a fund-raising letter from the World Wildlife Fund. "Every 15 seconds, an acre of Canada's wilderness is lost to logging, roads, sub-divisions and commercial development" (underlining in the original).[25]

* The World Wildlife Fund Canada further says that "every hour, at least 100 hectares of Canada's wilderness disappear—lost to logging, mining, hydroelectric dams and urbanization. If the current pace continues, we place our country's greatest asset at risk."[26]

* "When the logging industries in Canada, and in Melanesia, Russia and Brazil, continued to chop down the dwindling forests, the lungs of the entire planet became even more damaged and frail," warns a Greenpeace Canada mail-out.[27]

* "If nothing is done by us, our descendants will have few options," says a letter from the U.S. National Audubon Society. "We can project with some accuracy the eventual end of the natural world as we know it. That is, no trees. No wildlife. Climate changes so radical the tropics have migrated to the North Pole."[28]

The Audubon Society illustrates the changes in the environmental movement. Audubon still maintains an extensive system of bird and wildlife refuges but in recent years has expanded its reach to such issues as toxic waste and population control.

The society long ago terminated its Junior Audubon Clubs, which had taught children about birds. In 1990, it stopped publishing its *Wildlife Report*, a series of books on the condition of animal species and, a few years later, folded its bird magazine, *American Birds*.[29]

In 1991, Peter Berle, then Audubon's president, even tried to change the society's logo. The logo bore a picture of the great egret, a stately bird that Audubon had saved from extinction. Berle considered Audubon's "bird" image as stodgy, explained the *New York Times*, and he wanted people to know that Audubon was much more than birds.[30] (He replaced the egret with a blue flag.) His action caused an uproar, especially among longtime members, and he was forced to restore the great egret, although less prominently.

Newer environmental organizations do almost nothing except litigate and lobby. The Sierra Club Legal Defense Fund, for example, was created as an offshoot of the Sierra Club in 1971 after the Club stopped Disney Corporation from building a resort in California's Mineral King Valley. The Fund now employs forty lawyers who sue over issues ranging from endangered species to chemicals.[31]

Litigation is financially rewarding. Environmental groups in the United States can be compensated by taxpayers for legal costs when they sue the federal government. The Sierra Club Legal Defense Fund has received $1.8 million in tax dollars for its litigation on the spotted owl.[32]

Friends in High Places

Environmental groups can't maintain the barrage of predictions of disaster all alone. Other individuals and groups also spread the idea that calamity is around the corner.

Scientists as Activists

Paul Ehrlich of Stanford University has made a career out of predicting worldwide famine due to overpopulation. In 1968 he published *The Population Bomb*, in which he said that "massive famines" were likely in the 1970s.[33] These did not occur, but, undaunted, in 1990 he and his wife published *The Population Explosion*, predicting that "human numbers are on a collision course with massive famines."[34]

When the *New York Times* reported on Ehrlich's disagreement with a more optimistic social scientist, Julian Simon, he said, "Julian Simon is like the guy who jumps off the Empire State Building and says how great things are going so far as he passes the 10th floor."[35]

E.O. Wilson of Harvard University is trying to arouse public alarm over the loss of biodiversity. "Vast numbers of species are apparently vanishing before they can be discovered and named," he wrote in the *New York Times*. He went on to predict that 50 percent of all rain forest species may be lost by the middle of the next century.[36] Yet these figures (as we will see in Chapter 11) are guesses at best.

These scientists have the respect of the press and the public, but their claims are rarely based on their scientific knowledge. Stephen Schneider, a vocal proponent of the view that global warming will be severe, describes the dilemma that activist-scientists face. He told *Discover* magazine:

> On the one hand, as scientists, we are ethically bound to the scientific method, in effect promising to tell the truth, the whole truth, and nothing but ... On the other hand, we are not just scientists, but human beings as well. And like most people we'd like to see the world a better place ... To do that we need to get some broad-based support, to capture the public's imagination. That, of course, entails getting loads of media coverage. So we have to offer up scary scenarios, make simplified, dramatic statements,

and make little mention of any doubts we might have ... Each of us has to decide what the right balance is between being effective and being honest. I hope that means being both.[37]

Schneider's candor is refreshing, but it should warn us that we hear more from scientists than the plain facts.

The Media: Advocates and Proud of It

Time magazine science editor Charles Alexander stated publicly at a conference: "I would freely admit that on this issue [environmentalism] we have crossed the boundary from news reporting to advocacy."[38] A Cable News Network producer, Barbara Pyle, has said: "I switched from being an 'objective journalist' to an advocate in July 1980." On this date, she read the *Global 2000* report.[39]

Not all reporters have deliberately abandoned objectivity. But then it isn't necessary, since so many journalists share the views of environmentalists. In their book *The Media Elite*, Robert Lichter and his associates found that journalists reporting on nuclear power were far more "antinuclear" than scientists, including those who specialized in energy. The journalists quoted antinuclear sources far more than those who favored nuclear power.[40]

Stories about crises sell newspapers and push up television ratings. As one science reporter has observed, no one is likely to see a headline reading "Earth Not Destroyed; Billions Don't Die."[41]

Business: Out of Its Element

The direct cost of environmental legislation is often borne by businesses. But business opposition to environmental regulations is generally seen as being merely self-interested, and therefore is given little credibility. Thus, businesses can do little to challenge the apocalyptic claims of environmental activists. As a result, business lobbyists sometimes join rather than fight, hoping to wrest special advantages for their companies.

As the U.S. Clear Air Act of 1970 took shape, for example, some American auto manufacturers supported a provision that eliminated the air-cooled engine. By barring this technology, the law contributed to the disappearance of the Volkswagen "bug."[42]

In 1977, the U.S. Clean Air Act required power plants to control sulfur dioxide emissions. But rather than allow these utilities to use whatever method they wanted to reduce this pollution, the law required them to use special coal "scrubbers" to remove the sulfur dioxide. Why?

Eastern U.S. coal companies and their unions had protected their market. Without the law, many utilities would have bought low-sulfur western coal, and the eastern companies would have lost money. The results of this policy were much higher costs and probably dirtier air.[43]

The Environmentalists' Agenda

"I know social scientists who remind me that people are part of nature, but it isn't true,"[44] wrote National Park Service biologist David M. Graber. Instead, human beings are a "cancer," said Graber. "Until such time as Homo sapiens should decide to rejoin nature, some of us can only hope for the right virus to come along."

Graber's view of humanity diverges sharply from that of most people. In fact, many members of environmental groups would be amazed at such statements. Yet influential environmental advocates hold such views, and they influence what is taught in our schools. Parents should be aware of the following themes:

Private Property: Just a "Sacred Cow"

Many environmentalists consider private ownership to be the enemy of the environment. A newsletter of the Greater Yellowstone Coalition, an environmental group based in Montana, called private land rights a "sacred cow."[45] Jon Roush, president of the U.S. Wilderness Society, wrote in a letter to the *New York Times*: "Too many of us are still locked in that mindset that says the way to make money off a piece of land is to mine it, drill it or log it."[46] He recommended that trees be preserved instead. (That philosophy did not prevent him from selling 400,000 board feet of timber from his Montana ranch.)

As we will discuss later, the *absence* of private ownership rights explains many environmental problems. Publicly owned land is often littered and abused because there is no owner to insist on protection. Lakes are overfished and wildlife hunted to the point of extinction when there is no owner committed to maintaining the resource. Private ownership, in contrast, often encourages stewardship because the owner benefits from increasing the value of property, and suffers from neglecting it.

The Fragility of the Earth

Environmentalists love to illustrate the fragile nature of the earth.

* Paul Ehrlich, in an analogy frequently repeated in textbooks, has compared the Earth's ecology to the interconnected systems of an airplane. In his view, the organisms in an ecosystem are like the bolts which hold an airplane together. While the airplane may stay aloft in spite of the loss of a few bolts, after a point the plane will be so weakened that the loss of one more bolt will cause it to plunge from the sky. In a similar way, the analogy goes, the loss of too many species could damage an ecosystem to the point where it can no longer function.[47]

* One children's book, *A Great Round Wonder*, tells readers: "Imagine that the Earth is one gigantic spider web, where every string is connected to the rest. If you cut one string, no one may notice. If you cut several strings, the web will start to droop. And if you keep cutting, one day you will cut one string too many. Then the web will fall apart completely."[48]

❋ A science experiment for children suggests that they adopt an egg for the day. They are to carry it around with them, and try to bring it back to their next class undamaged. "The world is like an egg," they are told. "The world houses life, just as an egg can contain a baby chicken. The world sustains life, just as we can obtain nourishment from an egg. The world is strong, just as an egg's shell is tough enough to protect a developing chick. But the world is also fragile, just as a forceful blow will crack an egg's shell and cause its contents to spill out."[49]

These are effective images, but effective at what? —at terrifying our children about the imminent destruction of the Earth. As we will see, the Earth is in better shape than the books would have us think.

Only the Government Can Do It

Environmentalists often think that only government action can solve a crisis. The massive environmental damage caused by government central planning in socialist societies has not changed this view. To many, the Soviet Union and Eastern Europe are simply considered "different."

Western democratic governments are often no better. Governmental stewardship of resources is as bad as, or worse than, abuse by the private sector. In spite of decades of government management, the Atlantic cod fishery has been closed, and the Pacific salmon industry in Canada is in severe decline.

While profit-making businesses can cause pollution, over time private ownership discourages pollution. Since pollution wastes raw materials, companies can save money if they can use raw materials more efficiently and waste less. Competition spurs privately owned companies constantly to discover ways to produce more goods with less energy and fewer raw materials.

Economist Mikhail Bernstam has estimated that firms in socialist economies discharged more than twice as much air pollution as firms in Western market economies did[50] and used nearly three times as much energy to produce the same amount of goods.[51]

An Idyllic and Pastoral Past

Many environmentalists disparage modern life and romanticize the past. Margaret Mead, the famous anthropologist, once said, "Not war, but a plethora of man-made things . . . is threatening to strangle us, suffocate us, bury us, in the debris and by-products of our technologically inventive and irresponsible age."[52]

Herman Daly writes about the "corrosive effects of economic growth on community and on moral standards" and claims that "we have overshot the optimal scale of the human economy."[53] The implication is that we should return to a more idyllic past.

While many of us sometimes long for a simpler life, we must recognize that living in simple societies was precarious, due to disease, infection, spoiled food, and frequent famines. In the past, pollution was severe. In the fourteenth century, a Londoner was executed for burning sea coal, which had been outlawed to reduce smoke pollution. The Thames River was so clogged with human and animal waste that ships could hardly pass. In the early twentieth century, urban dwellers welcomed the automobile because it eliminated the horse manure that cluttered city streets.[54]

In their adulation of the past, environmentalists often assume that Native American tribes "walked quietly on the Earth." But many used fire extensively, creating prairie grasslands to attract buffalo, moose, and elk.[55] Even before they had horses and guns, Native Americans killed vast numbers of buffalo by herding them onto cliffs, where they plunged to their deaths.[56]

Nature, Not God

The grandeur of nature often takes the place of the grandeur of God. "It is not in God's house that I feel his presence most—it is in his outdoors, on some sun-warmed slope of pine needles or by the surf," writes Bill McKibben.[57] Joseph Sax describes his fellow environmentalists as "secular prophets, preaching a message of secular salvation." [58]

At times, the deification of nature leads to despising human beings. Stephanie Mills, author of *Whatever Happened to Ecology?* speaks of "debased human protoplasm."[59] E. O. Wilson says that it is a "misfortune" that a "carnivore primate and not some more benign form of animal" should now control the Earth.[60]

In sum, while the environmental movement has brought awareness of issues, it has brought with it some troubling baggage—values that are at odds with those held by most people. Exploring that conflict is beyond the purposes of this book, but parents, teachers, and students should be alert to the messages.

Notes

1 John McCormick, *The Global Environmental Movement* (London: Belhaven Press, 1989), 5.
2 Rachel Carson, *Silent Spring* (Boston: Houghton Mifflin, 1962).
3 Carson, 1–3.
4 Carson, 189.
5 Donella H. Meadows et al., *The Limits to Growth: A Report for the Club of Rome's Project on the Predicament of Mankind* (New York: Universe Books, 1972).
6 Meadows et al., 23.
7 Meadows et al., 56–9.
8 Dennis Avery, *Global Food Progress 1991: A Report From the Hudson Institute's Center for Global Food Issues* (Indianapolis: Hudson Institute, 1991), 12.
9 Council on Environmental Quality, *21st Annual Report* (Washington, DC: U.S. Government Printing Office, 1991), 311.
10 Avery, 12, 72.

11 See, for example, Gene Grossman and Alan Krueger, *Environmental Impacts of a North American Free Trade Agreement*, Working Paper No. 3914, National Bureau of Economic Research, Cambridge, MA, November 1991.

12 *Global 2000 Report to the President*, Vols. I, II, and III (Washington, DC: U.S. Government Printing Office, 1980).

13 *Global 2000 Report to the President*, Vol. I, 1.

14 "Toward a Troubled 21st Century: A Presidential Panel Finds the Global Outlook Extremely Bleak," *Time*, August 4, 1980, 54.

15 "A Grim Year 2000," *Newsweek*, August 4, 1980, 38.

16 Julian L. Simon and Herman Kahn, eds., *The Resourceful Earth: A Response to Global 2000* (New York: Basil Blackwell, 1984).

17 Simon and Kahn, 2-3.

18 Personal conversation between the General Manager of the Canadian Wildlife Federation and Liv Fredricksen.

19 Personal conversation between a Greenpeace member and Liv Fredricksen.

20 Greenpeace, *Annual Review 1995*, 11.

21 World Wildlife Fund Canada, *1996 Annual Review*, 22.

22 Adrienne Mason, *The Green Classroom* (Markham, ON: Pembroke, 1991), 29.

23 Christopher Boerner and Jennifer Chilton Kallery, *Restructuring Environmental Big Business* (St. Louis: Center for the Study of American Business, January 1995), 9, 30.

24 Lacey Phillabaum, "Greenpeace: The Mother Ship Takes a Blow" in *EarthFirst—The Radical Environmental Journal*, September-October 1997, 6.

25 World Wildlife Fund Canada, Fund-raising letter.

26 World Wildlife Fund Canada, *1996 Annual Review*, 4.

27 Greenpeace Canada, *1995 Annual Review*, 2.

28 Letter from Jan Beyea, a scientist for the National Audubon Society, sent in early 1994.

29 R. J. Smith, *No Regrets for Great Egrets* (PERC, Bozeman, MT, unpublished paper, 1995).

30 Anne Raver, "Old Environmental Group Seeks Tough New Image," the *New York Times*, June 9, 1991, A1.

31 Jonathan Adler, *Environmentalism at the Crossroads: Green Activism in America* (Washington, DC: Capital Research Center, 1995), 42.

32 Adler, 45.

33 Paul Ehrlich, *The Population Bomb* (Sierra Club, 1969), 36–37.

34 Paul R. Ehrlich and Anne H. Ehrlich, *The Population Explosion* (New York: Simon and Schuster, 1990), 17.

35 John Tierney, "Betting on the Planet," *New York Times Magazine*, December 2, 1990, 81.

36 Edward O. Wilson, "Is Humanity Suicidal?" *New York Times Magazine*, May 30, 1993, 24-29.

37 Jonathan Schell, "Our Fragile Earth," *Discover*, October 1989, 47.

38 David Brooks, "Journalists and Others for Saving the Planet," *Wall Street Journal*, October 5, 1989, A20.

39 Ronald Bailey, *Eco-Scam: The False Prophets of Ecological Apocalypse* (New York: St. Martin's Press, 1993), 169.

40 S. Robert Lichter, Stanley Rothman, and Linda S. Lichter, *The Media Elite* (Bethesda, MD: Adler & Adler, 1986), 166–219.

41 Michael Fumento, *Science Under Siege: Balancing Technology and the Environment* (New York: William Morrow and Company, 1993), 342.

42 Michael S. Greve and Fred L. Smith, Jr., eds., *Environmental Politics: Public Costs, Private Rewards* (New York: Praeger, 1992), 11.

43 Greve and Smith, 8.

44 David M. Graber, "Mother Nature as a Hothouse Flower," *Los Angeles Times Book Review*, October 22, 1989, 9.

45 *Greater Yellowstone Report* (Bozeman, MT: Greater Yellowstone Coalition), Summer 1989.

46 Letter to the Editor, *The New York Times,* January 7, 1996, 18.

47 Frank Baumann et al., *Science Probe 8* (Toronto: John Wiley and Sons Canada, 2nd ed., 1993), 463.

48 Shelley Tanaka, *A Great Round Wonder: My Book of the World* (Toronto, ON: Douglas and McIntyre, 1993), 46.

49 Susan V. Bosak, *Science Is... Second Edition* (Co-published Richmond Hill, ON/Markham, ON: Scholastic Canada/The Communication Project, 1991), 390.

50 Mikhail S. Bernstam, *The Wealth of Nations and the Environment* (London: Institute of Economic Affairs, 1991), 22.

51 Bernstam, 24.

52 Quoted in National Center for Policy Analysis, *Progressive Environmentalism: A Pro-Human, Pro-Free Enterprise Agenda for Change,* Task Force Report, April 1991, 3.

53 Herman E. Daly, "Consumption and the Environment," *Report from the Institute for Philosophy and Public Policy* (College Park, MD: University of Maryland School of Public Affairs), Fall 1995, 4–9.

54 William J. Baumol and Wallace E. Oates, "Long-Run Trends in Environmental Quality," *The State of Humanity*, ed Julian L. Simon (Cambridge, MA: Blackwell, 1995), 442–448.

55 Alston Chase, *Playing God in Yellowstone: The Destruction of America's First National Park* (Boston: Atlantic Monthly Press, 1986), 92–115.

56 John Canfield Ewers, *The Horse in Blackfoot Culture* (Washington, DC: Smithsonian Institution, 1980), 170.

57 Bill McKibben, *The End of Nature* (New York: Anchor, 1989), 71.

58 Joseph Sax, *Mountains without Handrails: Reflections on the National Parks* (Ann Arbor, MI: University of Michigan Press, 1980), 104.

59 Stephanie Mills, *Whatever Happened to Ecology?* (San Francisco, CA: Sierra Club Books, 1989), 106.

60 Wilson, 24.

Chapter 4

At Odds with Science

Don't be misled by titles like *Environmental Science* or *Earth Science*. Despite their names, these books may not be teaching science at all. Science sets out to discover what "is." Many environmental texts skip past the "what is" to arrive at the "ought to be."

For example, scientists don't know whether greenhouse gases are causing the Earth to get warmer. The acid rain scare has turned out to be exaggerated. Garbage disposal is not a crisis. But the environmental section of the teaching guide *Science Is...* encourages children to change their behaviour anyway: "If you've decided to do a few little things–like walking or biking instead of taking a car, or turning off the lights when you don't need them, or recycling—then you're already helping to stop the greenhouse effect, acid rain, energy waste, and landfill overflow."[1]

While global warming is treated as a fact in classrooms, scientists themselves are still exploring it as a question. They are using the existing body of scientific knowledge, from geology to atmospheric chemistry, to figure it out. Bit by bit, week by week, writing in specialized journals, their latest findings accumulate.

Scientists tell us, for example, that temperature measurements taken from satellites show no change in global temperatures in recent years, but bore holes (dug deep into the ground) in Canada and the United States show signs of warming temperatures over the past century. Another study suggests that air pollution might be cooling the Earth, and another examines how ocean currents affect temperatures. So, while it is too early to tell if the greenhouse effect will cause noticeable warming, gradually the pieces of the puzzle are being put together.

Unfortunately, this discovery process is largely neglected in the schools when environmental issues are discussed. Reading a typical textbook would lead you to believe that on most environmental issues the science is settled. But it is not.

* Children learn that one hundred species of plants and animals may be going extinct each day. In fact, no one even knows how may species there are now, and the estimates are guesses, partly based on studies of how many species disappear when the habitats of small islands are destroyed.

* Organic farming is considered safe because it doesn't use pesticides. But the fruits and vegetables we eat have many more *natural* carcinogens than are ever added through pesticides.

* Overpopulation is often pegged as the root of environmental problems. Yet economic studies have failed to show that rapid population growth causes economic problems or leads to depletion of natural resources.

The Scientific Method

To understand where environmental science veers from science, we need to recognize that over the years scientists have developed a process for learning what "is". This is the scientific method, and it works like this.

Scientists start by being curious about something. To use a simple example, suppose that they want to know the cause of fire. Gradually, they develop a hypothesis, a statement about the physical world that can be tested. For example, a scientist might develop a hypothesis about one piece of the puzzle: The scientist might propose that fire needs oxygen to burn.

To test hypotheses, scientists devise experiments. The scientist studying fire and oxygen might use three closed chambers. In each, the scientist might start a fire and then replace the air in each chamber with a different gas: in the first, carbon dioxide; in the second, nitrogen; and in the third, oxygen.

The scientist then observes the results. The fires in the chambers with carbon dioxide and nitrogen go out, but the fire in the oxygen chamber continues to burn. The experiment supports the hypothesis that fire needs oxygen to burn.

Scientists document their experiments and results precisely and submit their findings to scientific journals. If other scientists (their professional peers) find a paper to be of high caliber, it is published and becomes part of the scientific literature. More scientists can then review the experiments and perhaps repeat them.

If an experiment is repeated many times and produces the same results, scientists have established a scientific fact. The accumulation of many scientific facts leads to the development of a theory. This is a statement about the physical world that is supported by scientific experiments and other forms of verification but does not have sufficient evidence to establish it as a scientific law.

Ultimately, a theory may lead to the recognition of a scientific law. Sir Isaac Newton, the famous seventeenth century British scientist, for example, first stated the theory of gravity. However, only after many experiments did other scientists agree with Newton and consider the theory a scientific law.

The World As Laboratory

Of course, real science is rarely as simple or straightforward as this outline suggests. For one thing, not all scientific questions are testable in carefully controlled laboratory experiments. So scientists have developed techniques to discover facts "in the field." While these techniques are not as good as a controlled experiment, they can, when used rigorously, lead to greater understanding.

Some years ago people began to notice that trees in Western Europe, including England, were dying. Many people thought that the cause was "acid rain" (excessive sulfur dioxide and nitrogen oxides in the atmosphere). When scientists examined the forests more closely, however, they found that acid rain couldn't explain very much of the damage. Forests are affected by many factors—different kinds of pollution, cold weather, poor management, and insects. They concluded that abnormal weather had caused some damage. More important, they found that the diseased trees were exceptions. European forests were, in general, fairly healthy. The amount of wood they produced each year was rising steadily.[2] (We will look more carefully at acid rain in Chapter 15.)

In the mid-1980s, scientists developed a theory that chlorine from CFCs was reducing ozone in the upper atmosphere over the Antarctic. To test this theory, NASA scientists made expeditions into the stratosphere over the Antarctic in specially fitted high-flying airplanes. There they measured the levels of ozone and other chemicals. These expeditions supported the theory that chlorine from CFCs is depleting ozone, but they also supported the view that other factors, such as cold polar temperatures and the winds known as the polar vortex, affect ozone levels, too.[3] (We will look at ozone more closely in Chapter 14.)

Why Science Isn't Easy

Other factors make environmental science difficult—but stimulating.

Cause and Effect or Just Correlation?

Scientists want to understand what causes things to happen. Often it is possible to detect two things happening together, but it is difficult to know if one caused the other. The two events may be "correlated" but not linked by "cause and effect."

Over the past hundred years, the average global temperatures rose about half a degree centigrade. Over the same period, the amount of carbon dioxide in the atmosphere went up about 25 percent. Did the carbon dioxide cause the warming? Did the warming cause the rise in CO_2? Or did the carbon dioxide and temperatures just happen to go up at the same time? Scientists are still grappling with this question, as we shall see in Chapter 13.

Scientists have also looked back at the distant record, hundreds of thousands of years ago, by drilling deep holes in the ice. The ancient ice contains the carbon dioxide that was present in the atmosphere at that time, long before any greenhouse gases were unleashed by humans. Scientists can also estimate past temperatures from this ice. Again, there is a correlation between carbon dioxide levels and temperature. But in many cases the carbon dioxide came *after* the warming![4]

Computers—Shedding Light but Also Confusion

One way to cope with the complexity of the real world is to use computers. Scientists enter vast amounts of data about the real world and use sophisticated mathematical programs to simulate the complexity of weather and climate.

Many global warming predictions are based on models that attempt to simulate the workings of the entire Earth's atmosphere. This is an enormous task, since thousands of factors, from ocean currents to water vapor, influence the Earth's atmospheric and weather conditions. But how? Do clouds cool the Earth or warm it? They can do both. If greenhouse gases lead to an increase in clouds (as they might), the clouds could either warm or cool the Earth. Predictions are thus rather shaky.

Furthermore, simply because the Earth is so large, computer models treat large stretches of the Earth as if they were the same. For example, some computer models can't distinguish between forest and desert.[5] And one prominent scientist, Richard Lindzen, points out that the computer models cannot even successfully calculate the present average global temperature—let alone predict the temperature of the atmosphere 10 or 20 years from now.[6]

Theories in Conflict

For every scientific theory, usually several others exist that conflict with it. Scientists are constantly refining their theories in light of increased knowledge and experience.

For example, physics was full of uncertainty about fundamental theories and laws for more than half a century. When Marie Curie, late in the nineteenth century, observed that a rock containing the element radium (supposedly, inert matter) could create an image on a sealed photographic plate, she realized that matter was more complex than scientists had thought. At the time, physicists believed that matter only reacted at the chemical level, not at the atomic level. But, in fact, alpha particles from the radioactive radium had traveled through the protective cover and exposed the photographic plate.

The existing scientific theories could not explain what had happened, so Curie set out to discover the answer. She and her husband

Pierre proposed a mysterious source of energy within the atoms. Others, however, identified the alpha particle as the nucleus of the helium atom. And in 1905 Albert Einstein explained the source of the apparently enormous energy with his famous equation $E = mc^2$. It took about thirty more years to establish the theory firmly, and it led to the development of the atomic bomb.

Continuing the Search for Truth

When properly conducted, scientists' search for truth is governed by strict rules of conduct and ethics. Scientists make hypotheses, test them, and submit their findings for review and replication by other scientists. These scientific debates, while lively, are conducted free from political interference.

Environmental issues, however, are different. There is political interference. In 1992, U.S. Vice President Al Gore (then Senator) concluded that global warming was a fact. He wrote in his book *Earth in the Balance* that paying too much attention to the doubters "undermines the effort to build a solid base of public support for the difficult actions we must soon take."[7] His message: Agree with him or be quiet. Because of his prominence, American scientists had to listen, and Canadian scientists tended to follow suit.

But neither Al Gore nor any other politician is going to quash the scientific method. Ultimately, science, not politics, will answer the *scientific* questions surrounding global warming, species extinction, and other environmental issues.

Several years ago, Robert Balling of Arizona State University pointed out that knowledge about global warming was accelerating rapidly. Nearly half of all the major scientific articles or books about global warming since 1800 had been published in 1989 and 1990! He also noted that two scientists had concluded that if global warming was actually occurring, even a ten-year delay in reducing greenhouse gases would have a minuscule effect on future temperature (because the effect would occur so slowly). "We are learning more about the greenhouse effect every week, and we are certain to learn a great deal more in the immediate future," he wrote.[8] The sad part is that children aren't likely to obtain much of this knowledge in their classrooms.

Notes

1 Susan V. Bosak, *Science Is* (Co-published: Richmond Hill, ON/ Markham, ON: Scholastic Canada/The Communication Project, 2nd ed., 1991), 388.

2 National Acid Precipitation Assessment Program, *1992 Report to Congress*, Washington, DC, June 1993. Also K. Mellanby, ed., *Air Pollution, Acid Rain and the Environment* (Elsevier Applied Science Publishers for the Watt Committee on Energy).

3 Pamela S. Zurer, "Antarctic Ozone Hole: Complex Picture Emerges," *Chemical Engineering News*, November 2, 1987, 22–26.

4 Andrew Solow, "Is There a Global Warming Problem?" in *Global Warming: Economic Policy Responses*, ed. by Rudiger Dornbusch and James M. Poterba (Cambridge, MA: The MIT Press, 1991), 18.

5 Robert Jastrow, William A. Nierenberg, and Frederick Seitz, "An Overview," *Scientific Perspectives on the Greenhouse Problem* (Ottawa, IL: Jameson Books, Inc., 1990), 11.

6 Richard S. Lindzen, "Global Warming: The Origin and Nature of the Alleged Scientific Consensus," *Regulation*, Spring 1992, 89.

7 Al Gore, *Earth in the Balance: Ecology and the Human Spirit* (Boston: Houghton Mifflin Company, 1992), 39.

8 Robert C. Balling, Jr., *The Heated Debate: Greenhouse Predictions Versus Climate Reality* (San Francisco: Pacific Research Institute), 141–42.

Chapter 5

What Are the Costs?

Throughout North America, many people are trying to preserve the beauty of the land and the diversity of wildlife. Jane's friend David Cameron, who used to be a biology professor at Montana State University, is also a third-generation rancher. In addition to raising cattle and sheep, his family has a long tradition of protecting wildlife. Elk, deer, mountain lions, and bears thrive on his ranch.

A few years ago Dave decided to improve the wildlife in the area by bringing back the grayling, a native Montana fish that disappeared from nearby streams many years ago. Dave consulted with specialists and found a suitable place on the ranch to reintroduce the fish.

But then he learned that the U.S. Fish and Wildlife Service was considering listing the Montana grayling as an endangered species. Almost instantly, he changed his mind.

Once Dave had an endangered fish on his property, federal agents could prevent him from using his pastures for grazing. They could simply claim that his cattle would pollute the stream or otherwise harm the endangered fish. "I sadly bowed out," he says.[1]

Textbooks routinely support the U.S. Endangered Species Act and blithely recommend that Canada adopt a similar policy. Because the authors have little or no grounding in economics, they don't recognize that its severe penalties may have an effect exactly the opposite of its intention.

Without an understanding of economic principles, texts don't tell "the rest of the story." Here are a few more examples.

Ban CFCs

On January 1, 1996, production of chemicals known as CFCs became illegal in Canada. (Freon is the best-known of these chemicals.) The Montreal Protocol, an agreement by thirty-one nations to phase out the chemicals, had taken effect.

The Montreal Protocol was "one of the most significant environmental agreements ever attempted," says Ranger Rick's *Nature Scope*,[2] and other materials praise the agreement just as highly. But the textbooks leave out some important information. They don't tell children that:

* it now costs hundreds of dollars to have an auto air conditioner fixed so that it can use the new substitutes;

* the ban makes all kinds of cooling (not just air conditioning) more expensive, making Third World children more likely to die of infectious diseases because it will be more difficult to keep vaccines cold;[3]

* by raising the price of refrigeration, the ban will cause more people to get sick from food poisoning; and

* there is now a black market in illegally imported CFCs in the United States. "Law enforcement officials say the refrigerant has become the most lucrative contraband after illicit drugs," reported the *New York Times*.[4]

Recycle or Else

Recycling, too, is universally supported by environmental textbooks. But the textbooks leave out some facts.

* In Northern Ontario, a sparsely populated region, curbside recycling led to mountains of glass. No one had an economic incentive to buy the glass or even haul it away.[5]

* Recycling programs require the use of special trucks in addition to regular garbage trucks to pick up the separated materials and these extra trucks contribute to traffic congestion and air pollution.[6]

* University of Victoria chemist Martin Hocking has calculated that a ceramic mug must be used 1,000 times before it is as environmentally benign as a polystyrene cup.[7]

* Recycling paper doesn't save trees. If recycling paper increased dramatically, people who now grow trees for paper pulp would plant *fewer* trees.[8]

Don't Drive; Use Mass Transit

And then there is the automobile. Textbooks tell students that it is the bane of Americans' existence. Stop riding in a car, they say, and lobby for more mass transit. But that's not the whole story.

* People want to drive cars because they provide door-to-door convenience, especially for transporting young children.

* You can force people to pay for mass transit but you can't make them use it. Even in Vancouver, British Columbia, which has an

award-winning, tax-supported transit system, only 35.4 percent of commuters use transit to and from downtown.[9]

❀ The advent of the automobile in the early twentieth century brought enormous benefits. Farmland returned to forest because we didn't need so many fields for hay. City streets became cleaner without all that manure.

Yes, We Have Some Pollution

The textbooks fail to recognize that people respond to rewards and penalties. Environmental policies change the rewards and penalties, so people's behavior changes, sometimes dramatically.

The texts also fail to help children understand why we have pollution problems in the first place. Yes, some companies and individuals pollute. They do so because it's sometimes cheaper to let waste from their facilities enter the air or stream than to clean it up. But the picture is not entirely grim. Pollution is down:

❀ Between 1980 and 1993, airborne lead went down, on average, by 95 percent in Canada, while particulates declined by over 47 percent.[10]

❀ Since the mid-1970s, levels of pesticides, fertilizers, and chemicals in the Great Lakes have dropped dramatically.[11] For example, PCB levels fell 62 percent between 1980 and 1993.

Laws passed since 1970 have contributed to some of these improvements, but air pollution has been declining for years. Economist Robert Crandall points out that air pollution was declining faster in the United States in the 1960s *before* passage of the Clean Air Act, than it did after passage of the act.[12]

How could this be? Air pollution is often unburned fuel. Profit-making firms have an incentive, over time, to figure out how to use the fuel more efficiently, rather than wasting it by sending it up a smokestack.

Also, even before we had major environmental laws, courts discouraged severe pollution. A person has a right to be free from harm inflicted by others, and that includes injury by pollutants. Polluters can be sued in court by people who were harmed, and in the past they were. Industrial polluters were forced to compensate people whom they harmed with air and water pollution.

This common-law system discouraged pollution, but it was not perfect. When there were many sources of pollution (such as thousands of cars driving every day), the courts declined to blame any single individual or company, and left the correction of the problem up to local governments. In any case, today regulation has largely superseded this approach to pollution control.

"The Tragedy of the Commons"

Have you ever noticed that most homes and yards tend to be clean, while public parks and streets are often dirty? Have you ever wondered why we have no shortage of cats and dogs, while many other species are threatened with extinction?

Economics helps us understand these contrasts. When you or I own something, we have a strong interest in taking care of it. We have much less interest in taking care of things that we don't own or that "everyone" owns.

❧ We can keep our own yard clean and usually we can prevent other people from littering it. But, even if we clean up a public park, we can't keep others from making a mess of it as soon as we are done.

✴ We can take care of our pets. But no one can take care of whales in the ocean. In fact, whale hunters have an incentive to kill whales whenever they see them (rather than let them breed for the future). If they don't, other hunters may come along and kill the whale they avoided.

Many environmental problems, especially in Third World countries, stem from the "tragedy of the commons": when land is owned in common and anyone can use it, there is incentive to restrict use.[13] In the Sahel region of Africa south of the Sahara Desert, a person who built a water well in the past could control access to it. But then colonial and national governments began to build wells in the area. Their intentions were good; they wanted the wells to be available to all.

But people were attracted to the land around the government wells and began to graze more livestock than the area could support. They believed that if they didn't take advantage of the resources immediately, they would lose them to their neighbours. So while there was enough water, there wasn't enough grass. Overgrazing destroyed the soil for future pasture.[14]

When private ownership is adopted, environmental problems often diminish. The World Bank found that:

✴ soil erosion declined when hill farmers in Kenya obtained secure ownership of their land.

✴ when slum-dwellers in Bandung, Indonesia, owned their own homes, their investment in sanitation tripled.

✴ private rights to a portion of the fishing catch reduced over-fishing in New Zealand waters.[15]

Such positive examples are rarely discussed in children's textbooks.

Let the Government Do It?

The message in our children's textbooks is that people should change their behaviour. Since only government has the right to force people to change, the textbooks usually recommend that the government adopt a new law or regulation.

As we have seen, governments can't always bring about the behaviour they want. But there are other reasons as well to question the recommendation "let the government do it": governments are often worse polluters than private industry and government policies actually promote many environmental problems.

❧ Until recently, the Canadian federal government has encouraged the conversion of wetlands and marginal areas to cropland. The Canadian Wheat Board Act allows farmers to produce more grain if they have seeded a great deal of land and then let it lie fallow. Although this was not the intent of the regulation, the farmers have an incentive to cultivate marginal lands instead of leaving them in their natural form.[16]

❧ Public sewage treatment plants are notorious for inadequate facilities. In Britain, where water and sewage have been privatized, the beaches have become cleaner.[17]

❧ Farm support prices also encourage excessive use of pesticides.[18]

❧ Many government managed fisheries in Canada are in decline, including the west coast salmon fishery[19] and the east coast cod fishery, which was closed in 1992.[20]

So, putting your trust in governmental solutions can backfire. That's the "rest of this story."

Is Economic Growth Harmful to the Environment?

Not far from Jane's home in Bozeman, Montana, outside the city limits, you can buy a homesite in a development called Eagle Rock Reserve. But you must buy twenty acres and then use only three acres for your home. The rest of your twenty acres is set aside as wildlife habitat, primarily for elk. These homesites cost a lot of money—$150,000 per homesite—because the land is valuable and could be used to build many more homes. But some people are willing to pay the price. Why?

As people become more wealthy, they are willing to spend their money to preserve open space, wildlife, and environmental amenities. Indeed, many economists argue that one of the best ways to improve the environment is to encourage economic growth, which leads to higher incomes throughout society.

Gene Grossman and Alan Krueger, economists at Princeton University,[21] looked at the national incomes of many countries and at the levels of pollution in those countries. They found that when the average income of a country is very low, economic growth puts stress on the environment, initially increasing pollution. But after a certain level of wealth is reached, the environment begins to improve. At that point, people have a greater interest in protection and they have the financial ability to achieve it.

In addition, economic growth leads to conservation of resources. Resources—energy, rare minerals, and other nonrenewable raw materials—turn out to be more plentifully available than ever. (We will discuss this more in Chapter 7.) For example, the profit motive spurs producers to become more efficient in their use of raw materials. In the 1960s, when most soft-drink cans were made of steel, making one thousand cans required 164 pounds (74.5 kg) of metal. By 1990, the same number of cans could be made from only thirty-five pounds (15.9 kg) of aluminum.[22]

Why? Trying to reduce their costs so that they could stay competitive, producers switched from steel to aluminum, which is lighter, and they made many slight changes that allowed them to use less aluminum. (They continue to try to reduce the use of aluminum.) No government regulation had mandated conservation. The pressures of the marketplace caused the change.

Economics teaches us about human behavior—the "rest of the story." It sheds light on why we have pollution problems and why some proposed solutions won't work. But good economics, like good science, is largely missing in our children's classrooms.

Notes

1 David G.Cameron, Testimony before the Task Force on Private Property Rights of the Committee on Resources of the U.S. House of Representatives, July 17, 1995.

2 Judy Braus, ed., *Pollution: Problems and Solutions* in *Ranger Rick's Nature Scope* series (Washington, DC: National Wildlife Federation, 1990), 70.

3 See Tim Beardsley, "Better Than a Cure," *Scientific American,* January 1995, 88–95.

4 Judy Edelson Halpert, "Freon Smugglers Find Big Market," *New York Times*, April 30, 1994, A1ff.

5 Guy Crittendon, "The Blue Box Conspiracy," *The Next City*, Fall 1997, 34–40.

6 Laura Jones, "Trash in Schools," *Fraser Forum*, March 1997, 23–24.

7 Laura Jones, "Trash in Schools."

8 Jane S. Shaw, "Recycling," *The Fortune Encyclopedia of Economics*, ed. by David R. Henderson (New York: Warner Books, 1993), 459.

9 "Commuters stick with cars, resist transit use." *The Vancouver Sun*, September 8, 1997.

10 Boris DeWiel, Steve Hayward, Laura Jones, and M. Danielle Smith, *Environmental Indicators for Canada and the United*

States." Critical Issues Bulletin (Vancouver: The Fraser Institute, March 1997), 19.

11 E. Calvin Beisner and Julian L. Simon, "Editors' Appendix," in *The State of Humanity,* ed. by Julian L. Simon (Cambridge, MA: Blackwell Publishers, 1995), 469.

12 Robert W. Crandall, *Controlling Industrial Air Pollution: The Economics and Politics of Clean Air* (Washington, DC: The Brookings Institution, 1983), 19.

13 This term was coined by Garrett Hardin in "The Tragedy of the Commons," *Science,* Vol. 162 (1968), 1243–48.

14 J. Dirck Stryker, "Technology, Human Pressure, and Ecology in the Arid and Semi-Arid Tropics," in *Environment and the Poor: Development Strategies for a Common Agenda,* ed. by H. Jeffrey Leonard (New Brunswick, NJ: Transaction Books, 1989), 95.

15 *World Development Report 1992,* 12.

16 DeWiel, *et al.,* 40-41.

17 Elizabeth Brubaker, "Bring Back Our Beaches" in *The Next City,* Summer 1997, Vol 2, Number 4, 32–46.

18 Jane S. Shaw and Richard L. Stroup, 56.

19 Laura Jones and Michael Walker, eds., *Fish or Cut Bait!* (Vancouver: The Fraser Institute, 1997).

20 *Charting a New Course: Towards the Fishery of the Future—Report of the Task Force on Incomes and Adjustment in the Atlantic Fishery* (Ottawa: Minister of Supply and Services Canada, 1993), 21.

21 Gene M. Grossman and Alan B. Krueger, *Environmental Impacts of a North American Free Trade Agreement,* Discussion Paper in Economics, Woodrow Wilson School of Public and International Affairs, Princeton University, Princeton, NJ, February 1992, 5. This paper has been published in *The U.S. Mexico Free Trade Agreement,* ed. by P. Garber (Cambridge, MA: MIT Press, 1993), 13–56.

22 Lynn Scarlett, "Make Your Environment Dirtier—Recycle," *Wall Street Journal,* January 14, 1991.

Chapter 6

World Population: Will Billions Starve?

Herbert London, a professor at New York University, tells how one evening his ten-year-old daughter sat down at the dinner table and announced that she and her family were eating too much. By over-consuming, they deprived starving Cambodians of food, she said. London's daughter had learned at school that "there is a finite world food supply," and that Americans' over-eating means deprivation for others.[1]

Our schools teach children that people are starving because:

* the world's population is growing too fast;

* the world can produce only so much food; and

* the people of the Western nations are consuming too much.

Population Growth Forever?

The typical text begins its section on population showing world population climbing at an alarming rate. It usually includes a graph like this.

Typical Graph of the Increase in World Population

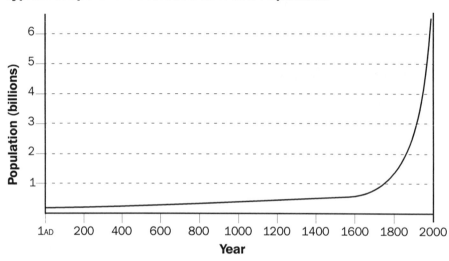

The graph ends around the year 2000, creating a frightening picture of unending growth. The writing supports this image.

The text *Canada Today* says: "The world's population is growing rapidly, and with it grows the demand for food. The greater is the population, the greater is the strain on the world's food supply."[2] Another text, promoting the concept "zero population growth," says: "Like populations of locusts, rabbits, or deer, at some point the human population must stabilize or decline."[3]

What the textbooks fail to show is that the *growth rate* of the world's population peaked in the mid-1960s and is slowing in most nations. They also fail to point out that the world's food supply has grown even faster than population has grown.[4]

In the 1960s, world population was growing at slightly over 2 percent per year, an unprecedented rate, but by the 1990s, the rate had dropped to 1.7 percent. It is expected to drop below 1 percent growth in the 2020s.[5] Thus, although no one knows for sure, some demographers think that by about 2100 world population will level off at between 10 billion and 12 billion people.

A more realistic graph, which extends farther into the future, would look like this.

Realistic Graph of the Increase in World Population

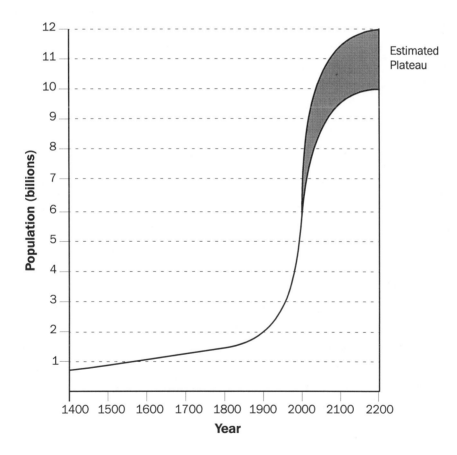

Demographers now think that the rapid growth of population during the twentieth century may be a one-time thing. Certainly, it reflects the dramatic decline in death rates in this century. Improvements in health care, sanitation, and nutrition have resulted in fewer women and children dying in childbirth, more children reaching maturity, and more adults living to old age.

Population levels climbed so rapidly because, until recently, people continued to have as many children as they did in the past, when only a few children in any family were likely to survive. Birth rates have lagged behind the dramatic declines in death rates.

But now, birth rates are going down, too. In Mexico between 1965 and 1987, the birth rate decreased by more than a third. In Asia, the birth rate fell from 2.3 percent in 1970 to 1.9 percent in 1990. Only in Africa did the birth rate increase slightly. In several countries in Asia, Singapore, Malaysia, and Japan, birth rates have fallen so low that government leaders are considering incentives to increase birth rates![6]

It Started with Malthus

Fears of overpopulation go back at least as far as Thomas Malthus, an early British economist. In 1798, Malthus sounded the alarm in *An Essay on the Principle of Population*. He argued that population would grow faster than food supplies, and thousands would starve.

Malthus thought that resources, including land for producing crops, were fixed. While food supplies could increase, they could not increase enough to keep up with rising population. Each new birth would mean that the same resources must be divided into ever smaller portions. Thousands of new births would mean thousands of new mouths to feed with those same fixed resources. Starvation would result when the supply of farmland was exhausted but population continued to increase.

Malthus did not anticipate how machinery, fertilizers, pesticides, modern seed-breeding techniques, modern transportation, and other factors would increase our ability to produce food. Today, Canadian farmers are held to strict quotas by the marketing boards preventing them from producing food at full capacity. And millions of acres of American farmland are deliberately kept out of food production.[7]

Human ingenuity keeps coming up with new technology, from new food varieties to new ways to raise crops. Such technology is likely to continue, says economist Julian Simon. "Tractors and wheeled irrigation pipes, which are making enormous contributions today, seemed quite unrealistic a hundred or fifty years ago."[8]

A major study from the Food and Agriculture Organization of the United Nations (FAO) indicates that overall demand for food will grow at a slower rate in the future, reflecting slower population growth and the fact that many people now have adequate diets.[9] The FAO study predicts that global capacity to grow more food will "not be a major obstacle" in providing enough food for the world's population.[10] On the contrary, some experts are worried less about population growth *per se* than that people are getting more wealthy. As incomes grow, demand for meat grows.[11] This will lead to major changes in agricultural production, but the changes reflect wealth, not hunger.

In spite of these findings, the authors of our children's textbooks still see the issue in Malthusian terms.

❈ While noting that "modern developments allow people to produce and process more food than ever before," one text warns that "the efficiency of the agriculture and food processing industries cannot increase forever ... Yet the Earth's population is steadily increasing—and with it, the demand for food."[12]

❈ In *Earthcycles and Ecosystems*, a children's book, Beth Savan writes: "human beings have multiplied too quickly, and we consume so many resources that we're running out of some of them."[13]

In later editions, by the way, Malthus was somewhat more optimistic than in his early writing. But that part of the message has not reached textbook writers.

Is Carrying Capacity Fixed?

Echoing Malthus, the texts perpetuate the idea that the Earth has a fixed "carrying capacity." Carrying capacity is a term used by biologists to describe how much land is necessary to support certain numbers of animals. Our textbooks indiscriminately apply it to people, too.

* "The reason for considering the wealth and lifestyle of people in different regions is that these factors affect the Earth's carrying capacity," says *Science Probe 10*. "What would happen if all of the more than 5 billion people in the world lived in the way that the average Canadian lives? ... The maximum population that the world can support will depend on the demand for resources that each person makes and the impact on the environment that each person has."[14]

* Margaret Fagan's text *Challenge for Change* says that: "As the human population continues to expand, the ability of the earth's biological systems to support it adequately is diminishing."[15]

But people, unlike animals, do not merely eat what food is available, and die if it isn't around.[16] People grow food and are capable of producing more of it if needed, so "carrying capacity" for humans is far different than for animals, if it has any meaning at all. Most scholars are confident that we have more than enough food to feed the world's growing population. (One expert claimed some years ago that the world could feed 47 billion people with a diet of the kind Americans were enjoying in the 1960s.)[17]

In the 1950s, scientists developed new varieties of wheat and rice that dramatically increased food production, especially in Asia. These advances became known as the Green Revolution. Today, the Green Revolution continues. While scientists don't expect any single "miracle" crop, the new varieties continue to proliferate. They range from high-protein corn to grains that thrive in acidic soils.[18] And yet, according to one text: "Critics of the Green Revolution claim that the increase in grain production has been achieved at the expense of social justice."[19]

Currently, world population is increasing at 1.7 percent annually, but production of wheat is increasing at 2 percent and rice at 3.5 percent.[20] Marketing boards restrict the amount that Canadian farmers can produce. They could increase their output if necessary, and would if permitted. Furthermore, the world currently has idle cropland that could be put under cultivation. The United States has about 60 million acres (24,281,136 ha) of unplanted farmland. Argentina has about 90 million acres (36,421,704 ha), now used for pastureland, that could be quickly cultivated.[21]

Feeling Guilty

These optimistic messages are drowned in a sea of blame. Instead of recognizing the role of modern technology in improving the lives of people all over the world, textbooks criticize the industrialized countries for their use of resources.

❧ A social studies textbook, *Canada Today*, states: "25% of the people in the world live in the first and second worlds [industrialized countries]. Found mostly in the northern hemisphere, the first and second worlds consume about 70% of the world's meat and 80% of its protein. They possess about 90% of its income."[22] This textbook also reprints a full-page advertisement for the Foster

Parents Plan of Canada picturing starving children. The advertisement reads: "Do you have the courage to care?" The editorial caption asks: "How would you organize your school or class to respond to an advertisement such as this one?"[23]

🌿 According to another text: "Approximately 25 percent of the people consume 70 percent of the food. Food tends to go to the people who have the most money. Food that could feed people is also used to feed farm animals and pets."[24]

🌿 The Canadian Junior Green Guide is more explicit: "If North Americans ate just 10% less meat, there would be more food available for 60 million more people each year. It just so happens that's about the same number of people who DIE of hunger in the world each year."[25] (Capitalization is in the original.)

These statements mislead our children. Whatever Canadians obtain from other countries they purchase from willing sellers. They don't "take" things. They possess wealth because they produce wealth. They efficiently turn resources into output, much of which goes to foreign countries. Without western technology, productivity, and generosity, the poor nations of the world would be poorer still.

Does Population Growth Cause Poverty?

Many texts claim that a slower growth rate of population would reduce poverty. "Africa's problems are related to its exceptional rate of population growth. The birth rate, 45 per thousand in the early 1980's, is much higher than that of any other continent," says the text *Canada in a Changing World*. It continues: "According to Edouard Saouma, director general of the Food and Agriculture Organization, 'Many African countries, if they do not take positive action to encourage a drop in fertility rates, are speeding headlong towards disaster.'"[26]

It is true that some nations with fast-growing populations are poor, but population growth is not the cause. Extreme poverty usually occurs because government policies prevent people from engaging in productive activities. In such nations rapid population growth can make life worse, but poverty is what makes population growth a problem. High levels of population do not themselves cause poverty, as recent studies have made clear.

❧ Evidence that population growth hurts economic development is "weak or nonexistent," reports Allen C. Kelley in a prominent economic journal, the *Journal of Economic Literature.*[27]

❧ "Concern about the impact of rapid population growth on resource exhaustion has often been exaggerated,"[28] say the prestigious National Research Council (NRC) and the National Academy of Sciences (NAS).

❧ Some of the richest countries in the world have high population densities and few natural resources. These include Hong Kong, Japan, and Singapore.

China: One Child or Else

The Chinese government's one-child policy has led to high levels of abortion, in some cases coerced abortions and sterilizations, and even to reported infanticide, reflecting a cultural preference for males. One text is straightforward about the disturbing conditions: "The armed forces wanted males and openly encouraged the murder of baby girls. Global outrage over this infanticide led the Central Committee to modify its strategy in 1984."[29]

But others give tacit approval. "Although the situation in China may seem like a great restriction on the freedom of some individuals, further expansion of the Chinese population would lead to far worse consequences for the entire population,"[30] says the Kendall/Hunt text *Biological Science: An Ecological Approach.*

Similarly, the text *Patterns of Civilization* notes the difficulties the Chinese face in finding ways "to provide for and develop their vast human resources." It states that "the Chinese government has encouraged people to marry later and have fewer children than in the past."[31]

In general, our children's texts approve of active government intervention to control population growth. The Glencoe text *World History: The Human Experience* explains that food production cannot keep up with population growth in many countries. It then points out that many of these countries are using population control measures and specifically cites Thailand, where over 70 percent of the families practice family planning aggressively pushed by the government.[32]

Experts are not really sure why birth rates are falling dramatically around the world. The dramatic declines in China's population growth rates started well before the "one-child" policy began in 1979. Some experts believe that the declines were due to major improvements in infant mortality (parents then had more confidence that their children would live to maturity) and to government campaigns urging fewer children and later marriages.[33]

In Singapore, birth rates fell in the 1960s and 1970s. Thomas Poleman of Cornell University points to government programs there, especially the decision to make large families wait the longest for new government housing, as a major cause.[34]

The declines also reflect families' changing wishes about family size.[35] Among the reasons behind these changes are economic growth and the shift away from agriculture in many developing countries.

❋ In countries where agriculture is the primary occupation, even very young children can be productive and families do not need to invest much in their education. (Before the mechanization of

Canadian agriculture, farm families were large and children helped work the fields.) Many children add to the family's labour supply and wealth.

❧ In industrialized countries, children must be educated before they can be productive. They don't add to the family's wealth until many years after they are born, and investing in their education is expensive. In these countries, parents tend to have fewer children.[36]

Why Do People Starve?

If there is enough food to go around, why do people starve? The primary answer is politics. In recent years, famines have swept through parts of Africa, as they did in China and the Soviet Union earlier in this century. Droughts have been a factor, but war, political strife, and government policies are the central cause.

Many countries "have suffered or are still going through severe disruptions caused by war and political disturbances," explains the Food and Agriculture Organization of the United Nations."[37] In Ethiopia and Somalia, for example, warring parties have used food as a weapon to starve regions of the country. When the rest of the world tried to help by sending food, poor roads, lack of storage facilities, and conflict between troops made it difficult to get food to those who needed it.

Even when war is not going on, government policies can hurt food production. This has happened in many countries in the world, but these policies are particularly severe in the Sahel region south of the Sahara Desert. Many African governments there control the price of grain and keep the prices paid to farmers low.[38]

Despite all these problems, African food production has increased in Kenya, Zimbabwe, the Ivory Coast, and South Africa in recent years. Crop production in Africa could double with new technology.[39] In any case, says Dennis Avery of the Hudson Institute, "Africa is a vestige of the hunger problem which once faced all of the Third World—it is not a forerunner of impending famine for the Earth."[40]

Talking to Your Children

With this background, you can readily answer questions that your children may ask about food and population. Here are some possible questions and answers.

❀ Are there too many people?

No. The Earth's "carrying capacity" is enormous. Human ingenuity is more than equal to the challenge of meeting the demands of a growing population.

❀ Does population growth cause starvation?

No. Food production has increased faster than world population, and this trend is likely to continue. Political strife and misguided governmental policies are the most important factors leading to starvation.

❀ Are Canadians consuming too much?

This is a moral question that each family must answer for itself. But the important point for your child's environmental education is that Canadians produce as much as they consume, and what they consume from other countries they purchase from people who sell it willingly. They don't "take" anything from anybody.

❀ Should governments try to control population?

Again, this is a moral question that each family will answer for itself. It appears that government programs to control population have had some success but that economic growth will be more important over the long run.

Activities for Parents and Children

Here are some activities and discussions that you can share with your children to develop a more accurate understanding of population and food problems.

Think about Earlier Generations

Many people these days are learning about their "roots" through genealogy. Your family's history can quell worries about overpopulation, too. Gather your children around the kitchen table with a large sheet of paper and develop a family tree for the past few generations. Talk about the past and present generations and their lifestyles.

Typically, past generations had a lot of children. Some of them died at early ages. Those who survived had to go to work when they were very young, and, for many, there was no such thing as retirement. People worked as long as they could—but they died earlier than they do today.

Few families traveled far from home because there were no cars or planes. Families seldom took vacations because parents had to work most of the year. Home entertainment consisted of reading, playing the piano, or, later, listening to the radio. Food was less available, with much less variety.

Discuss your family history. Compare it with the experience of other Canadians, as indicated by the table on page 80. As Canada's population grew, family size declined, and life expectancy rose. In economic systems characterized by private enterprise, more population does not reduce prosperity.

Family Size, Total Population, and Life Expectancy in Canada

	Average Size of Family	Total Population (in thousands)	Life Expectancy (year)
1901		5,371.3	
1911		7,206.6	
1921	4.3	8,787.9	59.37
1931	3.9	10,376.8	61.00
1941	3.9	11,506.7	64.58
1951	3.7	14,009.4	68.51
1961	3.9	18,238.2	71.14
1971	3.7	21,568.3	72.74
1981	3.3	24,343.2	75.39
1991	3.1	28,120.1	77.80

Source: *Historical Statistics of Canada*, page A255; *Canada Yearbook 1991*, page 88, 106; *Canada Yearbook 1997*, pages 77, 116, 174

A Trip to the Supermarket

Take your children on a trip to the supermarket. Discuss the foods that weren't available when you were your children's age. Did you have as many frozen foods? Did you have as many fresh fruits and vegetables during the winter? What about new varieties such as kiwi, starfruit, and bok choy? Think of some foods that were available to you but not to your grandparents. Discuss the improvements in transportation and technology that have increased the quantity, variety, and quality of foods. Compare the prices of chicken and lobster. Chickens are raised by farmers who must buy or grow the grain to feed them. Lobsters live in the ocean and people merely have to catch them. Yet lobsters cost more than chickens. Farmers can produce as many chickens as people are willing to buy, but lobsters are in limited supply.

During the Great Depression, one politician promised "a chicken in every pot"—that is, that someday every family would be able to afford to eat chicken. Today chicken is so inexpensive that it can be sold in fast-food restaurants. Stop at the produce section, where prices vary considerably from day to day. An early frost can stunt Okanagan fruit; and floods may wipe out Arizona's lettuce crop. When such natural disasters occur, supply goes down and the price goes up. Some people buy apples instead of oranges or use less lettuce. But the higher price also encourages producers to find or grow more oranges and lettuce, if they can. The result is that, while prices fluctuate, there is always a diversity of produce in most stores.

Plan a Garden

Imagine that the only food that your family will eat will come from your garden. Looking at a calendar, plan when you will plant, how long certain crops will take to mature, and when they will be harvested. At harvest time, what will you do with all the fresh food? How will you preserve it for the winter? How will the quality compare with that of fresh food?

Consider how many of your family's favorite foods would not be available if they had to depend upon just what their garden can grow. Point out how many foods come from other parts of the country or even other nations. Some apples come from Europe; some kiwis come from New Zealand; many fruits and vegetables come from Mexico and the United States.

Your children will learn that there is more to the abundance of food on our tables than simply growing it. They will learn the importance of food preservation, processing, and distribution.

Notes

1 Herbert I. London, *Why Are They Lying to Our Children?* (New York: Stein and Day Publishers, 1984), 31–32.

2 Angus L. Scully et al., *Canada Today, Second Edition* (Scarborough, ON: Prentice-Hall Canada, 1988), 405.

3 Peter Beckett, et al., *Science Probe 10* (Scarborough, ON: Thomson Canada, 1995), 447.

4 Indur M. Goklany, "Feeding the World's Billions Without Crowding Out the Rest of Nature" (Washington, DC: Department of the Interior, Office of Policy Analysis, November 1995).

5 Dennis T. Avery, *Global Food Progress 1991: A Report from Hudson Institute's Center for Global Food Issues* (Indianapolis: The Hudson Institute, 1991), 72, fig. 1-5.

6 Jacqueline R. Kasun, *Population and Environment: Debunking the Myths* (Baltimore, MD: Population Research Institute, 1991), 3.

7 Avery, 16.

8 Julian Simon, *The Ultimate Resource* (Princeton: Princeton University Press, 1981), 67.

9 Alexandratos, Nikos, *World Agriculture: Towards 2010* (Chichester, England: Food and Agriculture Organization of the United Nations and John Wiley & Sons, 1995), 124.

10 Alexandratos, 130.

11 Thomas T. Poleman, "Income and Dietary Change," in *Food Policy*, Vol. 20, No. 2 (1995), 49-159.

12 Frank Baumann, et al,. *Science Probe 8* (Toronto: John Wiley and Sons Canada, 2nd ed.,1993), 366.

13 Beth Savan, *Earthcycles and Ecosystems* (Toronto: Kids Can Press, 1991), 25.

14 Beckett, 457.

15 Margaret Fagan, *Challenge for Change* (Toronto: McGraw-Hill Ryerson, 2nd ed., 1991), 23.

16 See the discussion of carrying capacity in Simon, 177.

17 Colin Clark, *Population Growth and Land Use* (New York: Macmillan, 1968), 153.

18 Avery, 90.

19 Stewart Dunlop, *Towards Tomorrow: Canada in a Changing World* (Toronto, ON: Harcourt Brace Jovanovich Canada, 1987), 102.

20 Avery, 10.

21 Avery, 18.

22 Angus L. Scully, et al., *Canada Today* (Scarborough, ON: Prentice-Hall Canada, 1988), 413.

23 Scully, 422.

24 Myrtle Siebert and Evelyn Kerr, *Food for Life* (Toronto: McGraw-Hill Ryerson, 1994), 301.

25 Teri Degler and Pollution Probe, *The Canadian Junior Green Guide* (Toronto: McClelland and Stewart, 1990), 77.

26 Dunlop, 82.

27 Allen C. Kelley, "Economic Consequences of Population Change," *Journal of Economic Literature*, 26 (December 1988), 1685–1728.

28 Quoted in Julian Simon, *Population Matters: People, Resources, Environment, and Immigration* (New Brunswick, NJ: Transaction Publishers, 1990), 230.

29 Alyn E. Mitchner and Joanne R. Tuffs, *Global Forces of the Twentieth Century* (Edmonton: Reidmore Books, 1991), 248.

30 Milani, 932-3.

31 Burton F. Beers, *Patterns of Civilization* (Toronto: Prentice-Hall, 1984), vol. 2, 173.

32 Farah and Karls, 961.

33 Thomas T. Poleman, *Population: Past Growth and Future Control*, Working Paper, Department of Agricultural, Resource, and Managerial Economics, Cornell University, Ithaca NY, September 1994, 8.

34 Poleman, 8.

35 Lant H. Pritchett, "Desired Fertility and the Impact of Population Policies, *Population and Development Review*, March 1994, 55.

36 Avery, 70.

37 Alexandratos, 53.

38 Avery, 53.

39 Avery, 47.

40 Avery, 20.

Chapter 7

Natural Resources: On the Way Out?

Perhaps you remember, as we do, the energy crisis of the 1970s. Like the authors of our children's textbooks, people thought that there weren't enough natural resources to go around, and that there would be even fewer as the population grew and people were wasteful.

Neil Hrab was exposed to the fears when a high school student in Ontario. His teacher was leading a discussion about North American energy consumption. Mesmerizing the class, the teacher raised his hand and said: "If everyone in the world consumed as much energy as we do, then"—here he snapped his fingers—"all the energy in the world would be used up in the time it took me to snap."[1] Textbooks today repeat the message.

🍁 "Some experts estimate that if people continue to use petroleum, natural gas, coal, and uranium at present rates, most supplies will run out within the next 200 years," says the text *Journeys in Science*.[2]

* *Earth Science* writes: "World reserves [of copper] will be used up in about 60 years if present rates of use continue," and zinc will last "40 years at the present rate of consumption." Furthermore, "at present rates of use, world reserves of petroleum are estimated to last about 30 years and natural gas not much longer."[3]

* "Petroleum is particularly scarce," warns one geography text, saying that "some economists fear that only a 50-year supply may remain."[4]

These claims are not justified. World supplies of most natural resources are not running out. Fossil fuels and most minerals are more abundant than in the past—that is, they are more readily available and cheaper than they used to be. Most resources are so plentiful that they will last for centuries.

This news may come as a surprise, especially if you remember the high prices of fuel and the energy shortages in the late 1970s. How can we say with confidence that the world is not going to run out of its important nonrenewable resources? We will explain the reasons in this chapter.

Running on Empty?

Fear of scarcity pervades our children's texts. Students learn that there is only so much tin or coal or iron or oil to go around and, once used, it will be gone forever. The drumbeat is steady:

* *Science Directions 9* says that "coal, oil, and gas ... are in limited supply on Earth. They are non-renewable energy resources, and they are being used up."[5]

❋   "Once they [non-renewable resources] are used, they are gone forever," says the text *Journeys in Science.*[6]

❋   Another text says "energy comes from burning coal, oil, or gas" and asks: "What will happen when these supplies are used up?"[7]

❋   *Canada—A New Geography* states: "Resources such as minerals and fossil fuels are called non-renewable since they cannot be replaced once they are used up."[8]

One reason they will be gone, say the texts, is that Canada and the United States are using too much of these resources.

❋   "Rich western countries, with only 20% of the world's population, use 70% or the world's energy," says the curriculum supplement *Science Is . . .*[9]

❋   "The average person in a developed nation uses 80 times as much energy as the average person in a developing nation, who lives without electricity or a car,"[10] says another.

❋   "If we consume more than our rightful share of such resources as petroleum, future generations will blame us for squandering the Earth's limited wealth," says the geography text *Canada in a Changing World.*[11]

A children's book states that "the rich countries are using up most of the world's resources—the food, and the things that make energy, such as oil and gas."[12]

Youngsters are bombarded with instructions to conserve energy. Most of these are harmless and a few are useful. After all, our children should turn off the lights when they leave a room. But many texts also urge more taxes and regulations to cope with the supposed crisis.

❦ Beth Savan, in the children's book *Earthcycles and Ecosystems*, says that "lately, we've been dirtying up the atmosphere with exhaust fumes from cars, furnaces and power plants." She then suggests that children "[w]rite to government decision-makers and ask for laws that require people to use less energy."[13]

❦ "The supply of fossil fuels is being used up at an alarming rate," says the text *Biology, An Everyday Experience*. "Governments must help save our fossil fuel supply by passing laws limiting their use."[14]

Why They Are Wrong

It is true that resources are finite, but this is largely irrelevant to human experience. Specific natural resources are limited in quantity, but in most cases the services that they provide can be supplied by other resources as well.

Throughout history, people have feared the depletion of a vital resource only to find that when the price rose, they could switch to another resource and get the same service. During the Middle Ages in Europe, charcoal from wood was the primary source of energy. As wood became more scarce, the price rose and people began to search for a substitute. Eventually, they found it in a previously worthless rock—coal. In the mid-nineteenth century, whale oil was used for lamps. As it became more difficult to find whales in the oceans, whale oil prices began to rise, and people began to fear that whale oil would disappear. According to economist J. Clayburn LaForce, however, as the price rose, people began to look for substitutes and they found one in coal oil.[15] Indeed, the steady increase in the use of coal set people worrying, too. A prominent economist, W. Stanley Jevons, said in 1865 that he doubted England's prosperity could continue once its supplies of coal were exhausted.[16]

But as the most easily mined coal was used up, the price of coal began to rise and people began searching for additional sources of energy. (They also wanted one that burned more cleanly.) Farmers in western Pennsylvania had been cursed with a black liquid substance on their land that harmed their crops and pastures, driving down the value of their land. To a few entrepreneurs, this black liquid known as "rock oil" looked promising, and in 1859 the Pennsylvania Rock Oil Company of Titusville, Pennsylvania, successfully dug for oil. The gooey substance took the pressure off coal, and today coal is plentiful, even in England.

What People Really Want

Most textbooks miss the point about natural resources. The authors think that what is important is the resource and whether it is renewable or nonrenewable. But what we want is not the resource itself, but the service provided by using the resource.

People don't really want copper wire, petroleum, and electricity; they want communication over long distances, warmth in winter, and transportation to their homes and offices. These services can be provided by many different resources, especially as technology advances.

Consider copper. Copper is a highly efficient conductor of electricity, so it is widely used for wiring that supplies electricity to our homes and connects our telephones. Some people think that the world faces a serious copper shortage, and that this could stunt economic growth. But we don't rely on copper the way we used to, not because it is scarce but because other materials are proving more useful.

For telephone lines, we are beginning to use fiber optic cables instead of copper wire. These glass fibers, derived from ordinary sand, can carry many more messages at a time than copper wire can. Because fiber optic cables can replace copper today, there will be less need to use copper for communication. Communication satellites have also replaced copper wire. There is little reason to doubt that we will have ample supplies of copper for generations to come.

Prices Make a Difference

People shift from one resource to another in response to changes in prices. As natural resources become scarce, their prices increase. As prices increase, several things happen.

First, consumers begin to conserve. In recent history the price of oil has twice gone up dramatically. The first hike occurred after the outbreak of the Middle East War in 1973 and an oil embargo by oil-producing countries; the second occurred in the late 1970s after the overthrow of the Shah of Iran. (Both events were the result of political actions, not natural shortages.)

In both cases, the higher prices caused consumers to use less energy. They turned down their thermostats in winter, turned off the air conditioning in the summer, drove less, and tuned up their cars so they would run on less fuel. As time went on, they bought more fuel-efficient automobiles and increased the insulation in their houses. These measures didn't happen all at once, but they gradually reduced the demand for oil.

Consumers also shifted to substitutes. People can substitute warmer clothes for home heating, and can replace air conditioning with fans or fewer clothes. They can use other fuels such as coal and natural gas. In the 1970s and 1980s, people took just such steps.

The price rise also increased the incentive of producers to supply more oil. Before the embargo, the price of oil was so low that it did not encourage exploration for new oil reserves. When prices rose, oil exploration did, too. In addition, price increases stimulated producers to increase supply by figuring out how to get oil from fields that had been considered dry. New techniques like slant drilling, water extraction, and deeper drilling could pay off when the price was higher.

These changes caused the price of oil to stop climbing. In fact, in the mid-1980s, to the surprise of many people, the price of oil collapsed. It had been US$34 per barrel in 1981 but it was US$10 per barrel in early 1986[17] (about US$12 when adjusted for inflation). Today oil is readily available and relatively inexpensive—in spite of large new taxes that have been added to the price.

Another Misunderstood Idea: "Known" Reserves

Most of the predictions in our children's textbooks are based on a simple calculation that is used inappropriately. The textbooks report the "known" or "proven" reserves of important minerals or source of energy. They divide this figure by the consumption per year to predict how soon we will run out.

Oil Prices per Barrel, 1949–1993

Source: Energy Information Administration, *Annual Energy Review 1998* (Washington, DC: U.S. Department of Energy, 1998).

As every geologist knows, "proven" or "known" reserves is a very limited concept. It is not meant to describe all the reserves on the planet, but those that can be recovered economically at present prices.[18] If oil costs $25 a barrel, oil that can't be extracted for less than $25 isn't counted as a reserve because no one is willing to extract it. So "known" reserves at $25 per barrel exclude a lot of oil that we know about, that would be extracted at $30 or $40 a barrel, but not at $25.

If we began to deplete the "known reserves," prices would go up, at least temporarily. Petroleum companies would seek out additional sources, and "known" reserves would increase.

The U.S. Geological Survey (USGS) has developed estimates that reflect this fact. In addition to "known" reserves, the USGS estimates "ultimate recoverable" resources, which are 0.01 percent of the material in the top kilometer (six-tenths of a mile) of the earth's crust. It even includes the amount estimated to be in the entire Earth's crust. As the graph on page 92 indicates, when these estimates are used, the number of years until depletion of a resource goes up dramatically.[19]

For example, "known reserves" of copper are expected to last about 45 years but "ultimate recoverable" reserves would last about 340 years, and the amount in the Earth's crust represents 242,000,000 years.[20] These figures are largely ignored in the textbooks.

Talking to Your Children

The most important point your children should understand about natural resources is that they change over time. Natural resources aren't useful until human beings figure out how to use them, and human ingenuity is constantly finding how to use new resources or old resources in new ways.[21] As long as the human mind is free to be creative and ingenious, we should not worry about depleting our natural resources. Now you can answer some questions your children may ask.

Known Reserves and Estimated Ultimate Recoverable Resources

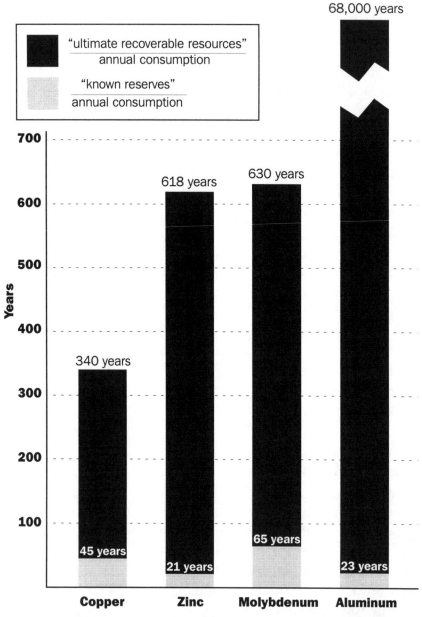

Source: David Osterfeld, *Prosperity versus Planning: How Government Stifles Economic Growth*. New York: Oxford University Press, 1992, 95, table 4-5, citing William Nordhaus.

✤ Are we running out of natural resources?

No. Most natural resources are plentiful. While some may become more scarce over time, price changes will cause people to find substitutes. The resources that we use will change over time. Materials that were previously unknown or neglected will provide the services we want.

✤ How much oil is left in the ground?

No one knows for sure. The textbooks claim that we may run out of reserves of oil and other raw materials in a specified number of years. But these estimates reflect only the reserves that can be obtained at current prices. If prices go up, "known" reserves will increase.

✤ Should we conserve natural resources?

Conservation of natural resources is a good idea but it should not be placed above all other considerations. People *inevitably* conserve when prices go up. They use less and look for products that provide similar services at lower cost. There is a natural tendency to conserve when something becomes scarce.

Activities for Parents and Children

Here are some activities and discussions that you can share with your children to help them develop a more accurate understanding of natural resources.

A Trip along the Telephone Wires

Ask your children to take an imaginary trip along the telephone wires. Discuss with them how their voice travels from your telephone to their grandmother's phone (or to another relative who lives across the country). Most children can understand that the voice is converted into a fluctuating electrical current that travels along copper wires and through switching stations. Tell them that the telephone network was originally like this but it has changed.

As the number of phones, fax machines, and computers increased in recent years, more and more phone lines were needed. The price of copper wire began to be a problem for the phone companies. Phone companies wanted to find a cheaper way to send the multitude of signals. So now that same call may travel from your house to a satellite station, where it is converted into microwaves and transmitted to a satellite in space and then transmitted back to earth near your grandmother's house, where it is converted back to electrical impulses and travels by copper wire to her telephone. Or the phone call may leave the house and be put on a fiber optic cable made of glass (which originally came from ordinary sand) and travel with thousands of other calls to a distant location. You and your children may wish to draw these different ways to transmit information.

Another way to illustrate these concepts is to take your children to an electronics store and have the manager show them all the products that can be linked by telephone (computers, fax machines, etc.). Or take your children to the phone company and have an engineer explain how the phone network in the country works. You can also point out the various advertisements on television (MCI, Sprint, etc.), which show how extensive our communication network is. Human ingenuity responding to higher prices has constructed a communication system that is less dependent on copper than in the past.

"Betting the Planet"

Your children may enjoy the story, "Betting the Planet," which appeared in the *New York Times* in 1990.[22] Ten years earlier, at the crest of a wave of public alarm over the rising price of oil and other commodities, economist Julian Simon offered to make a wager. He challenged anyone to select a commodity and name a future date. On that date, he said, the commodity would be cheaper than it was when the bet was made (assuming that general inflation was taken into account). If the material turned out to be more expensive, Simon would pay an agreed-upon amount. If it was cheaper, the other person would pay Simon.

Paul Ehrlich, the well-known advocate of population control, took up the challenge. He selected five metals—copper, chrome, nickel, tin, and tungsten—that he was sure would cost more in ten years because we would start running out of them. Simon bet that the prices would be lower.

By 1990, the five metals had fallen in real (that is, in inflation-adjusted) terms. Julian Simon easily won the bet. Simon wasn't simply lucky. He knew that the prices of all major commodities have fallen over time and saw no reason to expect that process to change. When materials appear to be scarce, prices go up, but these price hikes are usually temporary. Higher prices lead consumers to look for substitutes and spur producers to seek out new sources of supply. Over time, more supply and less demand cause prices to fall.

Another Way to Look at Materials

A policy analyst, Stephen Moore, has compiled an index that illustrates how cheap some metals are today. His index is based on how long it would take for a person to earn enough money to buy a pound of the metal. Instead of using the actual figure, he used 100 as the figure for 1990, and based all the other numbers on the 1990 figure.

In 1980, the figure for copper was 125. That means that a person had to work 25 percent more time to earn enough money to buy a pound of copper than he or she would in 1990. (If it took 100 minutes of work for the average worker in 1990 to buy a specific amount of copper in 1990, it would have taken 125 minutes in 1980.) The table indicates that the cost of copper in terms of hours worked went down dramatically during the past century.

Sit down with your children and a piece of graph paper. Using the numbers provided below, ask them to make a graph (it could be one graph or as many as three) showing how prices have changed for these metals.

Index for Comparing Changes in the Price of Metals

	Copper	Lead	Mercury
1890	928	683	1496
1900	944	651	1238
1910	568	513	1025
1920	278	324	619
1930	217	236	923
1940	158	184	1184
1950	135	215	248
1960	129	123	409
1970	155	109	532
1980	125	136	235
1990	100	100	100

Source: Stephen Moore, *Doomsday Delayed: America's Surprisingly Bright Natural Resource Future*, p. 30.

Discuss with your children why the price has decreased. There may be a number of reasons. Demand for copper, as we have seen, fell because substitutes were cheaper. Lead is known to be dangerous, so people have been looking for alternatives to use in paint and gasoline. Also, there may have been an increase in the supply of these metals. In any case, producers have more than kept pace with the demand for these metals. We can expect that progress to continue with these and with all major natural resources.

Notes

1 Personal fax from Neil Hrab, July 22, 1997 to Laura Jones.

2 Peter Beugger, Larry Yore, *et al.*, *Journeys in Science 6* (Toronto: Collier Macmillan Canada, Canadian ed., 1990), 89.

3 Samuel N. Namowitz and Nancy E. Spaulding, *Heath Earth Science* (Toronto: DC Heath Canada, Canadian ed.,1987), 75–79.

4 Stewart Dunlop, *Towards Tomorrow: Canada in a Changing World—Geography* (Toronto: Harcourt Brace Jovanovich Canada, 1987), 14.

5 Robert A. Douglas, *Science Directions 9* (Edmonton: Arnold, 1991), 157.

6 Peter Beugger, Larry Yore, *et al.*, *Journeys in Science 5* (Toronto: Collier Macmillan Canada, Canadian ed., 1990), 90.

7 Robert A. Douglas, *Science Directions 8* (Edmonton: Arnold, 1991), 143.

8 Ralph Krueger and Ray Corder, *Canada: A New Geography* (Toronto: Holt, Rinehart, and Winston, 1982), 496.

9 Susan V. Bosak, *Science Is...* (Co-edited by Richmond Hill, ON/ Markham, ON: Scholastic Canada/The Communication Project, 1991), 354.

10 James E. Davis and Phyllis Maxey Fernlund, *Civics: Participating in Our Democracy* (Menlo Park, CA: Addison-Wesley, 1993), 565.

11 Dunlop, 14.

12 Shelley Tanaka, *A Great Round Wonder: My Book of the World* (Toronto: Douglas and McIntyre, 1993), 43.

13 Beth Savan, *Earthcycles and Ecosystems* (Toronto: Kids Can, 1991), 47.

14 Albert Kaskel *et al.*, *Biology, An Everyday Experience* (Lake Forest, IL: Glencoe, 1992), 677.

15 J. Clayburn LaForce, "The Energy Crisis: The Moral Equivalent of Bamboozle," Original Paper 11 (Los Angeles, International Institute for Economic Research, April 1978).

16 Quoted in Julian Simon, *The Ultimate Resource* (Princeton: Princeton University Press, 1981), 93.

17 James D. Gwartney and Richard L. Stroup, *Economics: Private and Public Choice* (New York: Harcourt Brace Jovanovich, 1987), p. 653.

18 U.S. Bureau of Mines, *Mineral Facts and Problems* (Washington, DC: Government Printing Office, 1985), 3.

19 David Osterfeld, *Prosperity Versus Planning: How Government Stifles Economic Growth* (New York: Oxford Press, 1992), 95.

20 Osterfeld, 95.

21 To convey this point, Julian Simon entitled his book on population and natural resources *The Ultimate Resource*.

22 John Tierney, "Betting the Planet," *New York Times Magazine*, December 2, 1990, 52–53ff.

Chapter 8

Canadian Forests: A Wasteland?

Remember the child who felt sad because "they killed trees to make my bed"? Many environmentalists believe that logging is bad, and that clear-cutting threatens to destroy life on this planet. Our schools, guided by such views, give our children a one-sided picture of logging and a completely distorted view of what our forests are like.

Chemainus, like many other British Columbian towns, was once supported by a thriving forestry-based economy. The closure of the sawmill in 1983 sparked environmentalists to declare that the province was running out of trees, and that we were overlogging the planet.

Textbooks echo these warnings, misguiding a generation of children into feeling guilty about their furniture. "Green" propaganda becomes more important than facts, and exaggeration for the effect of teaching children to be environmentally sensitive becomes the norm. The truth is that the world has an abundance of trees, and that British Columbia's forest management practices are improving, although you won't learn that in school.

No Trees Left?

Our children learn that our forests are largely gone. They were cut down by greedy commercial interests and they will never be the same again.

* "Ninety percent of the forests have disappeared since Ontario was settled 150 years ago," according to the World Wildlife Fund in *Take Action*.[1]

* *Investigating Terrestrial Ecosystems* states that, "about one-third of the land area of the earth is forest. This is a generous figure, since it includes savanna and scrubland, where trees are few and scattered. Before humans began to exploit the forest, this figure probably stood at two-thirds." It further warns that Canadian forests "have degenerated to a dangerous point."[2]

* And *Journeys in Science* says that "five hundred years ago ... three-quarters of the area of North America was covered with forest. The European settlers who began arriving in the early sixteenth century cut down and burned vast areas of forest to clear the land for settlements and farms. Sometimes, the result was disastrous."[3]

* According to *Science Probe 8*: "Forest researchers ... think that we may not produce enough wood to meet the demand in the future."[4]

* "What if the forests that are cut down for paper are not replanted?" asks the Merrill text *Biology: The Dynamics of Life*. "Eventually wood would become a limited resource." (Just in case students miss the point, the text shows a picture of a clearcut forest.)[5]

But was clearing land for farms and using the wood to build homes "disastrous"? After all, in the nineteenth century, people wanted farms and homes more than they wanted pristine forests full of dangerous animals. And were the forests destroyed haphazardly, or were they harvested for good reason? What is the current state of our forests? The texts avoid these questions.

Are We Running Out of Trees?

The premise that the nation is running out of trees is simply untrue. Federal and Provincial governments own over 90 percent of forests in Canada. Every year, the government names the annual allowable cut for these Crown lands. This allowable cut is much less than the total new growth each year. And, in fact, the harvest levels are usually far below the allowable cut. Since 1970, the harvest of softwood exceeded the allowable cut only once, in 1989.

**Canadian Total Annual Harvest and Annual Allowable Cut
(by volume in millions of cubic meters)**

	Total Annual Harvest	Annual Allowable Cut
1993	169.3	230.7
1988	184.4	233.7
1983	149.6	207.1
1978	151.9	227.9
1973	140.5	228.4
Source: National Forestry Database, Canadian Council of Forest Ministers		

Government restrictions and geographical factors combine to make less than half of Canada's forestland available for commercial logging.[6] Lands that are theoretically available for commercial harvest are often inaccessible. Much of the forestland in British Columbia, for example, is hard to reach, covers mountains where it is difficult and dangerous to log, and is a long way from lumber markets. Textbooks rarely mention these vast forests that nobody wants to log. They focus on relatively small areas like the Carmannah Valley and Clayoquot Sound in the southwestern corner of British Columbia or along the coastline. These are the forests that receive the most press coverage but they are not representative of Canada's vast forestland.

Clearcuts: Destructive or Efficient?

Textbooks, environmentalists, and the media all agree that clearcuts are bad. Our children's texts provide photographs of especially unattractive examples of recently clearcut hillsides. During a skit presented to an elementary school in Vancouver, the BC Ministry of Environment-funded *Green Team* asked the class a riddle: "There were once thousands of trees and species for thousands of years, and now there are just stumps." The children are supposed to say what the team is describing, and they do: "A clear-cut."

In the same presentation, an itinerant caterpillar sings to an orphaned pine tree:

> Home, home on the range,
> Where the deer, and the bears,
>   and the caterpillars used to play,
> Where seldom is heard,
> An encouraging word,
> And the machines and the people came
>   and took all the trees away!"[7]

Children's books tell the same story. *Maxine's Tree,* a children's book, tells the story of a clearcut through the eyes of a five-year-old: "The mountainside across the valley was bare. Its trees had been cut and taken away. Nothing green was left. Only ragged burnt stumps were standing." Maxine's father explains that the forest will "be re-planted, but it won't be like an old-growth rainforest. It will be only a tree farm . . ."[8]

"This forest on the left has been clear-cut—all the trees have been completely cleared out," says the children's book *Earthcycles and Ecosystems.* "Large bulldozer-like machines drove into the area, the trees were chopped down with chainsaws, then huge machines cut off their branches"[9]

Take Action, a book endorsed by the World Wildlife Fund de-scribes clearcutting this way: "Using bulldozers and chainsaws, log-gers cut or knock down every single tree, whether it is wanted for lumber or not . . ."[10]

Most books of this type focus on the negative aspects of clear-cut-ting. While it is true that poorly managed clear-cuts can cause prob-lems like river damage and landslides, it is also true that clear-cutting has many advantages.

Clear-cutting is frequently the most economical way to harvest trees and it is a useful way to clear areas where trees have been dam-aged by fire, insects, or disease. In Sweden as well as Oregon and Washington, clear-cutting has been used to restore forests degraded by partial cutting.[11] Partial cutting can prevent certain light-loving species of trees like the Douglas fir from regenerating properly. As well, clear-cutting mimics the beneficial effects of forest fires.

Most importantly, clear-cutting is often safer than selective log-ging. In older, less uniform forests, trees may have dead tops and huge dead branches called "widow makers."[12] By clear-cutting we can log these areas with the least risk to loggers—a concern to their fam-ilies that the textbooks conveniently omit.

Why So Much Logging?

In Canadian history texts, our young people learn that greedy lumber companies exploited Canada's forests by overcutting timber, and that the environmental movement is saving the forests by pressuring the government into establishing parks and protecting forests.

It is true that many forests were heavily logged from early times until recently, but this logging should be put into perspective. When the first settlers arrived, they viewed forests as an impediment. Trees were cut down to make way for farms, towns, and cities. Early settlers did not consider timber a scarce resource. They never envisioned that there could be a shortage of wood. And, in fact, there never was.

When the country began to industrialize after 1850, wood became a valuable resource. Wood was used for fuel in early factories, for railroad ties and bridges, and for construction of houses, farms, and manufacturing centers. Logging changed. Instead of individuals clearing trees for private use, logging became an important part of the nation's industrial economy.

About a century ago, the end of the Gold Rush in the Yukon marked the beginning of the "timber rush" in British Columbia. Prospectors for gold now saw wealth in the trees. The government promoted the expansion of the logging industry, viewing forests as a source of revenue and employment, and a reason to immigrate to the relatively young and undeveloped province.

The forests seemed to be endless. The first generation of loggers used hand-held tools and horses to harvest trees one by one. Even had they wanted to, the technology did not exist at that time to bring about mass deforestation.[13] Logging camps full of young men armed with axes and saws barely left a mark on the forests. Tree-planting was not considered necessary, as there were trees as far as the eye could see. Indeed, had they wanted to replant trees, they would have found it a losing proposition. In the United States, Gifford Pinchot, who became the first director of the U.S. Forest Service, tried his hand at managing timber in North Carolina, with replanting part of his operation. But he couldn't make money at it.[14]

The fact that the loggers were working predominantly on Crown land also discouraged replanting. They didn't own the land but, rather, leased it. There was no guarantee that they would have access to any trees which grew in the future. Private corporations left regrowth up to the government, whose officials, in turn, left it up to natural regeneration—if they gave it much thought at all.

The government wasn't worried about running out of trees. Due to the primitive nature of technology, and the rugged landscape, the government's early attempts to compile forest inventories were inaccurate. The results confirmed the prevalent—and correct— impression that the forests were vast and that there was no danger of running out of trees. However, there was an exception to this optimism. Railroads needed ties and timbers, and they needed them in large quantities at the right time and in the right place. As a result, the railway companies experimented with tree nurseries. By 1880, plantation forestry was well-established in the eastern and southern states, and in eastern Canada.[15]

Taken as a whole, this history led to an impression of logging summed up by forestry critic and author Ken Drushka: "The lumber industry at the turn of the century operated on an ethic of 'cut the best, leave the rest and move on.'"[16] This image of greedy "cut and run" logging is found in our children's textbooks.

Changing Times

The 1950s were the glory years of the forest industry. Canada's postwar construction boom created a great demand for lumber for building homes, and growing population and a thriving economy boosted demand for other wood products as well. Military technology adapted to industrial purposes helped loggers harvest timber more efficiently. British Columbia's forests provided timber, employment, and tax revenues for the government.

Most of the forestry communities in North America were created in the latter half of the 20th century.[17] They provided steady employment and good wages for workers in the timber industry, and the towns with timber mills benefited from the healthy economy based on the forests. Company towns such as Powell River and Port Alberni (both of which grew up around MacMillan-Bloedel mills) were among the wealthiest in Canada in the 1960s and 1970s.[18] There began to be health concerns about mill pollution in the 1970s and 1980s, but demonstrations against the forest industry did not draw media attention through their violence until the mid-1980s.[19]

Planting Trees for the Future

While forests regenerate naturally if left alone, planting speeds up the process. Planting genetically superior species can increase the quality and quantity of wood.

Beginning around 1950, foresters became legally responsible for planting trees to replace those harvested from Crown land, but these laws were largely unenforced until the early 1970s. However, between 1975 and 1993, while the logged areas increased by 42 percent, the areas planted or seeded increased by 228 percent.[20]

Direct seeding involves scattering pine cones on the ground, and sometimes breaking them up to release the seeds. Planting involves manual placement of seedlings grown in nurseries. Planting is more expensive and more labour-intensive, but it is a far more successful method of forest regeneration. By the 1990s, foresters were replanting annually well over 400,000 hectares—an area two-thirds the size of Prince Edward Island. Although textbooks often blame big companies for exploitation of the forests, they grant them little credit for later attempts at forest restoration.

Canadian Annual Harvest and Annual Allowable Cut

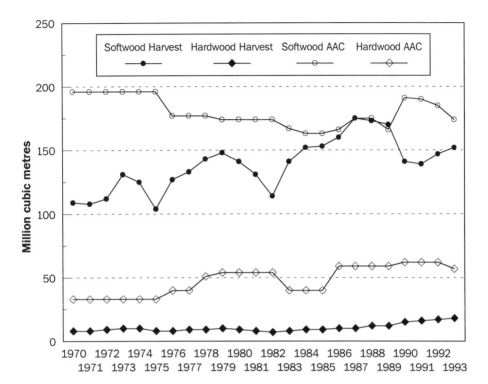

Talking to Your Children

The story of Canadian forests is a fascinating one. It is a story of settlers arriving in a heavily forested country where there were so many
trees that they were an impediment to settlement. These first settlers cleared the land and used the wood. They were followed by loggers who harvested the wood and sold it to build the economy of this
nation. Gradually, as wood became more scarce, prices rose. People
began to look for substitutes and the timber industry began to manage forests for the long term. Forests are regenerating.

Tree Planting in Canada: Trends in direct seeding and planting of harvested areas

	Direct Seeding by Area (hectares)	Planting by Area (hectares)
1993	34,000	418,000
1992	30,000	433,000
1991	43,000	463,000
1990	37,000	472,000
1989	43,000	434,000
1988	38,000	422,000
1987	37,000	393,000
1986	26,000	309,000
1985	26,000	261,000
1984	34,000	240,000
1983	37,000	212,000
1982	50,000	179,000
1981	43,000	161,000
1980	65,000	147,000
1979	39,000	143,000
1978	37,000	128,000
1977	43,000	122,000
1976	40,000	120,000
1975	34,000	127,000

Source: *National Forestry Database*, Canadian Council of Forest Ministers; Canadian Forest Service, Natural Resources Canada.

Now you are ready to answer some questions that your children may ask.

❋ Is Canada running out of trees?

No. The amount of wood grown increases every year, and every year more wood grows than is harvested. Companies consistently stay within the Annual Allowable Cut total, and forest cover has actually increased in southern Ontario from 25 percent to 29 percent since the mid-1960s.[21]

❋ Why were so many trees cut down ?

When the settlers arrived in Canada, there were so many trees that it was difficult to farm until some of them were cut. Later, wood was so widely available that it was used for building houses, for fuel in factories, ships and railroads, and for railroad ties and commercial buildings. It exported to many countries. In British Columbia, especially, it was the magnet that attracted immigration with the promise of jobs and even wealth. As long as wood was cheap and plentiful, people did not have an incentive to replant trees.

❋ What is the state of Canada's forests today?

Wood is plentiful. More wood is grown each year than is cut down. We are replanting harvested sites far more consistently than in the past.

Activities for Parents and Children

Here are some activities and discussions that will help your children get a more balanced picture of what has happened to North America's forests.

Is "Old Growth" Better than "New Growth"?

"Old-growth" forests are forests whose trees have not been cut or burned for a long time, perhaps several hundred years. New or "second-growth" forests have grown up after being logged or cleared by forest fires. The forests in Stanley Park in Vancouver, British Columbia, for example, are predominantly second-growth, and yet are considered so beautiful that they attract thousands of tourists every year.

Some textbooks suggest that ancient or "old-growth" forests are better than new or "second-growth" forests. If you live near forest-land, perhaps you and your children can see for yourself if this is the case. Find out if the forest you visit is "old-growth" or "new-growth." Ask a park or forest ranger to discuss the differences. Some animals such as the northern spotted owl, which nests in the cavities of old trees, thrive in old-growth forests, although they have also been found in younger forests. Small mammals and most large game animals such as deer and moose, however, are more plentiful in younger forests. These forests usually have a greater variety of trees and plant life because the forest floor gets more sunlight than in old-growth forests. Perhaps you can find both kinds of forest in your region. If not, your children can learn more about the differences through library research.

Keep in mind that forests that were never logged are not necessarily composed of old trees. Forests change. Before settlers came to Canada, forest fires were frequent. In fact, First Nations people often encouraged fires to make the land more attractive to game. So, even if the settlers had never cut down any trees, we would have forests with trees of many different ages, not simply "old-growth."

Visit a Lumberyard with Your Children

Take your children to the local lumberyard to learn how consumers and suppliers respond to changing prices of wood. As prices go up, people conserve wood. By buying less wood, they leave more for others. When wood prices go down, the opposite happens. People want to use more wood, and they conserve competing materials such as plastic and steel. Because people respond to changing prices, we are not likely ever to run out of wood.

At the lumberyard, you could enlist the manager's help.

✤ Ask him how the price of lumber has changed recently. Has it gone up or down? Why?

✤ Ask him to show your children the wide variety of wood products, such as plywood, hardwood veneers, particleboard, pressure-treated wood, wood pellets for wood stoves, bark for landscaping, and so on. When wood becomes expensive, suppliers develop products that make a limited amount of wood go farther. Particleboard, for example, uses small bits of cheap wood but is as strong as more expensive lumber. Hardwood veneers—thin layers of wood that are glued on top of less-expensive plywood—make attractive furniture cheaper than it would be if solid hardwood lumber were used throughout.

✤ Ask him to point out non-wood products that also extend the life of wood or enable us to use less wood. Paints and preservatives protect wood outside. Steel strapping and holders strengthen wood construction. Drywall replaces wood paneling inside homes. Steel studs are used in the walls of homes and office buildings.

Notes

1 Ann Love and Jane Drake, *Take Action* (Toronto: Kids Can, 1992), 50.

2 William A. Andrews and Donna K. Moore, *Investigating Terrestrial Ecosystems* (Scarborough, ON: Prentice-Hall Canada, 1987), 193–94.

3 Larry D. Yore *et al.*, *Journeys in Science 7* (Toronto: Collier Macmillan Canada, Canadian ed., 1990), 353.

4 Frank Baumann, *Science Probe 8*, 2nd Edition, The Wiley Science Program (Toronto: John Wiley and Sons Canada, 1993), 514.

5 Alton Biggs *et al.*, *Biology: The Dynamics of Life* (Columbus, OH: Merrill, 1991), 769.

6 FAO, "The Forest Resources of the Temperate Zones. Main Findings of the UN-ECE /FAO 1990 Forest Resources Assessment," quoted in M. Patricia Marchak, *Logging the Globe* (Montreal: McGill-Queen's University Press, 1995), 32.

7 *The Green Team*, Observation at William Van Horne Elementary School, Vancouver, June 1997.

8 Diane Leger-Haskell, *Maxine's Tree* (Victoria: Orca, 1990).

9 Beth Savage, *Earthcycles and Ecosystems* (Toronto: Kids Can, 1991), 28–29.

10 Ann Love and Jane Drake, *Take Action* (Toronto: Kids Can, 1992), 57.

11 Hamish Kimmins, *Balancing Act: Environmental Issues in Forestry*, Second Edition (Vancouver: University of British Columbia Press, 1997), 79.

12 Kimmins, 81.

13 Marchak, 3.

14 Roger A. Sedjo, "Forest Resources: Resilient and Serviceable," in *America's Renewal Resoures*, ed. by Kenneth D. Frederick and Roger A. Sedjo (Washington, D.C.: Resources for the Future, 1991), 87.

15 Ken Drushka, *Stumped: the Forest Industry in Transition* (Van-couver: Douglas and McIntyre, 1985), 26.

16 Ken Drushka, *Stumped: The Forest Industry in Transition* (Van-couver: Douglas and McIntyre, 1985), 31.

17 Marchak, 41.

18 Marchak, 94, 87.

19 Marchak, 92–93.

20 Environment Canada Website, Forestry.

21 Bruce DeWiel, Steve Hayward, Laura Jones, and M. Danielle Smith, *Environmental Indicators for Canada and the United States*. Fraser Forum Critical Issues Bulletin (Vancouver: The Fraser Institute, March 1997), 34–35.

Chapter 9

The Rain Forest: One Hundred Acres a Minute?

Around the globe at the equator lies a hot, humid, tropical belt of land, much of it covered by canopies of leafy trees. The understory teems with rich vegetation, exotic birds, a myriad of small mammals, and a multitude of insects. This is the rain forest. And just about every schoolchild learns that it is in danger.

* *Science Is...*, a teacher's resource guide, declares that "we lose 100 acres [40.5 hectares] of rainforest per minute. That's fast enough to destroy all the world's rainforests in just a few decades."[1]

* "Every year 250,000,000 (250 million) acres (101,171,400 ha) of tropical rainforest are cut down," says the *Kids' Ecology Book.* "That's almost 250 million city blocks or the size of England."[2]

* *Science Directions 9* writes about the "tropical forests, which are being cut and burned at an alarming rate."[3]

❖ "Deforestation is happening at such a rate that some people predict that the rainforests will vanish by early in the next century," reads *Journeys in Science*.[4]

It isn't just that forests are being converted to cropland, these books say. The soil is soon exhausted since its nutrients have been absorbed by the trees and other vegetation. "Thus, within a few years, land once covered by awe-inspiring forest is reduced to useless wasteland," sums up Prentice Hall's *World Geography*.[5] North Americans are partly responsible for this devastation, the books say.

❖ Cattle ranches are replacing the rain forest, says *Looking at the Environment*, by David Suzuki and Barbara Hehner. "Almost all the beef raised on this [former rain forest] land ends up as hamburgers in North American fast-food restaurants."[6]

❖ A geography text prints under a photograph of a woman eating a hamburger, : "Some environmentalists claim that in taking a bite from a hamburger, you might also be taking a bite from a rainforest. What is the link between hamburgers and rainforests?"[7]

The fact is, however, that Canada imports less beef from rainforest countries than we export to them.[8] Our fast-food restaurants are supplied predominantly by Canadian ranchers. Our consumption of hamburgers in Canada is having very little impact on the state of the Brazilian rainforests.

A More Objective Look

Deforestation usually refers to the complete conversion of forest to cropland or other uses. Sometimes the wood from the forest is logged; at other times, trees are burned to clear the land. Deforestation is a legitimate concern but the problem should be viewed objectively, not sensationally. Although there are differences of opinion as to the severity of the problem, and arguments that the extent of deforestation is exaggerated, most textbooks only tell the scary part of the story.

Some conversion of the rain forest is not a bad thing. As we saw in Chapter 8, Canada has experienced extensive forest clearing, beginning around the middle of the nineteenth century. Many prominent people, including timber magnate H.R. Macmillan, feared a "timber crisis."[9] They thought that the nation would run out of wood. But the label "timber crisis" is an exaggeration. As prices rose, demand for wood declined, and timber substitutes were developed. In addition, public and private efforts combined to encourage better forest management. Canadian forests today are healthy.

"It is clear," say resource economists Roger A. Sedjo and Marion Clawson, "that dynamic growing societies will generate pressures on and changes in the forest resource base."[10] The widespread clearing of tropical forests is likely to be temporary.

The textbooks are somewhat misleading about the estimates of rain forest clearing. Sedjo and Clawson, relying on numbers provided by the Food and Agriculture Organization of the United Nations, report that during the 1980s about 59,459 square miles (153,998 square kilometres) of forest were cleared per year.[11] This is about 0.8 percent of the tropical forest, and is in line with the textbook estimates.

But these figures include *all types* of forests and vegetation in tropical areas, not just tropical rain forests. Children aren't told that tropical areas have six vegetation zones: tropical rain forests, moist deciduous forests, dry deciduous forests, very dry forests, desert zones, and hill and low-mountain zones.[12] Tropical rain forests are less than half the total forest in every area except Asia.

❦ So when books claim that "100 acres a minute" (40.5 hectares) of rain forests are being destroyed, the actual figure is more like 21 acres (8.5 hectares) a minute.

❋ When they say that rain forests the size of England are being destroyed every year, the actual area is about one-sixteenth of the size of England.

Texts also mislead students by an almost complete failure to discuss the planting of new trees. In Asia, 10 percent of the total forest area is in forest plantations, and one acre of trees is planted for every two that are cut.[13] In Latin America, even though tree plantations represent less than 1 percent of total forest area, about one third of Latin America's output of wood for industrial use comes from them.[14] The table below gives a more complete picture.

What Causes Deforestation?

The books identify many causes for deforestation. The *Canadian Junior Green Guide* cites "four main reasons": commercial logging, cattle ranching, hydroelectric dams, and subsistence agriculture.[15] Others emphasize overpopulation and poverty, especially in Brazil,[16] and, as we have seen, overconsumption, especially of beef, by the developed world.

It seems to be easier to blame the Western world than to concede that the governments of some countries are bringing the problems on themselves. Yet Robert Repetto, an analyst with the World Resources Institute, an environmental think tank, points out a number of policies that are contributing to deforestation:[17]

❋ In Malaysia, the Philippines, and the Brazilian Amazon, sometimes the only way to obtain ownership of land is to clear it and cultivate it.[18]

❋ In Indonesia, the government gave companies generous tax concessions to encourage logging.[19]

Data on the World's Tropical Forests

	Tropical Forests[1]		Rain Forests			Tree Planting[1]	
	Percent of land area covered	Annual deforestation (percent)	Percent of total tropical forest	Annual deforestation (percent)	Ratio total tropical forest / deforestation[2]	Percent of total tropical forest	Ratio deforestation / tree planting[3]
Africa	24	0.7	16	0.54	184 / 1	0.57	32 / 1
Asia & Pacific	35	1.2	57	1.2	82 / 1	10.0	2 / 1
Latin America & Caribbean	56	0.8	49	0.42	234 / 1	0.94	12 / 1
Total	37	0.8	41	0.63	158 / 1	2.5	6 / 1

Source: United Nations, *Forest Resources Assessment 1990, Tropical Countries #112*, Food and Agriculture Organisation of the United Nations: tables 3, 4, 7, 8.

1 Includes all types of tropical forest: tropical rain forests, moist deciduous forests, dry deciduous forests, and very dry forests.
2 For example, in Africa, for every 184 hectares of total tropical forest, one hectare of rain forest was cut.
3 For example, in Africa, for every 32 hectares of tropical forest cut, one hectare was planted.

❋ Often "migration to forested regions has been seen as a means of relieving overcrowding and landlessness in settled agricultural regions ..."[20]

In 1989, Dennis J. Mahar, an economic advisor for the World Bank, reported on policies of the Brazilian government that encouraged deforestation.[21]

❋ Beginning in the 1960s, the government took major steps to open up the Amazon region to keep out immigrants from neighboring Peru and Venezuela.[22]

❋ The government started massive road-building programs (with the help of the World Bank).

❋ It subsidized settlers who would clear land for agriculture.[23]

❋ It subsidized loans for farming and created special tax breaks for cattle-raising.[24] (In spite of these extensive tax credits, few of the cattle ranches are actually profitable, says Mahar; John O. Browder of Tulane University says that without government subsidies, "producing rain forest beef would be a financial impossibility.")[25]

Such policies far outweigh the impact of Canadians eating hamburgers or using too much wood.

Some Good News

Some positive developments have occurred that should make children feel better about the future of rain forests around the world. They include:

❈   Timber volume in the temperate climates is increasing rapidly, including in Canada and the former Soviet Union.[26] In Canada and in the United States, more timber is grown each year than is cut.[27] The world is not running out of wood or trees.

❈   Wood production in Latin America is undergoing a major transition, say Sedjo and Clawson. Trees are being grown as crops in tree farms or plantations, where trees that are cut are continually replaced by new plantings.[28]

❈   Detrimental policies of governments and the World Bank are beginning to change, and private conservation organizations around the world are taking action to protect the rain forest. For example, they have worked with the governments of countries that have rain forests to create "debt-for-nature" swaps.

"Debt-For-Nature" Swaps

"Debt-for-nature" swaps are ways that private individuals around the world can help protect the rain forest or other areas of environmental concern. They emerged some years ago to give governments an incentive to protect resources.

Many countries in the tropics engaged in heavy borrowing, especially during the 1970s, and are having trouble paying back these debts. Private environmental organizations like the Nature Conservancy and the World Wildlife Fund raise funds and then offer to pay a portion of a country's debts to other governments or banks.

If they pay off a bond owed by the government, for example, they receive in return the right to the interest that the government pays on the bond. This interest can be used to protect an environmental resource. Twenty-one debt-for-nature swaps had been made by the end of 1991, most of them in Costa Rica and Ecuador.

No one knows how significant swaps will be. Economists Robert T. Deacon and Paul Murphy point out that they represent a small amount of money (about $100 million) compared to the total debt of these countries. Also, there is no way to make governments carry out their part of the agreement if they don't wish to. But such swaps do provide an avenue for protection of the rain forest that wasn't there before.[29] One swap between the World Wildlife Fund and Ecuador created a conservation fund that was twice as large as the government's budget for parks.[30]

In the years ahead, we may see other innovative ideas as concerned people around the world offer funds for protection of special places. If preserving the rain forest is important to people in the rest of the world, it seems fair for them to help do it.

"Lungs of the Earth"?

When forests are cleared by burning, the fires release huge quantities of carbon dioxide into the air. The books claim that this will increase global warming. And once the trees are cut down, they can no longer produce oxygen and absorb carbon dioxide through photosynthesis.

* *The Kids' Environment Book: What's Awry and Why* states that between 1 billion and 2.5 billion tons of carbon dioxide are added to the air every year as a result of deforestation. This is between one-fourth and one-half of all carbon dioxide released annually worldwide.[31]

* The Scott Foresman text *History and Life* says that the rain forests "currently produce about 40 percent of all the oxygen that we breathe." If they are destroyed, carbon dioxide will build up in the atmosphere.[32]

✤ The text *Journeys in Science* says that the clearing of the rainforests "may cause the amount of oxygen being released into the air to decrease."[33]

✤ *Take Action*, a children's book endorsed by the World Wildlife Fund, writes: "A South American tribal legend speaks true: 'The tropical rainforest supports the sky. Cut down the trees and disaster follows!'"[34]

It is true that burning trees adds carbon dioxide to the atmosphere. Burning releases carbon from the trees, which then combines with oxygen to form carbon dioxide. In 1989 Richard A. Houghton and George M. Woodwell estimated that deforestation could add between 0.4 and 2.5 billion tons of carbon each year (in the form of carbon dioxide) to the air. But these are guesses with a wide range of uncertainty, and they pale in comparison to the 100 billion tons that Houghton and Woodwell say are emitted by plants and soil through a process called respiration.[35]

Calling rain forests the "lungs of the earth," or saying that the rain forests produce 40 percent of the world's oxygen, implies that clearing the forests will affect our ability to breathe. And children take this message literally. Children have been known to make gasping sounds when they see paper littering the road—they have the idea that paper, which comes from trees, is taking oxygen out of the air.

Trees do contribute oxygen to the atmosphere through photosynthesis, but their contribution represents only a small part of the total amount of oxygen in the air. (Oxygen represents slightly more than 20 percent of our atmosphere.)

And while burning does add carbon dioxide, logging itself does not. (Some carbon dioxide is released from the soil after logging, however.) When trees are made into wood and used for construction of houses, their carbon is retained as long as the logs remain. The textbooks do not make this point.

Species: Extinct before They Are Counted?

Children are told that thousands of plant and animal species will become extinct due to the loss of the rain forests.

❋ "Thousands of species which humans have never even named have already vanished from the face of the earth," writes *Investigating Terrestrial Ecosystems*. "And dozens more join them every day. More species live in the tropics than in all the other biomes combined."[36]

❋ "Scientists estimate that no fewer than one out of every two species on our planet dwells in the rain forest," says Prentice Hall's *World Geography*. "Many of these species have yet to be discovered. It is also estimated that one species of plant or animal life becomes extinct every day due to the cutting and burning."[37]

❋ The World Wildlife Fund's *Take Action* predicts that "there will be no undamaged rainforests by the year 2070. Long before then, 60,000 plant species and more than a million animal species may become extinct."[38]

❋ Life-saving medicines will be lost. Linda Schwartz's book *Earth Book for Kids* says that the rain forests have plants that are used in 25 percent of all drugs and 70 percent of drugs used in cancer treatments.[39]

It is true that many medicines, perhaps one-fourth of all prescription drugs,[40] are derived from rain forest plants. But once the drugs have been identified, they can usually be made synthetically. It is possible, however, that some important genetic material could be lost if species disappear with the rain forest. Some steps are being taken to protect these resources. Drug companies recognize that the tropics may contain the raw material for future drugs.

In 1991, Merck & Co. arranged to pay $1 million to the Instituto Nacional de Biodiversidad (INBio), a conservation and science group in Costa Rica that is trying to identify and catalog the country's plants, insects, and microorganisms. In return, Merck received exclusive rights to review samples from INBio for possible commercial applications for two years.[41]

In spite of many claims, no one actually knows how many species are being lost in the rain forests or elsewhere in the world. This complicated issue is the subject of Chapter 11.

Talking to Your Children

You are now ready to talk with your children about the rain forest. You will find it easier now to answer some of their questions.

✤ Will the rain forest disappear?

No, although it will probably get smaller for awhile. Some tropical countries are experiencing what Canada experienced about one hundred years ago—widespread logging and conversion of forest to other uses. But that was a temporary phase for us, and it should be temporary for the rain forest, too.

✤ Are Canadians exploiting the rain forest by eating too much meat?

No. Canada imports less beef from Brazil than we export to it. Cattle can be raised in many different places, not just a former rain forest. Many cattle ranches in Brazil were created largely through government subsidies. These subsidies have more impact on deforestation than whether people eat hamburger or not.

✤ Is deforestation destroying the oxygen we need for breathing?

No. Vegetation produces oxygen through photosynthesis but its contribution is a small part of the total oxygen in the atmosphere.

✤ Does deforestation contribute to global warming?

Deforestation by burning does contribute some carbon dioxide to the atmosphere, and some people think the increases in carbon dioxide are causing warmer temperatures. No one knows how much carbon dioxide deforestation adds, however, and we're not sure that increases in carbon dioxide will cause significant global warming. (We'll discuss that in Chapter 13).

Activities for Parents and Children

Here are some activities and discussions that you might like to share with your children.

What Maps Can Tell Us

The maps in the figure on page 126 can reduce your children's fears about the loss of the rain forest. The round shape of the world causes maps based on some projections of the globe to convey an inaccurate impression of size so that areas near the equator sometimes look smaller than areas near the poles that are, in fact, about the same size. We have superimposed a map of Canada on a map of Brazil drawn to the same scale. This should help children envision just how big Brazil is. Destruction of the rain forest is a serious concern but your children should have an accurate view of this problem.

Living in a Poor Country

The textbooks sometimes cite subsistence farming or "slash-and-burn" agriculture as a cause of deforestation. But they don't really explain why such agriculture causes deforestation.

Size of Brazil Relative to Canada

Ask your children to imagine that the family lives in a country where the only way to obtain farmland is to clear it. The family clears a section of forest by cutting and then burning it. The fires put the nutrients that were in the trees back into the soil, which helps crops to grow. After a few years, some of the major nutrients are used up. It would be possible to restore some nutrients through the use of fertilizer and modern farming techniques[42] but the family could travel a few kilometres to another area and clear that land. Which will they do?

It may be easier to move away and clear more land than to nurture the soil in land that has already been cleared. In some places, lack of private ownership contributes to deforestation. If no one owns the land, no one will take care to replenish the soil.

Visit a Hardwood Lumber Yard

Most cities have lumber yards that specialize in hardwoods such as oak, mahogany, and teak. These woods are valued for their strength, durability or beauty, and are used for furniture and decoration. Some of these woods come from the rain forest.

Take your children to such a lumber yard and ask the owner or manager to show your children the different kinds of wood and tell them where they come from. If they come from Latin America or Asia, ask the manager to explain why the wood comes from so far away. Is the manager concerned that deforestation may lead to the disappearance of the wood? The manager may allay fears that too much wood is coming from the rain forest.

Notes

1 Susan V. Bosak, *Science Is...* Second Edition (Co-published by Richmond Hill, ON/Markham, ON: Scholastic Canada/ The Communication Project, 1991), 358.

2 Roma Dehr and Ronald M. Bazar, *Kids Ecology Book: Good Planets Are Very Hard to Find!* (Vancouver: Earth Beat, 1991), 45.

3 Douglas A. Roberts, *Science Directions 9* (Edmonton: Arnold, 1991), 265.

4 Larry D. Yore, Peter Beugger, *et al.*, *Journeys in Science 7* (Toronto: Collier Macmillan Canada, Canadian ed., 1990), 226.

5 Thomas J. Baerwald and Celeste Fraser, *World Geography* (Needham, MA: Prentice Hall, 1993), 250.

6 David Suzuki and Barbara Hehner, *Looking at the Environment* (Toronto: Stoddart, 1989), 68.

7 Stewart Dunlop, *Towards Tomorrow: Canada in a Changing World—Geography* (Toronto: Harcourt Brace Jovanovich Canada, 1987), 12.

8 Statistics Canada.

9 Ian Mahood and Ken Drushka, *Three Men and a Forester* (Madeira Park, BC: Harbour, 1990), 153–170.

10 Roger A. Sedjo and Marion Clawson, "Global Forests Revisited," in *The State of Humanity*, ed. by Julian Simon (Cambridge, MA: Blackwell, 1995), 332.

11 Sedjo and Clawson, 329.

12 See Food and Agriculture Organization of the United Nations, *Forest Resources Assessment 1990, Tropical Countries #112*, Tables 3, 4, 7, 8.

13 Food and Agriculture Organization of the United Nations, Tables 3, 4, 7, 8.

14 Sedjo and Clawson, 334.

15 Teri Degler and Pollution Probe, *The Canadian Junior Green Guide* (Toronto: McClelland and Stewart, 1990), 45.

16 See Baerwald and Fraser, 250-1, and Melvin Schwartz and John O'Conner, *Exploring a Changing World* (Englewood Cliffs, NJ: Globe, 1993), 243.

17 Robert Repetto, *The Forest for the Trees? Government Policies and the Misuse of Forest Resources* (Washington, DC: World Resources Institute, 1988), 1.

18 Repetto, 13.

19 Repetto, 16.

20 Repetto, 16.

21 Dennis J. Mahar, *Government Policies and Deforestation in Brazil's Amazon Region*, (Washington, DC: World Bank, 1989), 9.

22 Mahar, 11.

23 Mahar, 37.

24 Mahar, 13–20.

25 John O. Browder, "The Social Costs of Rain Forest Destruction," *Interciencia,* Vol. 13, No. 3, May/June 1988, 115–120 at 118.

26 Sedjo and Clawson, 333.

27 Evergreen Foundation, *The Truth About America's Forests,* Special Bonus Issue (Washington D.C.: Island, 1991), 4.

28 Sedjo and Clawson, 334.

29 Robert T. Deacon and Paul Murphy, "Swapping Debts for Nature: Direct International Trade in Environmental Services," in *NAFTA and the Environment*, ed. by Terry L. Anderson (San Francisco: Pacific Research Institute, 1993), 69–90.

30 Deacon and Murphy, 77.

31 Anne Pederson, *The Kid's Environment Book: What's Awry and Why.* (Santa Fe: John Muir, 1991), 71–8.

32 T. Walter Wallbark, et al., *History and Life* (Glenview, IL: Scott Foresman, updated ed., 1993), 766.

33 Yore and Beugger, et al., 346.

34 Ann Love and Jane Drake, *Take Action* (Toronto: Kids Can, 1992), 75.

35 Richard A. Houghton and George M. Woodwell, "Global Climatic Change," *Scientific American*, Vol. 260, No. 4, April 1989, 36–44.

36 William A. Andrews and Donna K. Moore. *Investigating Terrestrial Ecosystems* (Scarborough: Prentice-Hall, 1986), 285.

37 Thomas J. Baerwald and Celeste Fraser, *World Geography* (Needham, MA: Prentice Hall, 1993), 250.

38 Love and Drake, 71.

39 Linda Schwartz, *Earth Book for Kids: Activities to Help Heal the Environment* (Santa Barbara, CA: Learning Works, 1990), 114.

40 Deacon and Murphy, 73.

41 Deacon and Murphy, 74.

42 Roger A. Sedjo and Marion Clawson, "Global Forests," in *The Resourceful Earth*, ed. by Julian Simon and Herman Kahn (New York: Basil Blackwell, 1984), 151.

Chapter 10

North American Wildlife: On the Edge?

Eight-year-old Hunter Allen was fascinated by bats. One day he learned that bats had been found in the attic of a community center near his home. The people restoring the building wanted the bats to move out.

Hunter worried that the bats might be killed or have a hard time finding a place to live. But he had read in the National Wildlife Federation's magazine *Ranger Rick* that it is possible to make homes for bats. So Hunter wrote for instructions, got a few other Cub Scouts to help him, and asked a lumber company to donate some wood. They made "bat boxes" and, with the help of Hunter's mother, nailed five boxes on the side of the community center for the bats.[1]

Practical suggestions for helping animals, such as this one, are rare in our schools. The textbooks create an image of a world about to lose large numbers of species. They make the job of saving species or helping wild animals seem overwhelming and a task that only the government can handle.

Textbooks paint a grim picture of wildlife in North America.

✤ The geography text *Canada in a Changing World* states that "people have done much to reduce the list of species."[2]

✤ "In more recent times," claims *Science Probe 8*, "human activities alone have caused species to become extinct or disappear from an area. When people cause oil spills, drain wetlands, cut down forests, dam rivers, and build cities and highways, they also change habitats."[3]

✤ *Investigating Terrestrial Ecosystems* declares that "humans, through greed and carelessness, are driving many [species] to extinction."[4]

✤ "Hunting, trapping, and the destruction of habitat caused by human settlement and economic activity have resulted in the loss of hundreds of species," states Innovations in Science, a teaching resource package, in its section titled "Earth Team."[5] The books convey the impression that all hunting is bad, and that all development should be stopped.

Extinction: Mostly Out of Date in North America

Much of what our children learn is out of date. It is true that during the nineteenth century in North America, wildlife numbers declined. Some species, such as the passenger pigeon and the heath hen, disappeared entirely, and others, such as the grizzly bear, remain reduced in numbers. But the rebound of many species has been dramatic and largely unreported:

✤ The white pelican, considered threatened in 1978, was delisted by 1987 when 50,000 pairs could be found throughout Western Canada.[6]

❋   The population of pronghorn antelopes in the Rocky Mountains and the plains dropped from 30 million or 40 million to a mere 13,000 in 1930, but it has recovered to over one million today.[7]

❋   In sum, says Winston Harrington, writing for the research organization Resources for the Future, many game species are "more numerous today than 80 to 100 years ago"[8] and migratory birds such as the trumpeter swan, the whooping crane, and the peregrine falcon have made dramatic recoveries.[9]

A few animals, including the Vancouver Island marmot and the black-footed ferret, are still close to extinction. In most cases, however, the animals we hear so much about—the grizzly bear and the wolf, for example—are not in danger of extinction. Rather, populations are endangered in certain places.

Depletion and Restoration

The history of wildlife in North America is a lot like the history of its forests. It is a story of abundance followed by depletion, and depletion followed by restoration.

The texts recognize that loss of habitat and over-hunting led to the decline and extinction of animals in the 1800s. But they ignore the more fundamental reason: the absence of incentives to maintain wildlife populations. Early on, supplies of wild game seemed virtually inexhaustible, and no one thought it was important to restrict access to wildlife through laws or regulations.

In fact, Canada was largely built upon the fur trade. In the early days, fish and fur-bearing animals drew explorers and colonizers to Canada. The *coureurs de bois* and *voyageurs* paved the way for the settlers and industries that followed. The country was viewed as a limitless pool of resources that could be harvested at will.

Game animals provided early settlers with provisions vital for surviving through the harsh conditions. Unlike livestock, game animals were not fenced in and may have migrated over large territories. Property rights existed only for dead animals. Thus, settlers and hunters had no incentive—or ability—to conserve live animals. If they did, someone else could kill any animals they left. Thus, hunters had an incentive to kill as much game as possible.

As the population moved westward across the continent, settlers cleared the forests for farms, and the habitat for wildlife changed dramatically. Animals that require large areas in which to roam had a more difficult time. Grizzly bear territories extend for 30 miles, for example, and salmon use entire rivers. Settlers also hunted and trapped animals, and commercial hunters killed game to sell as food. Over time, this hunting reduced the numbers of many animal species, including the beaver, bison, passenger pigeon, wood duck, heath hen, and others. The common pool of wildlife became seriously depleted. Wildlife experienced the "tragedy of the commons" (see Chapter 5).

Only a few animal species actually became extinct. Charles Mann and Mark Plummer say that five birds disappeared from North America as a result of commercial hunting and forest clearing east of the Mississippi and around the Great Lakes. They were: the ivory-billed woodpecker, the passenger pigeon, the Carolina parakeet, the heath hen, and the Bachman's warbler.[10] Still, many populations were severely reduced in numbers. The stories of the passenger pigeon and the bison are particularly striking.

Passenger Pigeon

The passenger pigeon was so common throughout North America in the early 1800s that no one thought it could ever die out. In 1810, naturalist Alexander Wilson saw a flock in Kentucky that he claimed contained more than 2 billion birds. (He estimated the flock to be a mile [1.6 km] wide and 240 miles [386.24 km] long.)[11] The flocks darkened the sky as they passed over.

Since the birds required so much food and space, the advance of settlements and industrial expansion undoubtedly affected their numbers by reducing their habitat. But commercial hunting was a big factor, too. Hunters shot pigeons and shipped them east for sale, much as farmers ship chickens around the country today. During a forty-day period in 1869 three rail cars full of pigeons were shipped

---

The Spotted Owl: How Threatened?

Many people assume that the spotted owl is headed for extinction unless we make heroic efforts to protect it. But this is unlikely.

For one thing, the northern spotted owl—the subject of controversy in British Columbia and the Pacific Northwest—is a subspecies. The forests of southern B.C. are the northernmost extent of the subspecies' natural range, and its only habitat in Canada. There are two other spotted owl subspecies, the California, and the Mexican.

Second, the northern spotted owl may be more adaptable than we think. The northern spotted owl (like its relatives) nests in the cavities of old trees. People fear that if old trees are cut down, there may not be enough places for the owl to nest. But Lowell Diller, a zoologist for the Simpson Timber Co., has found high densities of spotted owls in redwood forests owned by Simpson, even though less than 2 percent of these forests are old-growth.[1]

For some people, what is really important is not the owl, but old-growth trees. In a now-famous statement, Andy Stahl of the Sierra Club Legal Defense Fund said in 1988: "Thank goodness the spotted owl evolved in the Pacific Northwest, for if it hadn't, we'd have to genetically engineer it."[2] Stahl was joking, but his comment reveals that the spotted owl is a tool for protecting old-growth forest.

The campaign to "save" the northern spotted owl has led to economic hardship for workers in the timber-based industries of British Columbia. People are having to travel farther abroad to find employment. Roslyn Kunin wrote in *The Province* that "the Chileans have an expression: 'Viva St. Spotted Owl.'" As fewer trees are logged in North American forests, markets have opened for Chilean forest products. And, says Kunin, "skilled B.C. workers are now heading south."[3]

to market daily from Hartford, Michigan. Nearly 12 million birds were shipped during that time. And over a two-year period nearly 16 million birds were shipped from another Michigan town.[12]

By 1890, the bird was rare. The last Canadian sighting was in Penetanguishene, Ontario in 1902.[13] The last passenger pigeon died at the Cincinnati Zoo in 1914.[14]

And this may be just the beginning. Already, the B.C. government is committed to preserving twelve per cent of the province in parks, reserves, and other non-commercial settings by the year 2000.

The Canadian Spotted Owl Recovery Team has released a report of regulatory recommendations to ensure the survival of the species. These range from doing nothing to preserving every hectare of spotted owl territory for the exclusive use of the owl and other indigenous species.[4] Perhaps a middle ground will be found.

Robert J. Smith, an environmental writer, has another idea. Instead of penalizing landowners for having spotted owls on their property, governments could pay people who prove that they have spotted owls on their land. "Such a program would be infinitely cheaper than taking billions of dollars of timber and private property, eliminating hundreds of thousands of jobs, and forcing huge numbers of people onto unemployment and retraining rosters," he writes.[5]

Notes

(1) Donald R. Leal, "Unlocking the Logjam Over Jobs and Endangered Animals," *San Diego Union-Tribune*, April 18, 1993, G4.

(2) Quoted in Randy Fitzgerald, "The Great Spotted Owl War," *Reader's Digest*, November 1992, 92.

(3) Roslyn Kunin, "Global jobs abound for those who have trade," *The Province*, March 19, 1996, A27.

(4) Dave Dunbar and Ian Blackburn, *Management Options for the Northern Spotted Owl in British Columbia* (Surrey: BC Environment, July 31, 1994) xii–xiii.

(5) Robert J. Smith, "The Endangered Species Act: Saving Species or Stopping Growth?" *Regulation*, Winter 1992, 87.

Bison (or Buffalo)

Great herds of bison (also known as the American buffalo) roamed the prairies during the early nineteenth century. In 1800, the plains bison were estimated to have numbered over 50 million.[15] Like the passenger pigeon, they were a common pool of animals that anyone could kill. With no one to protect them, they almost disappeared.

When bison became extremely rare late in the nineteenth century, the Canadian government stepped in. They were declared protected in 1893, and have been actively managed since the 1920s.[16] A herd of prairie bison was established in Wainwright, Alberta, by importing a herd from the United States, where the American Bison Society had been formed in 1905.

Wood Buffalo National Park, Canada's largest national park, was established in 1922 to protect the wood bison subspecies. In 1925, a transfer of prairie bison from Wainwright to the park in 1925 led to interbreeding and great population gains, but the rarer wood bison was almost lost as an independent species. Fortunately, in 1957, a pure herd was found in the park and isolated. It was transported to Elk Island National Park, where today it thrives.[17]

There are many thousands of bison in North America today, on both public and private lands. While national parks such as Wood Buffalo and Yellowstone protect bison herds, one reason the bison numbers are growing is that people want to eat bison meat, which is leaner than beef. Because the herds are owned, markets lead to their growth in numbers, not their destruction.

Alarm at the Turn of the Century

During the late 1800s, many people became alarmed at the disappearance of wildlife. Bison were rescued, as we have seen. The National Audubon Society was formed in the United States to protect birds, especially egrets, whose plumes often decorated women's fancy hats. The Audubon movement advocated legislation to protect birds and conducted campaigns to educate the public, trying to arouse moral indignation against the plume trade. Audubon also created a system of private wardens who protected wildlife in key areas and it established a network of private wildlife refuges.[18]

In response to the changing public mood, provincial and federal governments also took action. Prime Minister Sir Wilfred Laurier and Sir Clifford Sifton worked in co-operation with President Theodore Roosevelt to protect North American wildlife through international wildlife treaties and other policies.

Today, fees for hunting licenses support most provincial and state fish and game departments. Federal excise taxes on hunting guns and ammunition and fees for duck licenses have been used to acquire millions of hectares of federal wildlife refuge lands.

Friend or Foe?

Many Canadians are encouraging Ottawa to adopt legislation similar to the United States Endangered Species Act (ESA), which they perceive to be an effective way to protect endangered species. While some children's texts in the United States point out that the act has aroused controversy, the texts consider it at least a step in the right direction.

* The act "embodies an encouraging attitude toward nature that has now become public policy," says one American text.[19]

* The "power and controversy" of the act is illustrated by the story of the Tellico Dam, says another. (In 1978, discovery of the snail darter, a small fish that appeared to be endangered, halted construction of a dam in Tennessee. Congress passed a law allowing the dam to be built, anyway.)

✤ "The Fish and Wildlife Service has found that the most effective way to save most species is to protect their habitats,"[20] says another. Protecting endangered species "may mean restricting human use of some areas," it continues.[21]

Some textbooks recognize that the U.S. Endangered Species Act has been controversial, since it has prevented government agencies and private individuals from activities such as building and farming in certain areas.

What the books don't say is that the act may be harming the species it seeks to protect. Suppose a homeowner discovers a painting by Rembrandt in his attic. Most people would be thrilled to find such a treasure and would protect it. But suppose the owner was required to convert his home into a museum and display the painting for the benefit of the public, paying all the costs. Most of us would consider this unfair. And the homeowner might be tempted to burn the painting before anyone found out about it.[22]

Now consider what happens if a landowner finds an endangered species on his or her property—something the owner might view as valuable, like an Old Master painting. The landowner will have to protect the species—following strict rules of the U.S. Fish and Wildlife Service—without compensation.

These restrictions could lead some people to destroy such an animal before anyone finds out about it. (This practice has been described as "shoot, shovel, and shut up.") Or perhaps the landowner would do something to the land to make it unattractive for the species. While such action is deplorable, we should at least understand it. It helps explain why the U.S. Endangered Species Act has not been very successful in accomplishing its objectives.

Only 27 species, out of about 1,400 American species listed, had been delisted by early 1995. Of these, only eight could be described as "success stories." (Some of the delistings were for errors in the original listing).[23] At best, the act has led to a greater awareness of endangered species and has helped a few high-profile species, such as the whooping crane, but this kind of record cannot be called a rousing success.

Who Is Saving Species?

There is always hope that endangered species will recover. Some species have rebounded dramatically through public and private conservation efforts. Your children may not know about the following:

Peregrine Falcons

The peregrine falcon was close to extinction in the 1970s when the Canadian Wildlife Service developed breeding techniques at a facility in Alberta. There was some debate as to whether captive breeding, which involved human intervention, was necessary to restore falcons, but they persisted. Two university-affiliated breeding centres joined the effort, and from 1976 through 1988 over 800 young peregrines were released across eastern Canada.[24]

Through these efforts—and, most scientists believe, through the elimination of the use of DDT in North America—the peregrine has rebounded. Peregrines can be found nesting on skyscrapers and under major bridges.[25] The bird has been taken off the endangered species list and is now listed only as "threatened."

Bluebirds

Bluebirds nest in holes in old trees and fence posts. Bluebird numbers were declining in the 1970s because older trees had been cut down and because sparrows and starlings were competing for the spaces. In recent years, members of the North American Bluebird Society have put up thousands of bluebird nest boxes, and bluebird populations are recovering.[26] In 1996, the eastern bluebird was moved from the "vulnerable" to the "not at risk" category by the Committee on the Status of Endangered Wildlife in Canada.[27]

Ducks

Many organizations, some of them supported by hunters, protect and restore habitat for ducks. Although taxes paid by hunters enable state and federal conservation agencies to acquire duck habitat, private organizations are a significant force in habitat protection:

* Since 1937, Ducks Unlimited has preserved or restored 2.5 million hectares (6 million acres) of wetlands in Canada and the United States. This organization, which has 550,000 members, works with private landowners to develop duck nesting areas and preserve wetlands.[28]

* The Delta Waterfowl Foundation (headquartered in Deerfield, Illinois) protects ducks with its "Adopt a Pothole" program. It pays farmers in central Canada and the United States to maintain the shallow depressions or "potholes" in farmland that provide nesting places for waterfowl.[29]

* The Delta Wildlife Foundation (headquartered in Stoneville, Mississippi) works with farmers to maintain wetland areas. It sponsors and places boxes for wood ducks and helps restock Canada geese. It encourages other environmental actions, too, from planting food plots for deer to building and distributing bluebird nesting boxes.

Deer and Elk

In response to growing concern about the safety of wildlife, Banff National Park, encompassing 6640 square kilometres in Alberta, has built large underpasses which permit large animals such as deer and elk to cross the Trans-Canada Highway without danger. Both humans and wildlife benefit from this arrangement in Canada's most popular national park: the animals can avoid the traffic, and the traffic is no longer disrupted by crossing wildlife.[30]

Canada Geese

By the 1920s, the Canada goose had been hunted to near extinction in this country. In 1968, Ontario's Ministry of Natural Resources decided to try to save the bird while introducing wildlife to the urban areas of Lakes Ontario and Erie. No one anticipated how well the geese would adapt to their new environment. The two dozen geese reintroduced to the area thirty years ago have grown into a population of 300,000 today. In fact, governments in urban areas across Canada and the United States are now battling the problem of overpopulation of Canada geese. They have been donated to food banks, transported to rural areas, and promoted as desirable targets to hunters.[31]

Talking to Your Children

The state of wildlife in North America is much better than the textbooks imply. Despite the growth of cities and towns, an enormous amount of land has been converted from farmland to wildlife habitat, as we discussed in Chapter 8, and many people are devoting their lives to protecting wildlife. The outlook for wildlife preservation in Canada is more promising than our children are led to believe.

Now you are ready to answer some questions that your children may ask.

* Are we losing species in Canada?

    Yes, we have lost some and we may lose a few more. Some species, such as the Vancouver Island marmot, may not be able to recover, despite enormous effort. However, many animals *are* recovering. Others, such as wolves and grizzly bears, are endangered in some areas but doing well in others.

* Why did the passenger pigeon become extinct?

The passenger pigeon was once so abundant that no one thought protecting it was necessary. But much of the pigeon's forest habitat was cleared, and because the pigeon was part of the common pool of wildlife, the "tragedy of the commons" contributed to its demise. Anyone who held back from killing it for food could not preserve it for the future because someone else could kill it. With no owners to protect the pigeons, hunters killed them in great numbers. In addition, its habitat shrank as settlers turned wild land to farmland.

❧ Does Canada need an endangered species act?

No. At best, the U.S. Endangered Species Act has saved only a few species, although it has probably saved some populations. One reason for its poor record is that it penalizes people who find endangered species on their property. These penalties may make people try to keep such species away. Thus, the Act sometimes makes an enemy of the species it is designed to help. Canadians can take pride in not having passed similarly harmful legislation.

Activities for Parents and Children

Fortunately, there is plenty of good news. Many wild animals are increasing in number, and many people are helping restore wildlife populations. The following activities will give your children a more optimistic outlook.

Watching Wild Birds

Even small towns now often have a store that specializes in wild birds. You can buy bird feeders and seed there. The store personnel will tell you what kinds of seeds attract local birds and where the feeder should be placed to attract birds. Let your children know that millions of people feed birds each year. This is one way in which people voluntarily help protect birds.

If your children become interested in birds, they may want to buy or build nest boxes. For instructions on building bluebird boxes, they can contact the North American Bluebird Society, P.O. Box 6295, Silver Spring, MD 20916-6295. For information about purple martins, they can contact the Purple Martin Conservation Association, Edinboro University of Pennsylvania, Edinboro, PA 16444. For general information about bird-watching, they can subscribe to the magazine, *Birds of the Wild*, (5694, 4 Highway #7E, Suite 199, Markham, ON, Canada, L3P 1B4). Introducing your children to birds may start them on a lifelong hobby.

Hunting and Fishing

Millions of people love to hunt and fish. Since hunters and anglers want to make sure that wild game and fish have a place to live and breed their young, they support organizations, both public and private, that protect habitat necessary to wildlife. Ducks Unlimited and Trout Unlimited often have local chapters that could send a representative to speak to your children's school. You may wish to contact their national headquarters by writing to: Ducks Unlimited Canada, Box 1160 Stonewall, Oak Hammock Marsh, MB R0C 2Z0, or Trout Unlimited Canada, P.O. Box 6270, Station D, Calgary, AB T2P 2C8.

One Glass, Two Straws

Your children might like to do this exercise, but you may prefer simply to describe it to them. They will quickly get the idea. Imagine two very thirsty children, each with a straw in a single glass of soft drink. How long will it take them to finish the glass? Not very long. If one slows down, the other one will get most of the soft drink. This is an illustration of the "tragedy of the commons." When you are taking something that you want from a common pool, you are likely to take it as fast as you can. If you don't, someone else probably will!

Now suppose that each child has a separate glass, each half-filled with soft drink. In this case, the children are not under pressure to drink so fast. One child might wait a while before drinking it, perhaps putting it in the refrigerator for later. As long as the child is assured that he or she has a right to that half-glass, he or she won't feel pressured to drink it now. In effect, each child "owns" the soft drink in the glass. Each child now has private property.

You might put a number of soft drink cans in the refrigerator (six cans for each child) and see how fast this "common property" disappears. Later, put in a six-pack for each child, with each six-pack marked with the child's name. Now, the soft drinks will probably disappear more slowly. The children will feel secure that their "property" will be there when they want it.

Notes

1 Catherine Dee, ed., *Kid Heroes of the Environment* (Berkeley, CA: Earth Works, 1991), 63–4.

2 Stewart Dunlop, *Towards Tomorrow: Canada in a Changing World—Geography* (Toronto: Harcourt Brace Jovanovich Canada, 1987), 11.

3 Frank Baumann, *et al.*, *Science Probe 8* (Toronto: John Wiley Canada, 2nd ed., 1993), 463.

4 William A. Andrews and Donna K. Moore, *Investigating Terrestrial Ecosystems* (Scarborough, ON: Prentice-Hall Canada, 1986), 285.

5 Rod Peturson and Neil McAllister, *Innovations in Science, Teacher Resource Package* (Toronto: Holt, Rinehart and Winston, 1991), page ET-39.

6   J.A. Burnett, *et al.*, *On the Brink: Endangered Species in Canada* (Saskatoon, SK: Western Producer Prairie Books, 1989), 154.

7   Winston Harrington, "Severe Decline and Partial Recovery," in *America's Renewable Resources: Historical Trends and Current Challenges*, Kenneth D. Frederick and Rojer A. Sedjo, eds. (Washington DC: Resources for the Future, 1991), 238.

8   Harrington, 237–8.

9   Harrington, 238.

10 Charles C. Mann and Mark L. Plummer, *Noah's Choice: The Future of Endangered Species* (New York: Alfred A. Knopf, 1995), 75–6.

11 Robert M. McClung, *Lost Wild America: The Story of Our Extinct and Vanishing Wildlife* (Hamden, CT: Linnet, 1993), 33.

12 James A. Tober, *Who Owns the Wildlife? The Political Economy of Conservation in Nineteenth-Century America* (Westport, CT: Greenwood, 1981), 95.

13 Burnett *et al.*, 10.

14 McClung, 35.

15 Valerius Geist, "Bison," *The Canadian Encyclopedia*, James H. Marsh, Editor in Chief, (Edmonton: Hurtig, 2nd ed., 1998), 233.

16 Burnett, *et al.*, 65–66.

17 Geist, 233.

18 Robert J. Smith, *No Regrets for Great Egrets*, Working Paper 94–4, Political Economy Research Center, Bozeman, MT, 1994, 2–4.

19 Bernard J. Nebel and Richard T. Wright, *Environmental Science: The Way the World Works* (Needham, MA: Prentice Hall, 4th ed., 1993), 420.

20 Karen Arms, *Environmental Science* (Austin: Holt, Rinehart and Winston, 1996), 263.

21 Arms, 263.

22 Richard L. Stroup, *The Endangered Species Act: Making Innocent Species the Enemy* (PERC, Bozeman, MT, PS-3, April 1995).

23 Stroup, 2.

24 Burnett, *et al.*, 155–156.

25 Robert J. Smith, "The Endangered Species Act: Saving Species or Stopping Growth," *Regulation* (Winter 1992), 85, plus personal communication by the author.

26 Robert J. Smith, personal communication.

27 Canadian Wildlife Bulletin, 3.

28 Information from Ducks Unlimited, Box 1160 Stonewall, Oak Hammock Marsh, MB R0C 2Z0,Canada.

29 Information from Delta Waterfowl Foundation, 102 Wilmot Road, Suite 410, Deerfield, IL 60015, USA.

30 Beth Savan, *Earthcycles and Ecosystems* (Toronto: Kids Can, 1991), 31; *The Canadian Encyclopedia*, 169–70.

31 Bob Reguly, "Honk if you like city life" in *The Next City* (Summer 1997), 40–44.

Chapter 11

Where Have All the Species Gone?

Jane's son David was just learning to write. He was too young to read environmental textbooks. But he knew that elephants in Africa were being "*pocht*" (that is, killed by poachers).

The message starts in preschool or kindergarten, and it doesn't stop. "Just imagine what it will be like for you and your children to live in a world without elephants, giraffes, tigers, or monkeys,"[1] says a biology text.

The idea that all these animals will completely disappear is nonsense. But by exploiting our children's natural sympathy for animals, these books build up an impression that the world will soon be devoid of most of the animals that our children love.

The children's book *Earthcycles and Ecosystem,* written in 1991, says: "By the year 2000, one of every five species on Earth will have become extinct. People are largely to blame."[2]

Earthcycles and Ecosystems is not a textbook, but the texts march to the same drumbeat:

❋ "Extinction rates are estimated to be as high as 100 species per day," says the *Green Team Teachers' Guide* sponsored by BC Environment.[3]

❋ "Every week, more than 20 kinds of living things disappear from the Earth forever," says *Science Is . . .,* a science supplement.[4]

❋ "At least one species is lost forever every hour of every day; some estimates say as many as 45 species of plants and animals will die each day," writes Adrienne Mason in *The Green Classroom,* a book for teachers.[5]

❋ A tenth grade text, *Science: Ideas and Applications,* declares it "alarming . . . that in this century alone, over 200 plant and animal species have become extinct because of human interaction."[6]

People, of course, are responsible for this destruction. People crowd out species, destroying their habitat.

❋ "Each year more than 8,000 different kinds of plants and animals become extinct because people are cutting down forests, damming rivers and building cities," says the *Kids Ecology Book.*[7]

❋ "Humans disrupt the web of life by destroying habitat in many ways, such as filling in shoreline, draining marshes and clearing forests." The *Green Team* continues: "Habitat destruction is now the major cause of extinction."[8]

❋ *Take Action,* endorsed by the World Wildlife Fund, warns that "one species becomes extinct every 15 minutes." One reason is that "their homes are being destroyed by cities that gobble up wild areas like monsters in a video game."[9]

Many other animals are disappearing because of hunting.

* The black rhinoceros is hunted for its horn, which is ground up and used as a potion.

* The African elephant is pursued for its ivory tusks, which are used for jewelry.

* "Daggers made from rhino horns, jewelry fashioned from sea turtle shells, and fur coats made from jaguar skins are just a few of the wildlife products illegally sold each year," says Ranger Rick's *NatureScope*.[10]

While the texts are correct about the dangers to these animals, they do not explain why these animals are hunted to the point of near extinction or how to protect them.

Looking at the Numbers

When children think about endangered species, they think about elephants, giraffes, and other appealing creatures. Yet the sweeping claims about extinction also include very small, often microscopic, animals and plants—insects and fungi. While these are also important for ecosystems, children should know that they account for the major part of these high numbers. And, as we will see, the high numbers are based on a somewhat controversial theory.

The truth is, we don't know how many species are disappearing. We don't even know the number of species that exist. Scholars have identified and named 1.4 million species.[11] In 1980, the *Global 2000* report published in the United States by the President's Council on Environmental Quality estimated that there are between 3 and 10 million species.[12] But in 1991, Paul R. Ehrlich and Edward O. Wilson said that there may be one hundred million species![13]

The numbers have grown because there may be many more insect and other arthropod species than previously thought. But as Dennis Murphy, director of the Center for Conservation Biology at Stanford University, admits, "Nobody knows how many species there are."[14] Since scientists are uncertain about how many species there are, they are also unsure about how many species are disappearing.

In 1980, the *Global 2000* report predicted that "at least 500,000 to 600,000 species" would become extinct in the next 20 years.[15] In 1993, Julian Simon and Aaron Wildavsky reviewed the source of these figures.[16]

* They found that the *Global 2000* Report based its predictions on estimates by Norman Myers in his 1979 book, *The Sinking Ark*. But Myers did not provide any basis for this estimate.

* They concluded that "pure guesswork" is the basis of a figure— one hundred species a day—that many people have treated as a "scientific statement."[17]

Scientists have been trying to figure out if there is a reliable way to predict how many species will be lost when habitat disappears. A famous series of studies actually attempted to measure how many species were lost when habitat was destroyed. And these were some studies! (Frankly, it was difficult for the two of us, Michael and Jane, to believe the descriptions of this process. Yet these studies have been described in several recent books, most notably *Noah's Choice*, by Charles C. Mann and Mark L. Plummer.)

In the 1960s, several biologists, including Edward O. Wilson, decided to test out the relationship between species loss and habitat loss by actually destroying the habitat on some small islands. Before and after, they would count the number of species that had disappeared. So they hired exterminators to destroy living things on small mangrove islands (little islands usually smaller than a house) off the southern coast of Florida. The exterminators built scaffolding around the islands, draped them with nylon, and pelted them with methyl bromide and tear gas.[18] After they had done their deed, scientists did their counting. Based on these studies (and some others in which the researchers actually used chain saws to chop off portions of little islands),[19] the scientists began to estimate what percentage of species will disappear in an area if a certain percentage of habitat is lost. E. O. Wilson presents this rule of thumb: if 90 percent of a habitat is destroyed, 50 percent of the species are lost.[20]

But, the results of all these studies are so variable that it is not clear that this rule of thumb is valid even for islands. And, it may not apply at all to forests and other places that aren't cut off by water. Professor Lawrence Slobodkin, writing in the journal *Nature*, concluded that the many studies have shown that the theory is "useless for explaining or predicting actual cases."[21] Others defend the theory, but predicting future extinctions on the basis of this evidence is scientifically risky.

A Brighter Picture

When it comes to *actual* extinctions that we know about, the picture is brighter. It is true that some species and subspecies have disappeared during the past few centuries, from the dodo bird in the seventeenth century to the Bali tiger in the twentieth, and many bird species on the Hawaiian Islands have become extinct. But for the most part the recorded losses have not been on the massive scale claimed in our children's texts.

❧   Puerto Rico was almost completely stripped of its forest at the turn of the century. "Yet it did not suffer massive extinctions," writes Charles Mann. Only seven of the island's 60 species of birds disappeared.[22] Ariel Lugo, a scientist who has studied Puerto Rico for a decade, explains that crops provided cover for the birds and the forest regrew rapidly.

❧ During the nineteenth century, forests were extensively logged east of the Mississippi and around the Great Lakes. Only five birds became extinct, say Charles C. Mann and Mark L. Plummer in their book *Noah's Choice*. They were: the ivory-billed woodpecker, the passenger pigeon, the Carolina parakeet, the heath hen, and the Bachman's warbler.[23]

❧ A recent book prepared by the World Conservation Union, *Tropical Deforestation and Species Extinction*, also supports the idea that the rate of extinctions is low. "Despite extensive inquiries we have been unable to obtain conclusive evidence to support the suggestion that massive extinctions have taken place in recent times as Myers and others have suggested," the authors write.[24]

Saving Elephants and Tigers

When it comes to the exotic animals that our children really do care about, such as elephants, tigers, and rhinos, textbooks usually blame hunting. Yes, this is the immediate cause, but not the full story.

Consider the African elephant. Late in the 1980s, many people became worried about these giant creatures. In several African countries, governments had created national parks but could not keep away poachers, who wanted the elephant's ivory tusks. Since elephants can cause enormous damage (they can tear down trees and destroy a year's crop of corn in a night), many people living near elephants were letting poachers kill them, especially if the poachers gave rewards.

International conservation groups such as the World Wildlife Fund pushed for an international ban on trade in ivory. That ban was adopted in 1989, but elephant numbers continued to fall in some countries. In others, including Zimbabwe, Botswana, Namibia, and

South Africa, elephant populations were increasing, not falling. But international conservation groups ignored this fact.

Elephant populations were going up in these countries for a number of reasons, including effective law enforcement. In addition, in parts of Zimbabwe, elephants were being protected because local villagers had a sort of "ownership" of the nearby elephants.

They received the benefits when elephants were legally hunted, and do so today. Villagers receive meat from the elephant plus proceeds from the sale of elephant hides and from hunters' payments for tusks, as well as from other hunter fees. Even though elephants can be very destructive, villagers who profit from the elephants will protect them from poachers. (This "ownership" does not mean that wild animals must be domesticated like cattle and sheep in order to save them.)

In Kenya, in contrast, where many elephants are kept in large national parks, the poaching goes on—in spite of the ban on the ivory trade. The chief reason is that no one who benefits directly from the herd through the kind of "ownership" found in parts of Zimbabwe. Thus, the people who live near elephants are not eager to help park rangers protect the herds for the future.[25]

So, too, with the tiger in Asia. Many Asians want tiger pelts and tiger bones (which they make into potions), and are willing to pay handsomely for them. Governments, under pressure from environmentalists, are attempting to protect the tigers by setting up reserves and trying to keep out poachers. But they have been unsuccessful.[26] If villagers received benefits when the tigers were killed, tigers would more likely be protected.

Today, as things stand, the only way to derive income from the tigers is to kill them illegally. Legal hunting and selling are not the problem, despite what the textbooks say. The problem is that no one has a personal incentive to protect the tigers, so poaching occurs.

Wildlife preservation is a complex issue, involving the loss of habitat, the effects of introduced species, and other problems.

Protecting wildlife today sometimes requires active human intervention. Without such management, wild animals can sometimes destroy their own environment. What is missing in our children's texts is a recognition that animals will become extinct in the wild if no one has an incentive to protect them.

What People Are Doing to Help

Overall, however, there is good news about endangered species. As human population grows, so does the ability of people to develop ways to protect wild animals and plants. Around the world, individuals, environmental organizations, and governments are trying to save endangered species.

* The Nature Conservancy and the World Wildlife Fund have sponsored the debt-for-nature swaps discussed in Chapter 9. These reduce countries' debts in return for protection of animal or plant habitat.

* The Nature Conservancy purchases land all over the world in order to protect endangered species.[27]

* As we saw in Chapter 9, pharmaceutical companies have begun to work with organizations in tropical countries to identify and preserve plants that may become the basis for medicines.

* Many zoos and animal centers are trying to save species in danger of extinction through captive breeding. For example, the Exotic Wildlife Association, an international organization of game ranchers, owns 19,000 animals that belong to species that are threatened or endangered in the wild.[28]

Talking to Your Children

Now you can answer questions that your children may ask about endangered species.

✤ How many species are becoming extinct?

No one knows. The very high numbers (ten thousand a year, for example) are based on guesses about how many species there are. These numbers include not only familiar animals like the rhinoceros and the tiger but also countless species of insects, spiders, and fungi. These are important to ecosystems but children are probably most concerned about larger animals. Some of these, like the rhinoceros and some kinds of tigers, could become extinct in the wild.

✤ What are people doing to protect endangered species?

Around the world many people and organizations are protecting endangered wildlife. Governments have set aside parks, and groups like the Nature Conservancy purchase land that has endangered species on it. Zoos and universities conduct captive breeding programs to assure the continuation of some endangered animal species.

✤ Will the African elephant and the black rhinoceros disappear?

They will probably not become extinct, as long as there are organizations and zoos that will protect some of them. They may become extinct in the wild, however, unless some way is found for people who live near these animals to benefit from protecting them.

Activities for Parents and Children

Here are some activities to inform your children about programs that help save animals all over the world. Perhaps your children will want to get involved in some of them.

Visit a Zoo

Take your children to a zoo and ask the zookeeper to tell your children about its programs to breed endangered animals and reintroduce them into the wild. Perhaps the zookeeper can explain some of the difficulties in reintroducing animals into the wild. If this zoo doesn't have such programs, he or she can undoubtedly tell them about places that do. Ask the zookeeper how your children might get involved by volunteering their time to help animals.

The African Elephant

Children are rarely told that elephants are thriving in Zimbabwe and nearby countries. As this chapter indicates, elephants in these countries thrive because villagers have a stake in taking care of the herds. They do not actually "own" or domesticate the elephants, but they act like owners because they benefit by making sure that elephants continue to thrive.

Talk to your children about how people might act differently toward the elephant if they received the meat and hide from an elephant that is killed—and sometimes cash as well. Would they allow poachers to wipe out the elephant? Probably not.

You could also talk to children about ownership of other animals such as cows and chickens. Why, you can ask, don't we worry about the possible extinction of cows and chickens the way we worry about the possible extinction of elephants and tigers? After all, millions of people use these animals for food every day.

The answer, of course, is that animals become extinct when they have no owners with a stake in their future. While it would be difficult for wild animals to have "owners," they will be protected if people living near them have a stake in their future.

You may wish to share the story of successful wildlife conservation programs in Africa by introducing older children to *The Myth of Wild Africa* by Jonathan S. Adams and Thomas O. McShane (W. W. Norton, 1992).

Noah and the Ark

Read your children the story of Noah and the Ark from the Bible (Genesis: 6-9) or a Bible storybook. This story illustrates how one good man and his family saved them from catastrophe, making sure that the offspring of the animals would continue to populate the earth. Talk with your children about modern-day "Arks" created by people who take on the responsibility of stewardship. These include zoos, nature centres, wildlife refuges, and ranches that specialize in game. They include organizations such as the Nature Conservancy, which protects endangered species by creating preserves. Their actions are not the same as protecting animals in the wild, but they make an important contribution.

Notes

1 Kenneth Miller and Joseph Levine, *Biology* (Englewood Cliffs, NJ: Prentice Hall, 2nd ed., 1993), 1065.

2 Beth Savan, *Earthcycles and Ecosystems* (Toronto: Kids Can, 1991), 31.

3 Green Team, *Green Team Teachers' Guide "Eco Education Program"* (Victoria: BC Environment, March 1996), 13.

4 Susan V. Bosak, *Science Is ...* (Richmond Hill/Markham, ON: Scholastic Canada/Communication Project, 2nd ed., 1991), 356.

5 Adrienne Mason, *The Green Classroom* (Markham, ON: Pembroke, 1991), 51.

6 H. Murray Lang, Editor, *Science—Ideas and Applications* (Toronto: John Wiley and Sons, 1998), 43.

7 Roma Dehr and Ronald M. Bazar, *The Kids Ecology Book* (Vancouver: Earth Beat, 1991), 45.

8 Green Team, 14.

9 Ann Love and Jane Drake, *Take Action* (Toronto: Kids Can, 1992), 6–8.

10 Judy Braus, ed., *Endangered Species: Wild & Rare*, Ranger Rick's *NatureScope* Series, National Wildlife Federation, Washington, DC, 1989, 34.

11 Paul R. Ehrlich and Edward O. Wilson, "Biodiversity Studies: Science and Policy," *Science*, Vol. 253, 16 August 1991, 758–62 at 758.

12 U.S. Council on Environmental Quality and Department of State, *The Global 2000 Report to the President,* Vol. 2, 331.

13 Ehrlich and Wilson, 759.

14 Quoted in Charles C. Mann, "Extinction: Are Ecologists Crying Wolf?" *Science*, Vol. 253, August 16, 1991, 736–38, at 738.

15 U.S. Council on Environmental Quality and Department of State, *The Global 2000 Report to the President,* Vol. 2, 331.

16 Julian L. Simon and Aaron Wildavsky, *Assessing the Empirical Basis of the "Biodiversity Crisis,"* Competitive Enterprise Institute, Washington, DC, May 1993.

17 Simon and Wildavsky, 7.

18 Charles C. Mann and Mark L. Plummer, *Noah's Choice: The Future of Endangered Species* (New York: Alfred A. Knopf, 1995, 60.

19 Mann and Plummer, 61.

20 Quoted in Mann, 737.

21 Lawrence B.Slobodkin, "Islands of Peril and Pleasure," *Nature*, Vol. 381, May 16, 1996, 205.

22 Mann, 738.

23 Mann and Plummer, 75–6.

24 T. C. Whitmore and J. A. Sayer, eds., *Tropical Deforestation and Species Extinction* (New York Chapman and Hall, 1992), quoted in Simon and Wildavsky, 9.

25 Randy T. Simmons and Urs P. Kreuter, "Herd Mentality," *Policy Review*, Fall 1989, 46–9.

26 Eugene Linden, "Tigers on the Brink," *Time*, March 28, 1994, 44–51.

27 Information from The Nature Conservancy, 815 North Lynn Street, Arlington, VA, 22209.

28 Ike C. Sugg, "To Save an Endangered Species, Own One," *Wall Street Journal*, August 31, 1992.

Chapter 12

The Air We Breathe

You probably remember seeing a scene from a Sherlock Holmes play or movie eerily wrapped in London fog. We know today that the thick, grey smoke that swirled ominously around the lamp-posts in the nineteenth century wasn't just fog. It was air pollution at its worst. Black smoke hung over the city, created by dust from the low-grade coal used for heating in the crowded residential districts.

The fog eventually disappeared. Over time Londoners used cleaner coal and replaced coal with oil, electricity, and gas. London's last famous "killer fog" took place in 1962.[1] But our children's texts would make you think that those days are still with us.

❧ "In the London 'smog' of 1952, more than 4000 people died in the combination of smoke and fog that was trapped in the city. Los Angeles, located in a valley and with one of the highest concentrations of automobiles, is also prone to smog," concludes one science text.[2]

❧ "In earlier centuries, man added only slightly to the natural pollution of the atmosphere. Today, one very large industrial country may add more than 150,000,000 tonnes of gases, smoke, and dust to the atmosphere each year," says the text *Focus on Science*.[3] (The text does not mention that there are an estimated 1 million metric tonnes of atmosphere for every person on the earth.)[4]

❧ "Air pollutants are a serious menace to health. They are thought to be a factor in causing many respiratory diseases. Such diseases include pneumonia, bronchitis, emphysema, tuberculosis, and lung cancer," says *Earth Science*.[5]

❧ Air pollution "may well pose the greatest danger of all ... There is the growing fear worldwide that unless the harm is stopped, we may eventually destroy all life on our planet,"[6] says Edward F. Dolan in his book *Our Poisoned Sky*.

According to our children's books, the chief culprit in producing air pollution is the automobile.

❧ The text *Focus on Science* says that "man-made pollution has become a major problem only in this century. To understand how this has happened, we have only to look at the increasing numbers of motorized vehicles."[7]

❧ "Our cars emit many toxic substances, including large amounts of carbon monoxide, which interfere with the blood's ability to absorb oxygen, which in turn may threaten the growth and mental development of unborn babies," says *This Planet Is Mine*.[8]

But the Air Is Cleaner

Air pollution used to be a serious problem in parts of urban North America. Today, although a few cities such as Los Angeles and Denver still have serious smog, Canadians live in a pleasant atmosphere where smog is a rare occurrence, as do most Americans. Air quality has improved dramatically. Automakers have reduced emissions of pollutants; our homes mostly use natural gas and electricity, not coal; and industries have reduced the particulates from their smokestacks.

The Fraser Institute has reported on the change in airborne levels of pollutants between 1975 and 1994. As the following table indicates, lead went down by 97.0 percent, carbon monoxide by 73.3 percent, nitrogen oxide by 41.9 percent, and sulfur dioxide by 61.5 percent.

Air Pollution Is Decreasing Nationally

	Percent Reduction	Period
Total Suspended Particulates	−46.2%	1980–1993
Lead	−97.0%	1974–1994
Carbon Monoxide	−73.3%	1975–1994
Ozone	+31.3%	1979–1994
Nitrogen Oxide	−41.9%	1977–1994
Sulfur Dioxide	−61.5%	1974–1994

Source: Steven Hayward and Laura Jones, *Environmental Indicators for North America and the United Kingdom.* 1999 Fraser Institute Critical Issues Bulletin (April).

Air Pollution: How Dangerous?

Does this mean that there is no air pollution problem? No. There can be real effects on human health, especially on people who are already sick.

✤ In 1993, *Scientific American* cited two studies of Californians showing that people living in polluted areas have higher levels of chronic diseases, including bronchitis and asthma.[9]

* Researchers from the Harvard School of Public Health found
that in several cities increases in very small particles in the air
may be linked to an increase in the number of deaths over the
next few days. This correlation was found even though the total
particulates (that is, the portion of the air comprised of particles)
were well within federal standards.[10]

Given these facts, it is important to keep improving air quality. But
our children's textbooks are not very helpful about how to do it.

Automobiles: The Enemy

The textbooks treat the automobile as the enemy in the war against
pollution. They urge children to ride bikes, join car pools, or use mass
transit. We, the authors of this book, have seen the results.

Devin (Michael's eight-year-old son) was driving with his father
one day. He noticed that many cars had only one person. By using
cars so wastefully, he said, people were making pollution much
worse. Then a bus stopped nearby. Michael asked Devin to count the
number of people in the bus. It was just a handful. As he finished
counting, the bus suddenly took off in a cloud of black smoke. Devin
had to agree that cars may well be causing less pollution per person
than buses.

Such a "reality check" is not found in the books our children are
reading. The book *Earthcycles and Ecosystems*, published by the
Kids Can Press in Toronto, is especially pointed about cars.

* "There are about 400 million cars in use today around the
world."

* "You can smell (and often see) the pollution that gushes out of
car tailpipes."

❀ "They're the main source of pollution in the cities ... Automobile pollution is so bad in some cities that cars have been banned!"

❀ "They release carbon monoxide ... too much of it can make it difficult for people to breathe or can even kill them."

❀ "Car pollution doesn't stop when a car dies and gets hauled off to a junkyard. Rusting car bodies clutter the landscape, and piles of used tires can turn into an environmental disaster. On February 12, 1990, 13 million used tires caught fire and burned for 17 days at a tire depot near Hagersville, Ontario. Oil and dangerous compounds melted from the tires and seeped into the land and groundwater below, causing serious contamination."

❀ "How can you reduce car pollution? Try using muscle power instead of horsepower: walk, jog, cycle, or skate ..."[11]

Certainly riding bikes and car pooling are good ideas. But children should learn the other side of the story.

❀ Today's new cars emit 96 percent fewer hydrocarbon tailpipe emissions (that is, pollutants) than models of the early 1970s.[12]

❀ Most auto pollution is caused by a very small fraction of cars. Fewer than 10 percent of all cars are responsible for more than 50 percent of total auto pollution.[13]

❀ The private automobile provides enormous benefits. It enables millions of people to go where they want to go, when they want to go, and it moves them from door to door—benefits that are especially important for parents with young children.

To address air pollution effectively, it is necessary to focus on real pollution sources. Probably the biggest is poorly tuned vehicles. Luckily, the technology for such an approach already exists. Donald Stedman, a University of Denver chemistry professor, has developed a device that uses an infrared beam of light to measure pollutant emissions from vehicles as they drive by on the road or highway.[14]

The device can be fitted with a camera to record license plates. Stedman's invention, which is being used experimentally in about 30 places around the world, could identify the real polluters at considerably less cost than mandatory emissions programs and other regulatory schemes.

So far, this idea has been ignored in the textbooks.

Talking to Your Children

Air pollution is a serious issue. For hundreds of years, air pollution has been recognized as aesthetically unpleasant and dangerous to health. But air pollution has been declining over the decades. In most parts of the country, the air is clean most of the time. Children should be taught this side of the story, too.

Now you can answer your children's questions.

❋   Is the air getting cleaner?

Yes. According to Environment Canada and Organisation for Economic Cooperation and Development (OECD) data, all the major air pollutants except ozone declined from 1975 to 1997. That progress is continuing.

❋   Is air pollution dangerous?

Yes, it can be. Severe air pollution is harmful to people's health, especially those with asthma or other lung diseases. But the air today is much cleaner than it used to be.

Activities for Parents and Children

The following activities will help you and your children put today's air pollution problems into perspective.

Remembering the Good Old Days

Most of us, including our children, have a nostalgic view of the past. We imagine the nineteenth century as resembling prints of horse-drawn sleighs traversing a snow-covered country roads. But life before the automobile was anything but pristine.

When your children raise concerns about the air pollution created by cars, ask them if they would rather live in a world with "clean, nonpolluting" horses instead of polluting cars. Most children will jump at the chance. Sit down with your children and add to their list of household chores feeding the horse twice a day and cleaning the stall or corral. (Few children realize that horses create forty pounds of manure per day and that this "pollution" must be disposed of.)

Or, take your children to visit a local stable. Have the owner or manager show your children the stalls and what it means to "muck out a stall." Ask the owner to tell your children how much waste is produced by the horses and how the people who work at the stable get rid of it. Then ask your children to imagine every car on your block replaced by a horse. What would the street be like? How would it smell?

A Tale of Two Cities

Show your children the photographs of False Creek, Vancouver, British Columbia on page 167. These photographs were taken from the same location 72 years apart. In the early part of the century, many

False Creek, Vancouver, British Columbia in 1926 (top), and in 1998 (bottom)

Credits: The Vancouver Public Library; reproduced by permission (top);
Liv Fredricksen (bottom)

workers lived in close proximity to the mills, and the mills spewed pollution. Today, we have different land-use priorities.

Ask your children which city they would like to live in. Most will pick the picture of the clean Vancouver. Ask them if the people who lived in the dirty Vancouver liked living there. If not, ask your children why they think people lived there.

The reason, of course, was that jobs were available, and back then people needed jobs more than clean air. But gradually, changes took place in Vancouver's industrial and business economy. Today, the people of Vancouver have clean air and good jobs as well.

A Matter of Prosperity

While many factors contributed to Vancouver's cleaner air, one important factor that is often forgotten is the increase in the wealth of its citizens. The following chart shows income per person in 1926 and 1996 (adjusted for inflation). The average income was nearly four and a half times as high as in 1996 as it was in 1926.

Canadian Income per Capita (GDP, in constant 1986 dollars)

1926	1996
$4,654	$20,618

Sources: Statistics Canada, *Canadian Economic Observer Historical Statistical Supplement 1995/96*, Cat. #11-210; *Canadian Economic Observer*, Dec. 1997, Cat. #11-010.

In the early part of this century, Canada was much poorer than it is today. People were more concerned with making a living than having a clean environment. Today, however, because we have greater wealth than we had then, we are better able to clean the environment.

Many Third World cities are polluted today. As they become wealthier, they, too, will take additional steps to protect their environment. As people become more affluent, they will insist on less pollution, and they will be willing to spend money—sometimes through their taxes—to help clean the air.

Notes

1 Derek M. Elsom, "Atmospheric Pollution in the United Kingdom," in *The State of Humanity*, ed. by Julian L. Simon (Cambridge, MA: Blackwell, 1995), 476–490 at 478.

2 Douglas Gough and Frank J. Flanagan, *Focus on Science: Exploring the Natural World* (Toronto, ON: D.C. Heath Canada, 1980), 356.

3 Gough and Flanagan, 356.

4 Russell Seitz, "A War Against Fire: The Uses of 'Global Warming'," *National Interest*, Summer 1990, 55.

5 Samuel N. Namowitz and Nancy E. Spaulding, *Earth Science* (Toronto: D.C. Heath, Canada, Canadian ed., 1987), 497.

6 Edward F. Dolan, *Our Poisoned Sky* (New York: Dutton, 1991), 4.

7 Gough and Flanagan, 354.

8 Mary Metzger and Cinthya P. Wittacker, *This Planet Is Mine: Teaching Environmental Awareness and Appreciation to Children* (New York: Fireside, 1991), 18.

9 James M. Lents and William J. Kelly, "Clearing the Air in Los Angeles," *Scientific American* (October 1993), 38.

10 Philip J. Hilts, *New York Times*, July 19, 1993, 1.

11 Beth Savan, *Earthcycles and Ecosystems* (Toronto: Kids Can Press, 1991), 43.

12 J. G. Calvert *et al.*, "Achieving Acceptable Air Quality: Some Reflections on Controlling Vehicle Emissions," *Science*, July 2, 1993, 37–45.

13 Rick Henderson, "Dirty Driving," *Policy Review*, Spring 1992, 56–60 at 57.

14 Henderson, 56–60.

Chapter 13

A Hotter Planet?

"Imagine a world of relentlessly rising temperatures, where farmlands are scorched into desert and inland waters like the Great Lakes shrink in the heat. As global warming intensifies, the polar ice caps dissolve and ocean levels rise by more than 100 feet, swamping low-lying islands and coastal areas. Vancouver, Halifax, New York City, Amsterdam, Shanghai and other port cities are inundated. As the global floodwaters rise, more than a quarter of the world's population is displaced." *Maclean's* magazine continues: "Plenty of scientists believe that the growing accumulation of man-made gases in the Earth's atmosphere could someday push temperatures to dangerously high levels and bring cataclysmic changes to the planet."[1] Welcome to global warming.

A *Toronto Star* article reprinted in a science text, discusses the issue of global warming, and then warns that "there's an ice mass half the size of a continent, resting on a rock shelf that's a little below sea level on one side of Antarctica. If the Antarctic Ocean warms up a bit in 50 years, and laps enough at the bottom of the ice mass, the whole thing might slip off its rock and float into open water. "That would be like throwing the world's biggest ice cube into the world's biggest drink. That one event, if it happens, could push the sea level up several metres and cause coastal flooding such as we've never even dreamed."[2]

Is the Earth Getting Warmer?

Despite these frightening depictions, global warming should not keep your children awake at night. It is true that over the past one hundred years, the Earth has become slightly warmer, but only by about half a degree Celsius or 1 degree Fahrenheit. (The Intergovernmental Panel on Climate Change estimates that the increase was between three-tenths and six-tenths of a degree Celsius or one-half to one degree Fahrenheit.) But most of the warming occurred before most of the greenhouse gases were put in the atmosphere by human actions.

As for the future, scientists do not know if the Earth will continue to get warmer. If it does, the increase may be so slight as to be hardly noticeable. Clearly, apocalyptic claims of a rise in the sea level of twenty-five feet are no longer taken seriously, except perhaps by overly imaginative writers. Recent studies have predicted a possible rise in sea level of six to forty *inches*, not feet.[3] And one reputable study suggests that warming would *lower* sea levels. (Warming would lead to more snow in the Arctic, which would increase the size of the ice caps.)[4]

Temperature predictions, too, have moderated. In 1989, some scientists were predicting an increase in global temperatures of between 3.5 and 5 degrees Celsius (6.3 to 9 degrees Fahrenheit) as early as the middle of the twenty-first century.[5] In 1990, an intergovernmental panel of scientists projected an increase of 3 degrees Celsius (5.4 degrees Fahrenheit) by the year 2100.[6] The latest estimate, however, is that temperatures may increase by between 1 and 3 degrees Celsius (between 1.8 and 5.4 degrees Fahrenheit) by the year 2100.[7]

Global warming captured public attention because of some very hot summers in the 1980s, especially one in 1988. On a hot day James Hansen, who heads NASA's Goddard Institute, told a congressional committee that he thought that human actions were beginning to raise the world's temperatures—that global warming had arrived. It is true that some studies show that several years in the 1980s were the hottest on record.

But measurements of temperature taken by satellite (rather than measurements close to the ground), showed no warming between 1979 and mid-1996 (see figure, page 173).[8] In fact, there was a slight cooling trend, which can be explained by the 1991 eruption of the Mt. Pinatubo volcano in the Philippines. Volcanic dust kept out sunlight, cooling the Earth.

What Scientists Know

Let's look at what scientists do know. They agree that average world temperatures have gone up slightly since good record keeping began about one hundred years ago, probably about half a degree Celsius or about 1 degree Fahrenheit.[9] That increase, which is pretty small, may reflect natural variation in temperature.

And temperatures haven't been going up steadily. There was a significant decline in temperatures between 1938 and 1970. That decline led scientists in the 1970s to worry about a coming Ice Age. In fact, Stephen Schneider, a scientist now predicting severe global warming, urged in 1976 that people consider "massive world-wide actions" to hedge against the possibility of a new Ice Age.[10]

When people talk about global warming, they usually mean that temperatures will rise due to the "greenhouse effect." There is nothing sinister about the greenhouse effect. A number of gases, including water vapor, CO_2, methane, and others, keep the earth warm by trapping infrared rays that would otherwise be lost to

Changes in Earth's Temperature as Measured by Satellite

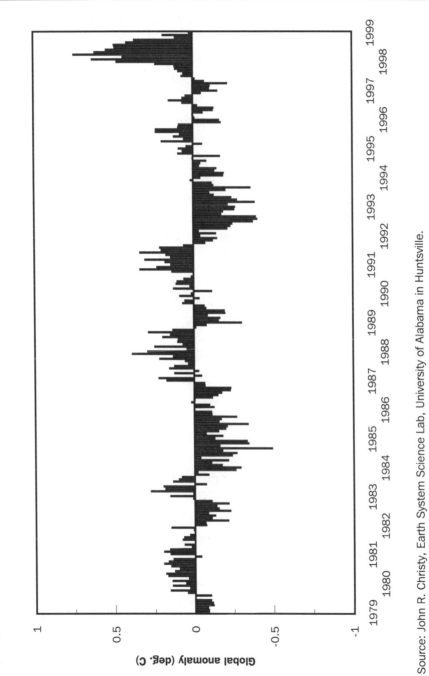

Source: John R. Christy, Earth System Science Lab, University of Alabama in Huntsville.

space. (Infrared rays are invisible rays of heat that are emitted by all objects that have temperature.)

This warming process is something like the buildup of heat that occurs in greenhouses, but it is not the same. Most warming in a greenhouse occurs because air is warmed and then trapped by the glass or plastic walls. In contrast, global greenhouse gases trap invisible rays of heat emitted from the Earth's surface.[11] Thanks to the greenhouse effect, the Earth is warmer than it otherwise would be.

Scientists who think the earth will get significantly warmer base their view on the fact that some greenhouse gases, especially carbon dioxide, are increasing in the atmosphere. Carbon dioxide is released when fossil fuels such as coal and oil are burned; and CO2 in the atmosphere has been going up since the start of the Industrial Revolution. It is believed to be about 27 percent higher than two hundred years ago.[12] Some other gases have been increasing as well.

But keep in mind that carbon dioxide, while extremely important, represents a very small part of the total atmosphere—about 0.035 percent or 350 parts per million. (In contrast, oxygen represents about one-fifth of the atmosphere or 200,000 parts per million!)

The Computer Did It

One reason why global warming has received so much attention is that computer models predict it. Climate models are simplified descriptions of the world's climate, written in mathematical formulas on computer programs. By changing the formulas, scientists can change climate predictions.

Some years ago, scientists decided to see what would happen if they assumed that CO_2 had doubled, as they thought it would by the middle of the twenty-first century. The result: Significantly higher temperatures, higher by between 2 and 6 degrees Celsius. The projections looked scientific. But scientists know that these computer models of the world's climate have strengths and weaknesses. Robert Jastrow, founder of NASA's Goddard Institute, and two colleagues point out that the models give such a rough picture of the Earth's climate that they miss entirely the effect of mountains such as the Rockies, the Sierra Nevadas and the Cascades. According to these models, the climate of heavily forested Oregon and the climate of the Nevada desert would be about the same, rather like equating the climate of the British Columbia rainforests with the climate of the southern Albertan Badlands.[13]

Another problem is that scientists are really guessing about how different aspects of the climate affect one another. For example:

* Water vapor is far more important than carbon dioxide in trapping heat. Carbon dioxide will increase temperatures significantly only if water vapor increases significantly. But will it?

* Clouds (composed of water vapor that has condensed into droplets) may increase if carbon dioxide goes up. Some clouds increase the warming effect and others decrease it by reflecting sunlight back into space.[14]

* Oceans and vegetation absorb CO_2, but how much, how fast, and for how long? No one knows.

If some of the early computer projections are correct, we should already have seen significant warming—an increase over the past one hundred years of 1.7 degrees Celsius (3 degrees F), says climatologist Patrick Michaels.[15] The actual increase, however, is only about half a degree Celsius. Recently, scientists have proposed that air pollutants such as sulfur dioxide may have slowed down the warming that would otherwise occur.[16] "It is still an open question," says Richard Peltier, a climatologist at the University of Toronto, "as to whether anything that is happening now can be attributed to the greenhouse effect."[17]

Another problem is that the pattern of warming does not follow the rise in CO_2. As the graph on page 177 shows, CO_2 concentrations in the atmosphere increased dramatically *after* World War II, but most of the temperature rise during the last century occurred *before* World War II. If the greenhouse theory is true, temperatures should have risen in tandem with the rise of greenhouse gases. They should not have fallen, as they did, between 1940 and 1970.[18]

And, temperatures in the Arctic, which should be getting significantly warmer if the computer projections are right, have been going down. Over the past forty years, they declined by 1.5 degrees Celsius (2.7 degrees F).[19]

A Warmer World: Some Benefits?

Children's textbooks, reflecting the popular view, discuss only the negative impacts of warming. But some scientists note that if the world gets warmer, that would not be all bad.

✤ "In fact," says Andrew Solow, a scientist at Woods Hole Oceanographic Institute, "there is some irony in the description of global warming as problematic, since it is not unreasonable to view human history as a struggle to stay warm."[20]

✤ Thomas Gale Moore, a prominent economist at the Hoover Institution, has even concluded that warmer weather would reduce deaths from heart disease and respiratory illness.[21] Cold temperatures lead to death more often than hot ones.

✤ More carbon dioxide in the air will benefit many plants. It causes more luxuriant growth, larger flowers, and greater crop yield.[22] Some scientists think that rising levels of CO_2 in the air have already contributed to the Green Revolution, that is, to the remarkable increases in food production of the past few decades.[23]

Changes in Temperature and Levels of CO₂, 1890–1998

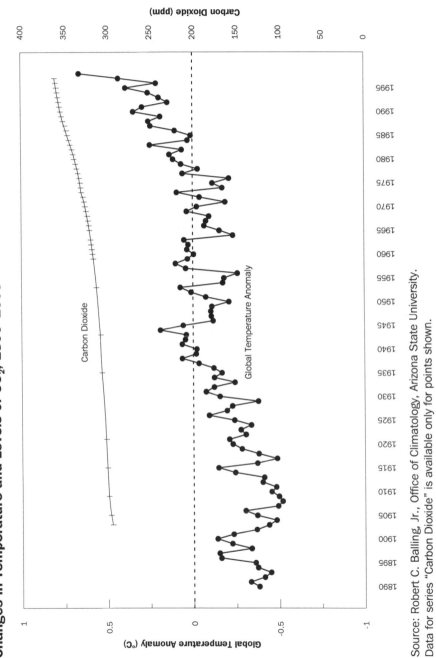

Source: Robert C. Balling, Jr., Office of Climatology, Arizona State University. Data for series "Carbon Dioxide" is available only for points shown.

Talking to Your Children

It is little wonder that our children are frightened. We would be, too, if we read the textbooks our children do. But now you can give your children a more balanced picture.

✸ Is the world going to get hotter?

No one really knows. Carbon dioxide keeps heat from being emitted into space and, because carbon dioxide is increasing in the atmosphere, temperatures may get warmer. However, the warming may be so small as not to be noticeable by the average person.

✸ Are human activities causing global warming?

Perhaps. By burning fossil fuels, humans add carbon dioxide to the atmosphere, and more carbon dioxide should keep more heat in the Earth's atmosphere. But the increase in warmth may be very small since many, many factors affect climate. Until recently, some scientists were more worried about a coming Ice Age than too much warming.

✸ Has the world been getting hotter?

Yes, a little. Scientists think that the Earth's average temperatures have increased by between three- and six-tenths of a degree Celsius or between one-half and one degree Fahrenheit over the past one hundred years. But the increase has been irregular, not steady, and it may simply reflect natural variation in temperatures over time.

✸ Is carbon dioxide harmful?

No. In fact, it is a beneficial part of the atmosphere. It provides food for plants. More carbon dioxide in the atmosphere should increase plant growth. This will increase the output of oxygen from plants through photosynthesis.

Activities for Parents and Children

The following activities should help reassure your children that the world is not "out of control" even if a modest amount of warming should occur.

Carbon Dioxide and Dinosaurs

Go to the library and check out books about dinosaurs. You might start with:

* K. Brasch, *Prehistoric Monsters* (Salem House, 1980), or

* J. W. Watson, *Dinosaurs and Other Prehistoric Reptiles* (Golden Press, 1970).

Show these books to your children and ask them to describe the trees and other vegetation that surrounds the dinosaurs. Then ask them if this world was warmer or cooler than the one we currently live in.

Now tell them that the Earth had an atmosphere that contained carbon dioxide levels that were five to ten times greater than now. The high CO_2 levels contributed to the rich vegetation. The earth was warmer and wetter, not burning up or drying out. (At other times, however, high carbon dioxide levels coexisted with cold temperatures.) The point is that the image of global warming that many people hold may be unnecessarily grim.

Take a Trip to a Greenhouse

What better way to learn about the "greenhouse effect" than to take your children on a trip to a commercial greenhouse? (Look under "Greenhouses" in the Yellow Pages.) Keep in mind that the "greenhouse effect" is a misnomer. The warming in a greenhouse occurs differently, as we discussed earlier in this chapter. But greenhouses create a warm, moist environment that encourages rapid plant growth. In addition, many greenhouses increase the CO_2 level in the greenhouse. As our children learn in basic science, plants use CO_2 to make food through photosynthesis. By increasing the CO_2 levels, the plants have more of what they need to grow vigorously.

Ask the greenhouse manager to explain how conditions in the greenhouse are controlled to help plants grow. Does this greenhouse add carbon dioxide? Why or why not?

A New Ice Age?

Doomsday predictions of climate change are nothing new. Your children may not be aware that in the mid-1970s many people worried about the coming Ice Age.

Take your children to the library and have them look up the following articles and book:

❋ Nigel Calder, "In the Grip of the New Ice Age," *International Wildlife*, July 1975.

❋ D. Colligan, "Brace Yourself for Another Ice Age," *Science Digest*, Feb. 1975.

❋ "Are We Headed for a New Ice Age?" *Current,* May/June 1976.

❋ *The Cooling*, by Lowell Ponte (Prentice Hall, 1976).

Indeed, in the early 1990s, after parts of North America experienced heavy snows and severe cold, a new interest in an Ice Age reemerged. Have your children look this one up, too: Michael D. Lemonick, "The Ice Age Cometh?" *Time*, January 31, 1994.

Notes

1 Mark Nichols, "Feeling the Heat" in *Maclean's* April 24, 1995, 52–53, 53.

2 Margaret Fagan, *Challenge for Change* (Toronto: McGraw-Hill Ryerson 1991), 246.

3 J. J. Houghton, *et al.*, eds., *Climate Change 1995: The Science of Climate Change.* Contribution of Working Group I to the Second Assessment Report of the Intergovernmental Panel on Climate Change. (New York: Cambridge University Press, 1996).

4 Gifford H. Miller and Anne de Vernal, "Will Greenhouse Warming Lead to Northern Hemisphere Ice-sheet Growth?" *Nature*, Vol. 355 (January 16, 1992), 244–246.

5 Stephen H. Schneider, "The Greenhouse Effect: Science and Policy," *Science*, Vol. 243 (February 10, 1989), 771–781 at 774.

6 R. Monastersky, "Global Warming; Politics Muddle Policy," *Science News*, June 23, 1990, 391.

7 J. J. Houghton *et al.*, *op. cit.*

8 R. W. Spencer and J. R. Christy, "Precise Monitoring of Global Temperature Trends from Satellites," in *Scientific Perspectives on the Greenhouse Problem* (Ottawa, IL: Jameson, 1990), 95–104, for figures through 1988; figures updated by R. W. Spencer.

9 See for example P. D. Jones, "Hemispheric Surface Air Temperature Variations: Recent Trends and an Update to 1987," *Journal of Climate,* Vol. 1 (1988), 654–660, and Philip D. Jones and Tom M. L. Wigley, "Global Warming Trends," *Scientific American*, August 1990, 84–91.

10 Quoted on the dust jacket of Lowell Ponte, *The Cooling* (Englewood Cliffs, NJ: Prentice Hall, 1976).

11 Sylvan H. Wittwer, "The Greenhouse Effect" (Burlington, NC: Carolina Biological Supply Company, 1988), 3.

12 Robert R. Balling, Jr., *The Heated Debate: Greenhouse Predictions Versus Climate Reality* (San Francisco: Pacific Research Institute for Public Policy, 1992), 23.

13 Robert Jastrow, William A. Nierenberg, and Frederick Seitz, "An Overview," *Scientific Perspectives on the Greenhouse Problem* (Ottawa, IL: Jameson, 1990), 11.

14 Aaron Wildavsky, "Introduction" to *The Heated Debate: Greenhouse Predictions versus Climate Reality*, by Robert C. Balling, Jr. (San Francisco: Pacific Research Institute for Public Policy, 1992), xxiv.

15 Patrick J. Michaels, "Crisis in Politics of Climate Change Looms on Horizon," *Forum for Applied Research and Public Policy* (Winter 1989), 15.

16 Summary for Policymakers of the Contribution of Working Group I to the IPCC Second Assessment Report 1995.

17 Nichols, *op. cit.*

18 Frederick Seitz, Robert Jastrow, William A. Nierenberg, *Scientific Perspectives on the Greenhouse Problem* (Washington, D.C.: George Marshall Institute, 1989), 19.

19 J. D. Kahl, D. J. Charlevoix, N. A. Zartseva, R.C. Schnell and M. C. Serreze, *Nature*, Vol. 361 (1993), 335–337, cited in *Are Human Activities Causing Global Warming?* (Washington, DC: George C. Marshall Institute, 1996), 33.

20 Andrew R. Solow, "Is There a Global Warming Problem?" in Rudiger Dornbusch and James M. Poterba, *Global Warming: Economic Policy Responses* (Cambridge MA: MIT Press, 1991), 7–28, at 26.

21 Thomas Gale Moore, "Health and Amenity Effects of Global Warming," *Working Papers in Economics E-96-1*, Hoover Institution, Stanford University (January 1996).

22 Sherwood B. Idso and Bruce A. Kimball, "Tree Growth in Carbon Dioxide Enriched Air and Its Implications for Global Carbon Cycling and Maximum Levels of Atmospheric CO_2," *Global Biogeochemical Cycles,* Vol. 7, No. 3, September 1993, 537–555.

23 J. Goudriaan and M. H. Unsworth, "Implications of Increasing Carbon Dioxide and Climate Change for Agricultural Productivity and Water Resources," in *Impact of Carbon Dioxide, Trace Gases, and Climate Change on Global Agriculture* (Madison, WI: American Society of Agronomy Special Publication Number 53, 1990), 111.

Chapter 14

Sorting Out Ozone

One evening before bedtime, Russell began to cry. He was worried about the ozone layer that surrounds and protects the earth. His father had told him that the air conditioner in the family car had chemicals that "eat" the ozone when they evaporate. Russell, a second-grader in Forest Hills, New York, felt hopeless.[1] But his father urged him to do something about it. And he did.

Russell started an environmental club at his school. His group, Kids Save the Ozone Project (Kids STOP), lobbied the mayor and city council in New York City to pass a law requiring chlorofluorocarbons (CFCs) in auto air conditioners to be recycled. The group even lobbied the president to urge him to support a worldwide ban on CFCs.

Russell became concerned about the ozone layer because it troubled his father, but many children learn in school that the thin layer of ozone in the stratosphere is being "eaten away" by man-made chemicals, primarily CFCs. Without ozone to protect us, students are told, the sun's ultraviolet (UV) rays will damage crops, cause skin cancer, and injure our eyes. One science book says that "'CFCs . . . are 'eating' holes in the ozone layer,"[2] and one children's book even shows little PacMan-like creatures eating the ozone molecules.[3]

Concern about ozone depletion has a basis in science. It is, in fact, a more genuine environmental worry than global warming or species extinction. But, fear of ozone loss is exaggerated. There is no ozone crisis.

Ozone: The Simple Version

Ozone depletion is a complicated scientific issue. But in our children's textbooks and other literature, the message is simple.

* "Without Earth's sunscreen, we'd be in big trouble," says the children's book *Earthcycles and Ecosystems*. "Farm crops would be damaged by the radiation and would produce less food. People would be plagued with skin cancer and eye diseases, caused by the increase in ultraviolet rays."[4]

* "The increase of ultraviolet light can threaten human and plant life," says *The Green Classroom*. "Ultraviolet light harms our eyes and immune systems ... [and] can increase the occurrence of skin cancer."[5]

* The science text *Challenge for Change* says: "Since ozone absorbs the ultraviolet rays, any reduction in its amount could lead to a greater degree of ultraviolet rays reaching the earth's surface with harmful effects. It is known that exposure to ultraviolet rays causes skin cancer, and the radiation may be harmful to other animal tissue and plant life."[6]

* Too many ultraviolet rays "can cause skin cancer and eye diseases. They can do terrible damage to crops and other plants—especially some of the ocean plants that sea creatures depend on for food," says a book for children.[7]

To understand this issue, we should start with oxygen. The normal oxygen that we breathe is composed of two atoms of oxygen (O_2). Ozone is a molecule composed of three atoms of oxygen (O_3). It is found in extremely small quantities high above the earth, most of it in the stratosphere, the atmospheric layer between ten and thirty miles up. Because most ozone is found there, the stratosphere is sometimes called the "ozone layer." But the amount of ozone is so small that if all the bits of ozone in a column of space in the stratosphere were compressed together, the ozone would be about one-eighth of an inch thick.[8]

This thinly scattered ozone absorbs some of the sun's ultraviolet rays, preventing them from reaching the atmosphere close to the Earth. These rays are invisible components of sunlight. Ozone absorbs only very short rays, which scientists call UV-B radiation.

The major worry is not stratospheric ozone itself but, rather, the radiation that is normally blocked by ozone. If ozone declines, more UV-B rays will reach the earth on a clear day. Too much of this radiation can cause sunburn, irritation of the eye's cornea, and skin cancer.

Ozone: Two Complex Issues

There are two ozone depletion issues. (And we're only talking about the ozone that exists many miles up in the stratosphere! Ozone close to ground is part of smog.)

First, scientists have been trying to figure out if the worldwide layer of stratospheric ozone is thinning. And, second, they have been trying to figure out the cause of what is known as the "ozone hole" above Antarctica. These are separate questions, although the textbooks tend to mix them up, creating confusion.

❧ "Unfortunately, the ozone layer is in danger. Little by little we are destroying it," says Beth Savan's children's book *Earthcycles and Ecosystems*, referring to the worldwide layer of ozone.

❋   It continues: "There's already a big hole in the ozone layer over Antarctica ... We destroy the ozone layer by producing chemicals that eat it up."[9]

The Global Ozone Issue

Let us begin with the question of the worldwide thinning. Ozone is an unstable molecule. It can break apart, forming oxygen and a free-floating oxygen atom. This is what "ozone depletion" means. Natural forces that break ozone apart include trace gases such as hydrogen oxides, nitrogen oxides, and chlorine.

But ozone is also constantly created. Sunlight reacts with oxygen, breaking the oxygen molecule (O_2) into free-floating oxygen atoms. When a loose oxygen atom joins an oxygen molecule, O_3 is formed again. Creation and destruction of ozone go on all the time. The ozone layer is not a solid that is "eaten away" by chemicals. It is not a fabric that is being "torn."

Natural fluctuations of ozone are very large. Over a few months, the amount of ozone can vary by 50 percent over parts of North America.[10] From day to day, the amount of ozone can vary by 25 percent.[11] Because these changes occur naturally, they arouse little concern. And because these fluctuations are so large, it is difficult for scientists to know whether the ozone layer is thinning over time or, if it is, what is causing the thinning.

The Antarctic Ozone "Hole"

In 1985, British scientists reported that during the period between August and October of 1984, the amount of ozone over Antarctica had dropped dramatically—by more than 40 percent from what it had been some years before. This loss extended over an area broader than the entire Antarctic continent. This reduction in stratospheric ozone became known as the "ozone hole."

In the textbooks, it is pretty scary. "In 1984, about 30 percent of the ozone was gone; in 1985, 50 percent; in 1987, 60 percent," says

The Kids' Environment Book. "On October 5, 1987, scientists recorded a level that was barely one-third of normal. By then the hole was
bigger than the continental United States and as deep as Mount
Everest is high."[12]

Our children are rarely, if ever, told that this thinning of the ozone
layer over Antarctica is temporary—that is, it lasts for only a short period of time each year—or that it probably reflects conditions unique
to the South Pole. And there is no ozone hole over the North Pole, even
though people have predicted one from time to time, and some loss of
ozone has occurred over the North Pole late in the winter.[13]

CFCs: Cause of It All?

Now, enter the supposed villains: CFCs. Many scientists believe that
these chemicals are both thinning ozone and directly contributing to
the ozone "hole." Let's see why they think this.

CFCs contain chlorine. In addition, they have an unusual property: they are inert. That is, they don't react easily with other chemicals. This makes them nontoxic and nonflammable.

Because they are so safe, they have been widely used, especially
for cooling in refrigerators and air conditioners, but in other ways as
well. They were found in aerosol propellants at one time, but their
use in Canada was banned in 1980 after concerns about ozone loss
first surfaced.[14] They were also used in the production of some plastic
foam products such as Styrofoam cups, plates, and fast-food containers, a point that some books emphasize.

Because these chemicals don't break apart easily, they stay in
the atmosphere a very long time. Gradually over many years, they
float up to the stratosphere, where they are finally broken apart by
sunlight, and their chlorine atoms are released.

These chlorine atoms, through complex chemistry, can change
two ozones (O_3) into three oxygens (O_2). Scientists theorize that a sin-

gle chlorine atom can break apart up to 100,000 ozone molecules.[15] In the atmosphere, however, other chemical reactions interfere, slowing but not stopping the process.

Are CFCs causing ozone to thin around the globe? And are they causing the ozone "hole"? Let us look at each ozone issue again.

The Global Ozone Issue

Scientists aren't sure how much the ozone is thinning. A panel of scientists convened by the National Aeronautics and Space Administration (NASA), the Ozone Trends Panel, reported in 1988 that ozone levels above the Northern hemisphere had declined by between 1 percent and 3 percent per decade.[16] These figures were later refined, updated, and published by a group headed by NASA scientist Richard Stolarski.[17]

In 1991, the U.S. Environmental Protection Agency (EPA) went further, announcing that the ozone layer above the United States had decreased by 4 to 5 percent between 1979 and 1990. However, this statement was based on an oversimplified analysis of satellite data. For one thing, there was an upturn after 1986. Second, the eleven and a half years of records may not be enough to distinguish human-caused decline from the natural sunspot cycle, says S. Fred Singer, the scientist who designed the instrument used on satellites to measure ozone.[18]

Further, the sun's eleven-year sunspot cycle affects the amount of ozone depletion. When the sun is at its strongest, there is more UV radiation in the stratosphere to break apart oxygen molecules, and more ozone is formed. When the sun is at its weakest, less oxygen is broken apart and less ozone created. One study concluded that "73 percent of the global O_3 declines between 1979 and 1985 are due to natural effects related to solar variability ..."[19]

Sorting out the "natural effects" is an enormous challenge. While chlorine from CFCs appears to be combining with ozone molecules to deplete ozone, the impact of natural forces on the increase and decrease of stratospheric ozone is also tremendously important. The most recent studies, taking into account chlorine, solar cycles, and volcanoes, can still only explain part of the loss of ozone that has been calculated for the period between 1979 and 1994.[20]

The Ozone "Hole"

Scientists have determined that the Antarctic ozone hole is related to a natural weather pattern. The vortex, a circular wind pattern around Antarctica, keeps warmer air from the tropics out during the winter, a time when the air temperature above Antarctica falls to minus 80 degrees Celsius or lower. It is so cold that ice clouds can form in the stratosphere (which, during the winter, is completely dark).

When the sun becomes visible above Antarctica in early spring, the sun can trigger chemical reactions involving the ice crystals, ozone, and chlorine. The source of most of the stratospheric chlorine is CFCs, although there are some natural sources of chlorine, too.

Chemicals that have been "holding" this chlorine release it. The chlorine reacts with ozone, depleting it. As the season progresses, however, the vortex breaks up and the ozone layer is replenished with a fresh supply of ozone-rich air from the tropics.[21] So, it appears that the direct cause of the ozone "hole" is chlorine in the stratosphere. But natural conditions play an important part, too.

The Big Fear: Cancer

If the ozone is thinning, will more UV radiation reach the Earth? And, if so, will it increase skin cancers?

In theory, the answer to both questions is yes. But, as we have seen, we aren't sure there is depletion or, if so, how much. More important, there is little evidence that UV radiation is increasing.

In fact, some scientists have measured just the opposite. The major study of UV radiation reaching the United States showed a slight decrease in UV radiation between 1974 and 1985. While this was a limited study, it shows the opposite of what one would expect if the ozone were thinning.[22] A more recent study showed an increase in UV radiation at a station in Toronto, but the study was based on only four years of measurements, and for two of those years there were problems with the information.[23]

A National Oceanic and Atmospheric Administration scientist reports that UV rays have decreased by between 5 and 18 percent during this century (possibly due to increased clouds and haze).[24] These studies suggest that the danger from ultraviolet radiation, at least in parts of North America, may be lessening rather than increasing.

Skin cancer rates have been increasing since World War II, probably due to changes in lifestyle. Just 50 years ago, people still wore bathing suits that covered much of their bodies. Dr. Frederick Urbach, a Temple University dermatologist, says that recent increases in skin cancer rates "are due to people spending more time outside, not more UV."[25] Fortunately, this type of skin cancer is easily treated. The death rate from nonmelanoma skin cancer is less than 1 percent.

As for melanoma, a very dangerous cancer of the skin, its relationship to sun exposure isn't clear.[26] A study by Richard B. Setlow of Brookhaven National Laboratory and his colleagues concluded that the effect of sunlight on melanoma was almost entirely through either visible light or the UV-A part of the light spectrum, not the very short UV-B wavelengths that are blocked by ozone. In other words, ozone and melanoma appear to have little to do with each other.[27]

UV Radiation: In Perspective

The most important fact that the textbooks fail to mention is that ozone depletion, if it is occurring, is similar to increasing one's exposure to ultraviolet light by moving closer to the Equator or higher up a mountain. There, the angle of the sun is more direct and people are exposed to more ultraviolet light.

❧ If the ozone level above North America has decreased by 4 or 5 percent, as the U.S. EPA estimated (but rather carelessly) in 1991, the effect would be about the same moving about 100 kilometres (sixty miles) south, say from Vancouver to Victoria. Moving south increases one's exposure to UV radiation about the same amount as a 4 or 5 per cent decrease in ozone.

❧ A scientific paper pointed out that a person who moves from Oslo, Norway, to San Francisco experiences an increase in UV exposure of 100 percent and increases his or her risk of skin cancer by 250 percent.[28]

What about Crops?
Another worry is that plants could receive too much UV radiation. But Alan Teramura, a leading expert on the effects of UV radiation on plants, points out that plants are remarkably adapted to withstand changes in UV exposure. Even if ozone declined by 20 percent, he says, we "wouldn't see plants wilting or fruits dropping unripened from their vines."[29] Although some plants could be damaged, others would be unaffected or produce greater crop yields.

What about Algae?
When there is an ozone "hole" over Antarctica, the amount of UV radiation does increase significantly there. Some textbooks suggest that plankton, the tiny algae in the water around Antarctica, may not be able to cope with so much radiation. Since other animals feed on these algae, their loss could affect the entire food chain.

Osmund Holm-Hansen, director of polar research at the Scripps Institute of Oceanography, studied these algae. He and his colleagues concluded that the ozone hole would decrease their growth by less than 4 percent while the hole was overhead, and would reduce annual growth by only 0.2 per cent (two-tenths of a percent) at most.[30]

What about Birds?

Keep in mind that when the ozone "hole" occurs in the spring, levels of UV radiation rise to about what they are in the Antarctic summer. This is the level of UV radiation that most migratory animals experience, anyway. Summer is the time that most migratory animals are there.

Ban CFCs, Raise Risks

Textbooks insist that drastic measures were needed to avoid further loss of ozone, and they applaud the Montreal Protocol, the 1987 international agreement to phase out CFCs. Canada was the first country to sign the updated protocol in 1990, which required the phase-out of CFCs by the year 2000. The Canadian government beat this deadline and by the end of 1997, the production and importation of CFCs officially ended, except for essential uses.[31]

The costs and risks of eliminating CFCs are rarely mentioned.[32] Most texts imply that the task will be easy and will have no harmful effects. They omit some important facts:

* CFCs are nontoxic chemicals that have saved lives and improved our standard of living. They keep our food safe and our homes, cars, and factories comfortable.

* Substitutes are less efficient. Refrigerators and auto air conditioners must use more energy to produce the same amount of cooling. This means burning more fossil fuels and more pollution. Hardly an ideal solution for the environment!

✵ Rapid adoption of substitutes makes the chance of serious problems more likely. One substitute known as HCFC 123 caused tumors in rats. The tumors were not cancerous, but it led one producer of industrial refrigeration systems to hold off on using it until it had been tested further.[33] Several substitutes produce a substance, TFA, that is toxic to plants, and some scientists worry that it could accumulate in wetlands.[34]

✵ Because substitutes cost more and do not work as well, there is now a multi-million-dollar black market in Freon (the best-known CFC). According to the *New York Times,* Freon is being smuggled into the United States, where CFCs were banned in 1996.[35]

✵ Maintaining auto air conditioners will be costly, because they will have to be retrofitted to use the substitutes.

Canada, the United States, and other industrial countries may be able to cope with more expensive refrigerators and troublesome car air conditioners. But developing countries, which are supposed to phase out CFCs early in the next decade, will experience more severe problems.

✵ Lack of refrigeration is already a serious health problem in many countries. If refrigeration becomes more costly, more people may unknowingly eat contaminated food. And more people may go hungry because food cannot be safely preserved.

✵ The most difficult problem in providing children with life-saving vaccines is keeping them cold. Lack of CFCs makes the job even harder.[36] Many countries still use kerosene fuel for portable refrigerators.[37] It will be more difficult to replace such dangerous refrigerators with cheap, safe ones.

❉ Old methods of food preservation, such as salting and smoking meats and fish, add potentially cancer-causing substances. These could put people at risk for cancers more dangerous than the skin cancer cited in the textbooks as a risk from ozone depletion.[38]

Talking to Your Children

Responsible scientists still have more questions than answers about ozone. But we do know some things about it. Here are some questions that you can answer now.

❉ Is the ozone layer disappearing?

No, it is not disappearing. Scientists think that there may be a decline in ozone caused by some chemicals, but this decline is so small that it is hard to distinguish from natural changes.

❉ What happens if the ozone layer thins?

A thinner ozone layer means that more ultraviolet radiation will reach the Earth on a clear day. However, a significant increase in ultraviolet radiation hasn't been measured, except temporarily over Antarctica due to the ozone "hole." And keep in mind that people increase their exposure to the sun's ultraviolet rays voluntarily by moving closer to the Equator and moving to higher altitudes. These changes are often much greater than any increase in exposure that may have been caused by ozone loss.

❉ What is the ozone hole?

The ozone hole is a large thinning of ozone above the Antarctic. It occurs each year in the Southern hemisphere's spring, when the winds of the polar vortex keep out ozone-rich air. As the season progresses, and the vortex dissipates, the "hole" closes up again. It is not permanent. When it occurs, more ultraviolet radiation reaches the South Pole and the surrounding area.

❧ What are CFCs?

CFCs or chlorofluorocarbons are chemicals that have an unusual property. They are inert, which makes them very safe. However, it also means that they don't break apart easily. Scientists have found that gradually over time they float up into the stratosphere, where sunlight breaks them apart, releasing chlorine. Scientists believe that the chlorine reacts with and depletes stratospheric ozone.

Activities for Parents and Children

As you can see, ozone issues are complicated. Here are some activities that will help your children understand these issues better.

Changes in Exposure
People make far greater changes in their exposure to ultraviolet rays than any change that may be caused by ozone depletion. Exposure to ultraviolet radiation changes as people move from north to south (in the Northern Hemisphere) and as they move to higher elevations. Your children can compute the changes in exposure to ultraviolet radiation.

For every hundred kilometres (sixty miles) traveled south, UV exposure increases by 5 percent. If your family travels from Edmonton to Calgary, which is about 300 kilometres south, how much will UV exposure increase? *UV exposure will increase by 15 percent. No one thinks that human exposure to UV radiation exposure has gone up anywhere near this much as a result of ozone loss.*

For every 45 metres (150 feet) of elevation, UV exposure increases 1 percent. If your family travels from Halifax, Nova Scotia, which is at sea level (32 metres), to Denver, Colorado, which is at an elevation of 1609 metres (5,280 feet), how much will your UV exposure increase? *Exposure will increase by more than 35 percent. Again, this is far more than any estimate of increased exposure to humans that may have occurred through ozone loss.*

Your Summer Vacation

Ask whether the family would be willing to give up a vacation trip to the mountains or to the beach because of the danger of increased UV exposure. This could lead to a discussion of trade-offs and choices.

If they aren't worried about increased UV radiation exposure by traveling, how much should they worry about the current state of the ozone? There is no definite answer here. The point is to think about the choices we make.

Children should be aware that regardless of the state of the ozone, basking in too much sunlight is not a good a thing. Physicians say that children should avoid sunburns by sunbathing less and by wearing sunscreen lotion whenever they are in the sun.

Alternatives to CFCs

Discuss the pros and cons of spending huge sums of money to convert to CFC substitutes. Air conditioners and refrigerators will become more expensive. This might not bother Canadians too much, but what about people in poorer nations? Should their ability to have refrigeration and air conditioning be restricted? Would your family be willing to give up those things?

Notes

1 Catherine Dee, ed., *Kid Heroes of the Environment* (Berkeley, CA: Earth Works, 1991), 79.

2 Susan Bosak, *Science Is...* (Co-published by Richmond Hill, ON/Markham, ON: Scholastic Canada/The Communication Project, 2nd ed., 1991), 361.

3 Tony Hare, *The Ozone Layer* (New York: Gloucester Press, 1990), 15.

4 Beth Savan, *Earthcycles and Ecosystems* (Toronto: Kids Can, 1991), 46.

5 Adrienne Mason, *The Green Classroom* (Markham, ON: Pembroke, 1991), 79–80.

6 Margaret Fagan, *Challenge for Change* (Toronto: McGraw-Hill Ryerson, 2nd ed., 1991), 23.

7 Teri Degler and Pollution Probe, *The Canadian Junior Green Guide* (Toronto: McClelland and Stewart, 1990), 19.

8 Sharon Roan, *Ozone Crisis: The 15 Year Evolution of a Sudden Global Emergency* (New York: Wiley, 1990), 8.

9 Savan, 46.

10 S. Fred Singer, "My Adventures in the Ozone Layer," *National Review* (June 30, 1989), 36.

11 "Daily Total Ozone As Measured by TOMS During 1980," chart prepared by M. R. Schoeberl, Goddard Space Flight Center, NASA, in *Science Summary* by Fluorocarbon Program Panel, Chemical Manufacturers' Association, Washington, D.C. (April 1989), 19.

12 Anne Pedersen, *The Kids' Environment Book: What's Awry and Why* (Santa Fe, NM: John Muir Publications, 1991), 33–4.

13 J. D. Mahlman, "A Looming Arctic Ozone Hole?" *Nature*, Vol. 360, November 19, 1992, 209.

14 Minster of Industry, Science and Technology, *The Canada Yearbook 1992* (Ottawa: Statistics Canada, 1991), 25.

15 Richard S. Stolarski, "The Antarctic Ozone Hole," *Scientific American*, Vol. 258 (January 1988), 32.

16 Richard A. Kerr, "Ozone Destruction Worsens," *Science*, Vol. 252, April 12, 1991, 204.

17 Richard Stolarski, *et al.*, "Measured Trends in Stratospheric Ozone," *Science*, Vol. 256, April 17, 1992, 342-349.

18 S. Fred Singer, "What Could Be Causing Global Ozone Depletion?" in *Climate Impact of Solar Variability*, ed. by K.H. Schalten and A. Arking, NASA Publication 3086 (Washington, DC: NASA, 1990).

19 Linwood B. Callis *et al.*, "Ozone Depletion in the High Latitude Lower Stratosphere: 1979-1990," *Journal of Geophysical Research*, Vol. 96, No. D2, (February 20, 1991), 2921–37, on 2931.

20 Susan Solomon *et al.*, "The Role of Aerosol Variation in Anthropogenic Ozone Depletion at Northern Midlatitudes," *Journal of Geophysical Research*, Vol. 101, D3, March 20, 1996, 6713–6728.

21 Susan Solomon, "Progress Towards a Quantitative Understanding of Antarctic Ozone Depletion," *Nature,* Vol. 347, September 27, 1990, 347–354.

22 Joseph Scotto *et al.*, "Biologically Effective Ultraviolet Radiation: Surface Measurements in the United States, 1974 to 1985," *Science*, Vol. 239 (1988), 762–4.

23 J. B. Kerr and C. T. McElroy, "Evidence for Large Upward Trends of Ultraviolet-B Radiation Linked to Ozone Depletion," *Science*, Vol. 262 (November 12, 1993), 1032-4, and John Maddox, "Can Evidence Ever Be Inconclusive?" *Nature*, Vol. 369, (May 12, 1994), 97.

24 Shaw Liu et al., "Effect of Anthropogenic Aerosols On Biologically Active Ultraviolet Radiation," *Geophysical Research Letters,* January 3, 1992, 2265.

25 Quoted in Ronald Bailey, *Eco-Scam: The False Prophets of Ecological Apocalypse* (New York: St. Martin's Press, 1993), 131.

26 The National Research Council studied the relationship and could not decide what connection there is between sun exposure and melanoma. National Research Council, *Causes and Effects of Changes in Stratospheric Ozone: Update 1983* (Washington, DC: National Academy Press, 1984), 189.

27 Richard B. Setlow *et al.*, "Wavelengths Effective in Induction of Malignant Melanoma," *Proceedings of the National Academy of Sciences U.S.A.*, Vol. 90 (July 1993), 6666.

28 Arne Dahlback *et al.*, "Biological UV-Doses and the Effect of an Ozone Depletion," *Photochemistry and Photobiology*, Vol. 49 (1989), 621–5.

29 Quoted in Bailey, 128.

30 Osmund Holm-Hansen *et al.*, "Ultraviolet Radiation in Antarctica: Inhibition of Primary Production," *Photochemistry and Photobiology*, Vol. 58, No. 4 (1993), 567–70.

31 Minister of Industry, Science and Technology, *The Canada Year Book 1992*, (Ottawa: Statistics Canada, 1991), 25, and personal communication with Ed Wituschek, Environment Canada, April 26, 1998.

32 Roger LeRoy Miller and Alan D. Stafford, *Consumer Economics in Action* (St. Paul, MN: West, 1993) does indicate the problem (p. 24).

33 Amal Kumar Naj, "CFC Substitute Might Be Toxic, Rat Study Finds," *Wall Street Journal*, July 2, 1991.

34 Steven E. Schwarzbach, "CFC Alternatives Under a Cloud," *Nature*, Vol. 376, July 27, 1995, 297–8.

35 Julie Edelson Halpert, "Freon Smugglers Find Big Market," *New York Times*, April 30, 1995, A1 ff.

36 Gary Stix, "Keeping Vaccines Cold," *Scientific American*, February 1996, 14–16.

37 Tim Beardsley, "Better Than a Cure," *Scientific American,* January 1995, 88–95.

38 Bailey, 138.

Chapter 15

Acid Rain

Sixteen-year-old Dan Shuman of Dover, Pennsylvania, noticed that the trees in his backyard were dying. And when he fished, he caught fewer trout and bass in the lakes and streams near his home. He suspected that acid rain was to blame.

He read in a fishing magazine that Dickinson College provided acid rain monitoring kits. So Dan recruited fifteen energetic Boy Scouts and raised money from several sports clubs. (The testing kits were $20 each.)

With his volunteers and kits, Dan set out to monitor twenty-two streams in the area. After a year of testing streams, Dan sent the information to Dickinson College for analysis. The college reported that the water was contaminated by acid rain.[1]

Yes, Dan and his crew of Scouts may have found that the streams they tested were contaminated with acid rain, but they did *not* find proof that acid rain was killing fish. And, the likelihood that his trees were dying from acid rain is slight. As we shall see in this chapter, while acid rain does exist, it does not have the widespread effects that are claimed for it.

Dead Fish, Dying Trees

"Acid rain is now the most controversial form of air pollution in the developed world," declares one text. "Factories spew forth sulphur oxides and nitrogen oxides, which dissolve in rain before returning to earth as sulphuric and nitric acids." It continues to say that "the result is a corrosive solvent 1,000 times as acidic as natural rain."[2] Other texts may not be so dramatic, but they convey the same message.

✳   *Innovations in Science* cautions that "acid rain ... pollutes lakes and rivers, damages forests and farmland, corrodes limestone and metal structures, and affects the health of humans, plants, and animals."[3]

✳   *Investigating Terrestrial Ecosystems* says that "recent studies suggest that acid rain is affecting growth and regeneration of forests."[4]

✳   "Trees in the maple forests of Quebec are dying, and some people are predicting the end of the maple syrup industry," as a result of acid rain, according to the geography text, *Canada in a Changing World.*[5]

✳   "It is now feared that acid rain will cripple or destroy the maple sugar industry in eastern Canada," says *Journeys in Science.*[6]

✳   "Acid rain has produced serious effects in the northeastern United States, Canada, and Scandinavia," says *Earth Science.* "Many lakes have become so acid that fish can no longer survive in them."[7]

Our children learn that air pollution from cars and coal-burning power plants in the midwestern states are carried by winds to the northeastern states and Canada. There, acidic rain and snow pollute lakes, streams, and the ground. Forests, fish, and crops are dying and buildings and statues are crumbling. Rarely do textbooks indicate that there is any question about the cause-and-effect relationship between acid rain and dying forests and lakes. Textbooks and other materials suggest experiments to dramatize the perils of acid rain.

❦ *The Canadian Junior Green Guide* instructs children to compare seeds sprouted in vinegar to seeds sprouted in water. Not surprisingly, the seeds exposed to vinegar don't grow.[8]

❦ Other textbooks suggest making a heavily acidic solution and spraying it on living plants. After several weeks, children observe that the plants wither and die.

❦ A book for children called *Ecology* instructs children to use a fish tank to create a closed system that has fish that produce carbon dioxide and grass that produces oxygen. The child experimenter sends sulfur dioxide gas into the air in the tank through a tube. Soon, the grass and fish die due to the acid rain that has been created in the mini-environment.[9]

❦ A *Teacher's Place Activity* located on the Environment Canada website instructs the teacher: "Pour vinegar onto five paper towels and place around the classroom before students come in. Note their reaction when they enter the class. Note their reaction to the odour when they enter the class. Tell the students what you did, and explain to them that you wanted them to experience the discomfort of a pollutant in their environment. Transition the class' thoughts to what it would be like for aquatic life in a pond or lake with increasing acid levels."[10]

These lab experiments are not accurate representations of the complex cause-and-effect relationships that surround acid rain.

❈ In the *Canadian Junior Green Guide* experiment, students are using vinegar with a pH level of 3. Acid rain in North America typically has a pH of 4.6. This means that the water used in the experiment is about forty times more acidic than the average acid rainfall.

❈ In the other projects, student are not told how to calculate or control the pH level of the acidic water.

What, Exactly, Is Acid Rain?

The term "acid rain" sounds ominous. It makes us think of rain so contaminated that it resembles car battery acid, and, in *Projects for a Healthy Planet: Simple Environmental Experiments for Kids*, Shar Levine and Allison Grafton actually claim that "acid rain has been recorded with the same pH as battery acid."[11] But, in fact, the term simply means rain that has a higher concentration of hydrogen ions than natural rain. It occurs when clouds or raindrops pick up substances from vehicle exhaust and coal-burning power plants that form acids when dissolved in water. This moisture can be transported over some distance before it falls as "acid rain."

Most *natural* rainfall is slightly acidic because of natural carbon dioxide and nitrogen oxides in the air.[12] But pollutants can, indeed, make rain more acidic. Electrical power plants and automobiles emit sulfur dioxide and nitrogen oxides into the air when they burn coal and gasoline. These chemicals combine with water vapor to produce dilute sulfuric and nitric acids in rain.

Scientists measure acidity on a scale from 1 to 14. This scale, known as the pH scale, measures the concentration of hydrogen ions. A value below 7 indicates that the liquid is acidic; a value above 7 indicates that it is basic or alkaline. This scale is logarithmic; that means that one number represents a value ten times more acidic than the number just above it. For example, 4 represents a value ten times more acidic than 5 (or 100 times more acidic than 6).

Normal rain has a pH of about 5.0. Acid rain typically has a pH of 4.6, and the most acidic rain in North America (found in western Pennsylvania and nearby areas) has an average pH of 4.2.[13] That is similar to the acidity of tomato or apple juice.

The pH Scale and the pH Levels of Acid Rain and Some Typical Household Substances

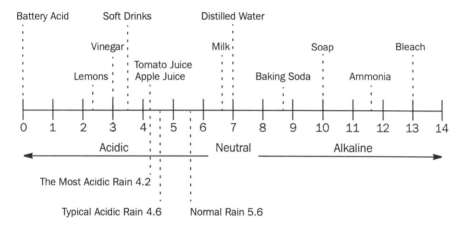

What Scientists Say

In the late 1970s, many people became alarmed about acid rain. A few small lakes, especially in Nova Scotia and in Adirondack Park in upper New York State, were found to be acidic. Fish couldn't live in them, yet people remembered a time when some of these lakes did have fish. What had happened?

About the same time, people also began to see forests with many dead and dying trees, especially in Europe. They suspected, incorrectly, that the cause was acid rain resulting from sulfur dioxide emissions from European power plants.

The fear aroused at that time entered the textbooks. Unfortunately, the more complete story that has emerged from scientific studies has not replaced it.

Rarely do any books even hint that there is a large body of evidence that counters the apocalyptic claims about acid rain. Yet this evidence exists. It was collected by the US government.

This ten-year study, the National Acid Precipitation Assessment Program (NAPAP), cost more than $500 million and involved hundreds of scientists and technicians and resulted in hundreds of reports. US Congress authorized the program in 1980 to find out what harm acid rain may be causing. A final report was issued in 1990, and its conclusions, which countered many of the previous assumptions about acid rain, are equally relevant to the situation in Canada.

The scientists found that while acid rain may be harming some lakes and some trees, it is a much smaller problem than most people believed.[14] In fact, it may be beneficial for some agricultural crops and trees. The "Assessment Highlights" of the report came to these conclusions:

❋ In its nationwide survey of waters, less than 5 percent of the lakes and 10 percent of the streams were found to be "chronically acidic." However, this acidity was not necessarily caused by acid rain.

❋ Florida, which receives minimal acid rain, not the Northeast, has the highest percentage of acid lakes (23 percent). These lakes appear to be acidic due entirely to natural processes—the lakes are surrounded by highly acidic soils, for example.

❋ A special study of the Adirondack Lakes, where high acidity had aroused great concern, found that up to 30 percent of the small (two- to ten-acre) lakes in the region are acidic. But many of the lakes have natural organic acids, which can make the water acidic regardless of the acidity of the rain.

✤ "There is currently no widespread forest or crop damage in the United States related to [acid rain]," said the report. "Some areas may benefit through nutrient enrichment by nitrogen and sulfur deposition."

✤ Scientists discovered some harm to high-elevation red spruce in the Appalachians when acid rain was present with other factors such as stress from extremely cold winters. These forests account for only a small fraction of one percent of eastern woodlands.

The NAPAP study also found:

✤ While acid rain contributes to corrosion of building materials, the magnitude "has been difficult to assess."

✤ Sulfate particles in the air, which lead to acid rain, reduce visibility in some places by causing haze.

A later report from NAPAP studied the problems of European forests.

✤ The effects of air pollutants "are small compared with other stresses affecting tree condition," the report said. (These include abnormal weather conditions and insect damage.)

✤ Overall forest productivity has increased in Europe since the nineteenth century.[15]

Unfortunately, most children in our schools have never heard of NAPAP's findings. The *Teacher's Place Activity* on a federal government website was updated as recently as 10 April 1997, more than six years after the NAPAP study published its conclusions. But the NAPAP study was ignored. Environmentalists seem to work harder at scaring students than at correcting their mistakes.

Those Acid Lakes

Acid rain does not always make lakes acidic. Often, rain falls onto nearby ground and slowly moves through the soil before it enters the lake. If that soil is alkaline—that is, if it has many pieces of limestone in it—the limestone will neutralize the acid.[16]

So, while the NAPAP study found that some Adirondack Lakes are acidic and cannot support fish, one important reason is that the lakes are not surrounded by alkaline soil. If acid rain falls on the streams that feed into these lakes, they gradually become acidic because the surrounding soil does not neutralize or buffer the acidic water.

Nova Scotia has highly acid lakes and streams.[17] Many of them have been recorded with pH levels of 4.7 or lower. The culprit is unlikely to be acid rain, however, since, like Florida, rainfall over Nova Scotia tends to be much less acidic than that over the Adirondacks.

What could be the explanation? Edward C. Krug, a soil scientist who worked on the NAPAP project, offers one. Citing a 1986 study conducted by Environment Canada, he notes that Nova Scotian forestry practices at the turn of the century involved mass burning. In fact, the southwestern 90 percent of the province was "literally burned down to the underlying granite bedrock leaving behind alkaline ash."[18]

Thus the lower pH levels that came about following reforestation efforts may be natural for the area. Krug points out that Kejimkujik Lake in southwestern Nova Scotia had a pH of 4.0 in 1850. After logging and regional burning, pH levels rose to 5.0, but since the regeneration of the surrounding forests, the lake has dropped to 4.8.[19]

In the United States, too, NAPAP researchers found evidence (by studying fossils of algae) that some Adirondack Lakes were acidic in preindustrial times but temporarily lost some of their natural acidity during the late 1800s.[20] (The fact that the Iroquois word "Adirondack" means "bark-eater" also suggests that fish were not plentiful.)

The researchers also found that some Adirondack lakes lost fish for other reasons than acid rain. Changes in water levels caused by beaver-made dams or human-made dams and the introduction of predators explained some losses, for example. Out of the 409 Adirondack lakes that contained brook trout in the past, 282 (about two-thirds) still contain brook trout. Of the 127 that no longer support brook trout, only 44 (about one-third) apparently lost the trout because of acid rain.[21]

One of the studies prepared for NAPAP said that the acid lakes in the Adirondacks could be neutralized by adding lime to the lakes. This would cost $170,000 per year or a total of $500,000 per year for the entire Northeast.[22] This would have corrected the biggest problem caused by acid rain. But the U.S. Congress didn't seriously consider this alternative.

Controlling Acid Rain

Our children's materials recommend stronger laws to control acid rain but seldom consider whether the costs are worth the benefits.

* *Pollution: Problems and Solutions* (a Ranger Rick's *NatureScope* title) warns that these laws may meet opposition from lobbyists who ask for more proof. But it cautions that "many researchers feel that coming up with such proof may take too long or may not be possible at all."[23]

* A science text discusses who should pay the cost of the necessary smokestack scrubbers—industry or the taxpayers.[24]

In 1990, the U.S. Congress did, in fact, pass laws to control acid rain. Canada is committed in principle to similar actions. Amendments to the U.S. Clean Air Act required all major electric utilities to reduce their sulfur dioxide emissions by 50 percent by about the year 2000. These regulations are being phased in gradually but they will still speed up the reductions that would have occurred as old power plants were retired.[25] In 1990 it appeared that the regulations would cost companies and electricity consumers from $2.7 to $4 billion per year.[26]

But the U.S. Congress also instituted an innovative program that allows utilities to reduce the costs of adding scrubbers. Although all major utilities must cut back on their emissions, those that can control emissions cheaply can put on extra controls and obtain payment from utilities that can't reduce emissions so cheaply. This "trading" has made the regulations less costly than they would have been, while still achieving the same overall goals.

Talking to Your Children

Fortunately, acid rain is much less troubling than most people think. With the background in this chapter, you can answer your children's questions.

🍁 What is acid rain?

Acid rain is rain that has picked up substances from vehicle exhaust and coal-burning power plants that create acids when they are wet. It has a higher concentration of hydrogen ions than normal rain.

🍁 Can acid rain kill fish?

Yes, in relatively rare circumstances where the soils around the streams and lakes do not neutralize the excess acid. Such lakes can become too acidic to support fish. A number of small lakes in the Adirondacks are too acidic to support fish and the cause may be acid rain. It is possible, however, that the acidity of lakes in

Nova Scotia and the Adirondacks is primarily due to their natural environment. The acidity of lakes or streams is not a serious problem in most of Canada.

❧ What causes acid rain?

Acid rain is caused primarily by coal-burning electric power plants and vehicles that burn fuels containing sulfur dioxide and nitrogen oxides. However, natural causes (specifically, carbon dioxide and nitrogen oxides in the air) make most rain slightly acid.

❧ What should be done about acid rain?

In 1990, US Congress passed amendments to the Clean Air Act that required electrical utilities to reduce their emissions of sulfur dioxide. This may slightly reduce the number of acidic lakes. It will not restore most of the acidic Nova Scotian or Adirondack Lakes, but may have some other beneficial effects, such as improving visibility in some places, reducing the acid in some soils, and slowing the degradation of metal and stone on the exteriors of buildings.

Activities for Parents and Children

You may wish to use experiments to introduce your children to acid rain. The experiments that follow are closer to "real world" conditions than the experiments recommended in the texts.

Learning about the pH Scale

To understand the debate over acid rain, children should understand the concepts of acid and base. These are measured on a scale called the pH scale, which runs from 0 to 14, with 7 representing substances that are neutral.

You can illustrate the concept, using pH paper. It can be obtained from a "laboratory chemicals" company (look under "Chemicals" in the Yellow Pages). Ask for pH indicator strips with a pH range of 0–14. (A box of 100 strips will cost about $25.) Michael and his son Devin tried these experiments. *But we emphasize that these experiments require adult supervision!*

Understanding Acid and Base

❧ Materials needed: distilled water (not spring water), a clean glass, a straw, and pH paper.

Put about half a cup of distilled water in a clean glass. (Do *not* shake the water before the test.) Test the water using the pH paper. It should measure 7 on the pH scale (neither acidic nor basic).

Using the straw, ask your children to blow gently in the water for three or four minutes. Test the water again with the pH paper. This time it should measure slightly acidic. The reason is that our breath has carbon dioxide in it. The carbon dioxide reacts with water to make carbonic acid. Normal rain water is slightly acidic because the rain reacts with carbon dioxide in the air, forming carbonic acid.

❧ Materials needed: pH paper, small amounts of materials such as lemon juice, vinegar, ammonia, apple juice, cola, or baking soda.

Children should draw a line on a piece of paper with equal divisions from 0 to 14. Ask them to test the common household items above and record the pH readings on their scale.

From Acid to Base

❧ Ask your children to take about one tablespoon of vinegar and mix it with a half cup of distilled water. Have them test this solution. It should measure about 3 on the pH scale. Now ask them to collect about two tablespoons of very fine ash from the barbecue or fireplace. Mix the ash with the vinegar solution. When it is dissolved, test the solution. The pH level should increase.

Explain to your children that the ash is basic, and it has neutralized some of the acid.

Visiting a Garden Center

Take your children to a local garden center or nursery. Ask the owner or manager to discuss differences in soils and how plants react to them. Ask this person to tell your children about plants that thrive in acidic soil, and those that will die in such soil. Then have the manager show your children the different products available to treat soil so that it will be the right pH for specific plants.

Notes

1 Catherine Dee, ed., *Kid Heroes of the Environment* (Berkeley, CA: EarthWorks, 1991), 67–9.
2 Norman Myers, *GAIA, An Atlas of Planet Management* (New York: Anchor Books, 1984), 118.
3 Rod Peturson and Neil McAllister *Innovations in Science*, (Teacher Resource Package). (Toronto: Holt, Rinehart and Winston, 1991), ET-43.
4 William A. Andrews and Donna K. Moore, *Investigating Terrestrial Ecosystems* (Scarborough, ON: Prentice-Hall, 1986), 194.
5 Stewart Dunlop, *Towards Tomorrow: Canada in a Changing World Geography* (Toronto, ON: Harcourt Brace Jovanovich, 1987), 10.
6 Larry D. Yore, Peter Beugger, et al., *Journeys in Science 7* (Toronto: Collier Macmillian Canada, Canadian ed., 1990), 354.

7 Samuel N. Namowitz and Nancy E. Spaulding, *Earth Science* (Toronto: D.C. Heath Canada, Canadian ed., 1987), 81.

8 Teri Degler and Pollution Probe, *The Canadian Junior Green Guide* (Toronto: McClelland and Stewart, 1990), 23.

9 Martin J. Gutnik, *Ecology* (New York: Franklin Watts, 1984), 22–26.

10 Environment Canada, *Teacher's Place* (http://www.doe.ca). 10 April 1997.

11 Shar Levine and Allison Grafton, *Projects for a Healthy Planet: Simple Environmental Experiments for Kids.* (Toronto: John Wiley & Sons, 1992), 20.

12 D. W. Schindler, "Effects of Acid Rain on Freshwater Ecosystems," *Science*, Vol. 239, January 8, 1988, 149–157, at 149.

13 J. Laurence Kulp, "Acid Rain," in *The State of Humanity*, Julian Simon, ed. (Cambridge MA: Blackwell, 1995), 524.

14 National Acid Precipitation Assessment Program (NAPAP), "Assessment Highlights," Sept. 5, 1990 (National Acid Precipitation Assessment Program, Washington, DC, September 5, 1990), 4–7.

15 NAPAP, 1992 Report to Congress, June 1993, 72.

16 J. Laurence Kulp, "Acid Rain: Causes, Effects, and Control," *Regulation*, Winter 1990, 43.

17 Edward C. Krug, "The Great Acid Rain Flimflam," in Jay H. Lehr, editor *Rational Readings on Environmental Concerns* (New York: Van Nostrand Reinhold, 1992), 40–41.

18 Krug, 41.

19 Krug, 35–43.

20 Edward C. Krug, "Fish Story," *Policy Review*, Spring 1990, 44–8, and Kulp, 44.

21 The U.S. National Acid Precipitation Program, *1990 Integrated Assessment Report* (Washington, DC: The NAPAP Office of the Director, November 1991), 33.

22 Krug, 48.

23 Judy Braus, editor, "Pollution: Problems & Solutions," Ranger Rick's *NatureScope* (National Wildlife Federation, Washington, DC, 1990), 33.

24 Dean Hurd et al., *General Science: A Voyage of Discovery* (Englewood Cliffs, NJ: Prentice Hall, 1992), 500.

25 NAPAP, September 5, 1990, 19.

26 NAPAP, September 5, 1990, 14.

Chapter 16

Not a Drop to Drink?

Their local creek was so polluted that it was uninhabitable for fish and amphibians. It was a dumping ground for used tires, rusted car parts, and litter. The Grade 6 students at the elementary school near the river in Windsor, Ontario, wanted to do something about it.

They appealed to the Canadian Wildlife Federation for funding and, armed with rubber gloves and garbage bags, helped the community remove tonnes of debris from the river. Fish and wildlife now thrive in the river basin where students and volunteers have planted trees, erected bird shelters, and built bridges and walkways. The children have restored the river to a place that the local wildlife and community can enjoy.[1] Their success is testimony to the power of individuals working together to protect the environment.

A Flood of Crises

Some of our children's educational materials encourage positive action like the children's stream cleanup project. For example, *Rang-*

er Rick's NatureScope suggests that children contact the Adopt-A-Stream Foundation[2] to find out how they can restore a polluted waterway.

All too often, however, our children's texts treat water pollution as crises, not as a manageable problems. They fail to teach why we have water pollution.

First "Crisis": We Are Running Out of Water

Many textbooks observe that while three-fourths of the earth is covered with water, most of this water can't be used because 97 percent is salt water in the oceans and seas. Of the three percent that is fresh water, 2 percent is locked in the polar ice caps. This leaves only 1 percent available for use by plants, animals, and man.[3] Although most textbooks state the fact that Canada has an abundance of fresh water, the impression is that there is not enough on the planet for world use, and that Canada needs to manage its water supply as carefully as some of the more drought-plagued countries.

❧ After condemning the wasteful western lifestyle, one text warns: "Some scientists say that, within a few years, we will no longer be able to find all the fresh water we need. Perhaps it would be more accurate to say the fresh water we want."[4]

❧ The geography text *Towards Tomorrow: Canada in a Changing World* suggests that "there is evidence that Canadians are about to enter a period of water scarcity."[5] In fact, however, Canada currently consumes only about 1.5% of its total available renewable freshwater resources.[6]

❧ "Since the earth has so little fresh water, care must be taken not to use large amounts needlessly." The text goes on to say: "Global studies show that humans are now removing fresh water from the land faster than the water cycle can replace it. In North America we use about twice as much water as the water cycle returns ... sooner or later a limit will be reached."[7]

Second "Crisis": Our Drinking Water is Contaminated by Chemicals

❀ "Groundwater is also vulnerable to pollution," writes the science curriculum supplement *Science Is...* "Just dumping common, everyday things on the ground can pollute groundwater because the Earth is like a sponge that soaks everything in. A couple of litres of paint, motor oil, or gasoline can seep into the Earth and pollute hundreds of thousands of litres of groundwater. Pesticides and fertilizers can seep into the ground and affect groundwater. Toxic chemicals from dump sites and even the salt used on slippery winter roads can affect groundwater supplies."[8]

❀ The text *Focus on Science* knows exactly where to lay the blame: "Unfortunately, man has abused his once-abundant supply of clean water. He has dumped fertilizers, road salt, untreated municipal sewage, and industrial wastes into the lakes and rivers, sometimes by accident, but often out of convenience."[9]

❀ "Although Canada has an abundance of fresh water, the quality of this water has been threatened by human activities ... Toxic (poisonous) chemicals are found throughout Canada's river basins," writes the text *Canada: Exploring New Directions*.[10] "Nowhere are they more prevalent than in the Great Lakes basin, where over 800 different chemical compounds have been discovered in the water! Many of these have found their way into water as a result of years of neglect and ignorance. Only recently have these invisible and odourless poisons been detected. As monitoring equipment improves, more and more are found each year."

Third "Crisis": Oil Spills

✤ "Oil spills are also a serious threat to the environment, particularly the oceans" writes *Earth Science*. "Ocean currents can move an oil spill some distance away from the point of the spill. Oil spills can be washed ashore, fouling beaches and marshes." [11]

✤ "Up to 6 million tonnes of oil are dumped into the world's oceans every year. Oil seeps out of boats that use it as fuel or carry it from port to port, and it flows into the sea from factories on the shore." The children's book *Earthcycles and Ecosystems* continues: "A large oil slick can cover many square kilometres (miles) of ocean, and it can last for up to ten years." [12]

An Empty Faucet?

For most Canadians, water is cheap and abundant. In fact Canadians have the cheapest water rates of any industrialized country in the world. [13] But occasionally after a series of dry years, some towns and cities impose regulations limiting the use of water—banning car washing and limiting the hours for watering lawns.

Such restrictions reinforce the impression that we are running out of water. In fact, they usually stem from governmental decisions that set the price of water too low.

The amount of water in the Earth's ecosystem is always the same; it is constantly being recycled through evaporation and precipitation. The Earth "has more than enough water to meet human demands," says Terry L. Anderson of Montana State University. The problem, he explains, is that "water is often found in the wrong place at the wrong time." [14]

Frequently, water is in the "wrong place" because it is cheaper than it should be, and this causes people to overuse it. Our children's texts urge water conservation but they don't explain that low prices discourage conservation. Realistic pricing would change this situation. When water does become more expensive, people usually respond by using less of it. Industries can produce the same products with vastly different amounts of water.

* Some electric utilities use 170 gallons (765 litres) to produce one kilowatt-hour of electricity.

* But it's possible to produce the same amount of electricity with less than two gallons (nine litres)![15]

Similarly, farming can use a great deal of water or just a little. Higher prices would encourage farmers to conserve and perhaps to change the crops they grow. They could decrease their production of alfalfa and increase production of safflower or canola, for example.[16] Wiser policies could make more water available for everyone, rather than having water restrictions year after year.

A Government Failure?

The government provides water and sewage treatment throughout most of Canada. While this gives Canadians with the cheapest water in the industrialized world, it does not provide the best sewage treatment. The state of Washington frequently complains about Victoria's habit of flushing poorly treated wastes directly into the ocean. Many other Canadian cities share the practice.

Indeed, throughout the world, governments are often reluctant to invest the capital required to improve sewage-treatment plants. In the 1980s, it was estimated that bringing the British sewage system up to European code would cost $54 billion. This would have hiked taxes, and almost guaranteed an election loss to whoever put such a policy in motion. So Britain chose to privatize water supply and sewage in 1989. This move led to higher water rates for some, but it has also led to the clean-up of many beaches and waterways.

The idea of privatizing water and sewage was discussed in Quebec as early as 1993, and Ontario is slowly experimenting with the policy. Private water bills would indeed rise, but taxes would likely go down (or the deficit would be reduced), and the environment would become cleaner. It could be a welcome trade-off.[17]

Ticking Time Bombs?

Landfills containing chemicals are pictured as ticking time bombs that will eventually pollute groundwater and surface water by seeping out.

❋ "There are over 1000 man-made chemicals which find their way into our rivers and lakes. They are pumped from factories and leak from dumps," says the text *Canada: A Growing Concern.* "The entire neighbourhood of Love Falls, New York was abandoned when it was discovered that chemicals were leaking from a nearby dump and were causing cancer and birth defects." (In fact, while chemical wastes can poison water supplies, long-term hazards from the most famous waste sites, including Love Canal in New York State, have not been scientifically confirmed by epidemiological studies.)

❋ "In many parts of the United States, wells have been shut down and people are using bottled water," says the Merrill text *Biology: Living Systems.*[18] (The text does not report where in the United States this is occurring or whether it is for a very short time or a long period.)

Chemical wastes *can* pollute our water. But our children need to be taught that pollution problems are more complex than simply "bad guys" dumping chemicals.

Some texts attempt to spread the blame. "We all contribute to polluting Earth's waters," says one, citing the pollution caused by flushing toilets, washing hands, brushing teeth, and watering lawns.[19] The downside of this approach is that it instills guilt in children for everyday activities.

A better way to look at water pollution is to recognize why it occurs. Streams, rivers, and groundwater are essentially a common pool. Just as people tend to litter in public spaces, people allow waste to enter a commonly owned waterway.

If water weren't entirely a common pool, the picture would be different. In England and Scotland, it is possible to own rights to fish in streams and rivers. If fish are killed by pollution, fishermen can sue the polluter in court. In fact, the Anglers Conservation Association in England has obtained damages or injunctions for its members in hundreds of cases.[20] Ranchers in western Canada who have private trout streams flowing entirely within their property are careful to prevent pollution. However, private protection of other streams is rare, since fishing rights are not owned in Canada.

Over the years, it appears that there has been improvement in the cleanliness of our waterways. In 1990, an expert from Resources for the Future reviewed most of the available studies of water quality. He concluded that there had been "some improvement," although it "has not been dramatic." However, he noted "local success stories of substantial cleanup."[21] (Another review noted significant reductions in chemicals such as DDT and PCBs in the Great Lakes since 1970.[22])

It is hard to know how much has been accomplished since there was little information about water quality conditions when the act was passed, and thus no basis upon which to judge later progress.[23] Either way, textbooks are quick to demand more laws. One says:

"In the past governments have been slow to spend the large amounts of money needed to clean up the polluted waters. They have also been reluctant to pass and enforce tough anti-pollution laws to stop polluters."[24]

Nearly everyone agrees that most "point sources"—identifiable places where pollution enters a stream or river—have been controlled. But water that runs off fields, homes, buildings, parks, and farms, picking up natural and synthetic substances, still pollutes streams and rivers. This "non-point" source pollution is much harder to control.

Slicks and Spills

Oil spills can cause immediate—and very serious—harm to the environment, especially to fish, birds, and animals like otters that live near the ocean. But our children's books don't tell the full story of these spills.

Texts like *Earth Science* imply that the beaches may never be clean again.[25] This is not, in fact accurate. Canada's largest oil spill occurred in 1970 when the Liberian tanker *Arrow* struck a rock in Chedabucto Bay, Nova Scotia. After a $3.9 million dollar operation to clean up the 16,000 tonnes of bunker oil, the local ecology was found to be in good shape. The lobstering season opened on schedule, and the herring catch was up.[26]

A 1990 U.S. government study of six highly publicized oil spills around the world also concluded that water and beaches recover fairly quickly after even big spills.[27] The Congressional Research Service (an arm of Congress) found, for example, the following:

❦ When the *Argo Merchant*, an oil tanker, was grounded off the shore of Massachusetts in 1976, the EPA administrator at the time called it "the biggest oil spill disaster on the American coast in our history."[28] In fact, however, pollution damage was small. The Congressional Research Service (CRS) reported a "general scientific consensus that classifying the incident as an ecological catastrophe had no factual basis."[29]

❧ In 1979 an oil well in the Bay of Campeche, Mexico, exploded. Oil and gas spewed from the pipe and the platform burned up. This turned out to be the largest oil spill in the history of offshore drilling or tanker transportation. Yet by the end of 1980, said the CRS, the only oil left was "scattered patches of tar mats along the Texas barrier island beaches,"[30] and some of these may have been natural oil seeps.

❧ In sum, the environmental impact of the spills studied was "relatively modest and ... of relatively short duration,"[31] said the CRS. It also found that "short-term impacts on marine animal life are dramatic but recovery of species populations in almost every case studied has been swift."[32]

In addition to perpetuating exaggerated fears, the books are misguided about policy. After discussing the *Exxon Valdez* spill in Prince William Sound, Alaska, in 1989, the kids' book *Earthcycles and Ecosystems* asks: "How else can you use less oil? A great deal of oil in North America is used by industry, to power factories, to heat buildings and to make products such as plastics. You can't do much on your own to reduce oil used in these ways. But you can make your concerns known to government."[33]

The implication of this line of argument is that laws against offshore drilling will avoid oil spills. In fact, they will do the opposite—they will encourage them. The *Exxon Valdez* was carrying oil that had been drilled in Alaska. Bans on off-shore drilling encourage more *on-shore* drilling. That means more shipping of oil in ocean vessels to reach refineries.

Talking to Your Children

Experts think that water quality is improving in Canada and the United States. It is, however, difficult to be sure. Although raw data on Canadian water quality exist in a federal database, the information is not in a format that can be used to evaluate water quality on a national level.

We do know of specific examples of major improvements in water quality. Sometimes, as related at the beginning of this chapter, people have joined together to clean up a body of water so that people can swim and fish in. As for water availability, we know that there is enough water for everyone.

Now you can answer your children's questions.

❧ Are we running out of water?

No. The amount of water on the Earth stays the same, and Canada consumes only about 1.5 percent of its available fresh water.[34] However, some places do not have enough water for people to live comfortably during droughts. This is usually because governments provide water at less than its cost, leading people use large amounts of water, often wastefully. In the western United States, for example, higher water prices might cause farmers to shift from alfalfa, rice, or cotton, to crops that use less water. Then, more water would be available for other uses.

❧ Is our water getting more polluted?

Probably not. It appears that many lakes and streams have better water quality than they used to. Laws require industry and sewage plants to clean their water before sending it to streams or rivers. But the laws do not really address the water that flows over streets and fields, picking up pollutants. Primarily because of this pollution, some bodies of water remain seriously polluted.

Activities for Parents and Children

The following activities will help your children think realistically about water supplies and water pollution.

Reading a Utility Bill

Ask your children to look at the two sample utility bills below, which charge residents for water, sewage, and trash pick-up.

Utility Bill #1			Utility Bill #2		
Reading Date 1/22/99		Reading 465462	3/31/99	4/30/99	
Water Rate/ 625 Gal.	Sewer Rate/ 625 Gal.	Consumption	Trash Rate/ Can	Number of Cans	Trash Charge
$0.011	$0.008	1912	$1.50	6	$9.00
	Charges			**Charges**	
	Water	$21.38		Water	$15.00
	Sewer	$15.30		Sewer	$10.00
	Trash	$15.00		Trash	$9.00
Date Due 3/15/99	Amount Due	$51.68	Date Due 5/30/99	Amount Due	$34.00

Ask them to compute the price per gallon of water from the information on these two water bills. They will quickly notice that Bill #2 lumps water together with other services and doesn't charge on the basis of the amount of water you use. (That bill does charge for trash volume, however, as we will discuss in chapter 19.)

Discuss with your children how these two billing procedures can influence how a person or family will use water. Which is more likely to encourage conservation? *(The first bill, because you can reduce your water bill by using less.)* Which leads to more usage? *(The second, because usage doesn't affect the amount you are charged.)*

Now compare your own water bill to the two above. Would the family save money if everyone in your family conserved on water?

On a Shopping Trip

Ask the manager of a plumbing supply store to show your children the many products that homeowners can purchase to purify their tap water. The manager could also show the children water softening equipment and explain what it is used for. At home, discuss these products that help people get cleaner or better water.

At the grocery store, show them the kinds of bottled water for sale. Have them note a typical price per gallon. Back home, ask your children to compare the price of bottled water to the price of tap water, using your water bill (if it supplies these figures). They will probably find that the price is much higher at the store.

Ask your children why people are willing to pay more for bottled water. For one thing, the higher price is for drinking water or specialized water such as distilled water, while the water from the faucet has many uses. In addition, some people want a certain kind of taste in their water and they are willing to pay for it.

The point of these discussions is to show that people can take action on their own to ensure that their drinking water is to their liking.

Rivers and Streams

When you are in the country, stop at a river or stream. Point out that in most places in the country, no one "owns" the water in the stream, unless it is a small stream on private property. Fishermen can fish in the stream but they do not "own" the right to fish in clean water. If someone pollutes the stream, users of the water have little recourse.

In contrast, if someone dumped trash in your backyard, you could sue that person for polluting your property (so people rarely do such a thing). Similarly, if people owned a stream, they could sue polluters to protect their property.

This process works in England, where the right to fish is something that a person can own. Do you know of any private fishing lakes or ponds? A visit to them might help explain why public streams and lakes are often dirty.

Notes

1 Canadian Wildlife Federation Bulletin, 4.

2 Judy Braus, ed., "Pollution: Problems & Solutions," *Ranger Rick's NatureScope* (Washington, DC: National Wildlife Federation, 1990), 65. The Adopt-a-Stream Foundation at the Northwest Stream Center is located at 600, 128th St. S.E., Everett WA 98208 USA (206-316-8592).

3 See Snyder *et al.*, 546, for example.

4 William A. Andrews and Sandra J. McEwan, *Investigating Aquatic Ecosystems* (Scarborough, ON: Prentice-Hall, 1987), 3.

5 Stewart Dunlop, *Towards Tomorrow: Canada in a Changing World-Geography* (Toronto: Harcourt Brace Jovanovich Canada, 1987), 150.

6 Boris DeWiel, Steve Hayward, Laura Jones, and M. Danielle Smith, *Environmental Indicators for Canada and the United States*. Critical Issues Bulletin (Vancouver: The Fraser Institute, March 1997), 40.

7 Andrews and McEwan, 3.

8 Susan Bosak, *Science Is . . .* (Co-published by Richmond Hill, ON/ Markham, ON: Scholastic Canada/The Communication Project, 2nd ed., 1991), 374.

9 Frank Flanagan, *Focus on Science: Exploring the Physical World* (Toronto: D.C. Heath, 1979), 269.

10 Leonard A. Swatridge and Ian A. Wright, *Canada: Exploring New Directions* (Markham, ON: Fitzhenry & Whiteside, 1990), 242.

11 Samuel N. Namowitz and Nancy E. Spaulding, *Earth Science* (Toronto: Holt, Reinhart and Winston, Canadian ed., 1991), 495.

12 Savan, 64.

13 Elizabeth Brubaker, "Bring Back Our Beaches," *The Next City*, Vol 2, #4, 46.

14 Terry L. Anderson, "Water Options for the Blue Planet," in *The True State of the Planet*, ed. by Ronald Bailey (New York: The Free Press, 1995), 267–294 at 275.

15 James D. Gwartney and Richard L. Stroup, *Introduction to Economics: The Wealth and Poverty of Nations* (Fort Worth: The Dryden Press, 1994), 543.

16 Anderson, 284.

17 Brubaker, 32–46.

18 Raymond F. Oram, *Biology: Living Systems*, Annotated Teacher's Edition (Columbus, OH: Merrill, 1989), 753.

19 Ralph M. Feather, *Earth Science* (Lake Forest, IL: Merrill/Glencoe, 1993), 535.

20 Terry L. Anderson and Donald R. Leal, *Free Market Environmentalism* (San Francisco, CA: Pacific Research Institute, 1991), 148.

21 A. Myrick Freeman III, "Air Pollution Policy," in *Public Policies for Environmental Protection* ed. by Paul R. Portney (Washington, DC: Resources for the Future, 1990), 97–149, at 120.

22 E. Calvin Beisner and Julian L. Simon, "Editors' Appendix," in *The State of Humanity,* ed. by Julian L. Simon (Cambridge, MA: Blackwell Publishers, 1995) 469–475.

23 Roger E. Meiners and Bruce Yandle, "Clean Water Legislation: Reauthorize or Repeal?" *Taking the Environment Seriously*, ed. by Meiners and Yandle (Lanham, MD: Rowman & Littlefield, 1993), 73–101, at 76.

24 *Canada: A Growing Concern*, 230.

25 Snyder *et al.*, 586.

26 Shell Canada Ltd. "Canada's largest oil spill: A case study" in Margaret Fagan, *Challenge for Change* (Toronto: McGraw-Hill Ryerson, 1991), 200.

27 James E. Mielke, "Oil in the Ocean: The Short- and Long-Term Impacts of a Spill," *Congressional Research Service Report for Congress*, July 24, 1990 (90-356 SPR).

28 Mielke, 18.

29 Mielke, 19.

30 Mielke, 22–24.

31 Mielke, Summary.

32 Mielke, Summary.

33 Savan, 65.

34 DeWiel *et al.*, 40.

Chapter 17

Don't Eat That Apple!

Leigh, a sixth-grader, planted a garden. But it wasn't an ordinary garden. It was "organic." Leigh fertilized the plants with compost rather than chemicals and applied no pesticides while they were growing. (She did use a bug killer for the aphids on the vegetables when they were harvested.)

Leigh went to the trouble of planting a chemical-free garden because she had been taught that agricultural chemicals were dangerous. They "poison birds, animals and water supplies and also get in the food," she explained.[1] Leigh had probably read about pesticides in her textbooks.

* *The Kids' Environment Book*, which talks about the 2.5 billion pounds (1.1 billion kilograms) of "toxic gunk" on our crops,[2] and recommends organic gardening or, at least, buying organic foods.

* Or *This Planet Is Mine*, which says that the "lack of toxic substances" makes organic foods safer. "Logically, what's less risky for humans to consume is also a safer choice for the environment," this book states.[3]

231

Our children's books treat farm chemicals as dangerous by-products of technology that should be banned or severely restricted. To many authors, pesticides are killers and should be eliminated at all costs:

* The text *Earth Science* warns that "the poisons that pour into rivers and lakes—and even into the oceans—become concentrated in fish in percentages large enough to make the fish unfit to eat ... Insecticides have been responsible for killing fish in rivers."[4]

* "It is estimated that as many as 1.5 million people suffer poisoning by pesticides each year, because they do not use the necessary safety precautions to prevent exposure to these dangerous substances," says the text *Food For Life*.[5]

* Anne Pedersen advises that if you can't grow your own garden "the next best thing is to buy *organic* produce ... It's usually more expensive and maybe doesn't look quite as picture-perfect ... but it's probably safer."[6]

The Other Side of the Story

Chemicals have transformed farming. Pesticides have nearly eliminated the ancient scourge of insect infestation, and fertilizer allows farmers to restore the nutrients that plants take from the soil as they grow. An Environment Canada publication, citing a Hudson Institute book, says that pesticides are reducing cancer rates because their use has introduced more fruits and vegetables into the North American diet.[7]

But chemicals have disadvantages, too. Pesticides that harm insects can also harm humans and animals. The nutrients from fertilizers, while vital to crops, also spill over into waterways, where they encourage the growth of algae that can smother other plant life and fish. Some chemicals may reach pools of underground water that provide drinking water.

These days, what worries people the most is whether pesticide residues on food can cause cancer. Some scientists think that small amounts of pesticide left on food—amounts usually measured in parts per million or parts per billion—increase the risk of cancer. Yet the evidence for this is extremely weak. In 1996 a U.S. National Academy of Science report said that levels of chemicals in Americans' diet are "so low that they are unlikely to pose an appreciable cancer risk."[8] Canadian regulatory standards are even more stringent than those in the United States.[9]

DDT: Scare Number 1

Much of the fear about pesticides stems from concern about one product, DDT. The fear began with Rachel Carson's 1962 book *Silent Spring*. Carson treated DDT as a dangerous chemical that had killed wildlife and might be causing cancer to humans. Carson's attack on DDT shocked the world because it contradicted what everyone had believed about this "miracle" chemical.

DDT had saved thousands of lives by killing mosquitoes that carried malaria and typhus. By the time it entered commercial use in 1947, says historian Thomas R. Dunlap, it "had a reputation for effectiveness, power and safety unmatched by any other material."[10] Unlike most insecticides of the day, it caused no acute harm to people and its effect was long-lasting, so that repeated applications were not necessary. DDT appeared to be so safe that farmers, foresters, and municipal authorities quickly adopted it after the war.

Clearly, DDT was safe for people to use in the short run. But what about the long run? DDT builds up in the tissues of animals and people, and Carson raised concern that it could cause cancer.

This fear has been refuted to most scientists' satisfaction. In 1989, three public health scientists who had followed nearly one thousand people for a decade reported in *Science* magazine that they had found "no relation between either overall mortality or cancer mortality and increasing serum DDT levels [that is, levels of DDT in body fluids]."[11]

The strongest case against DDT was not that it caused cancer in humans but that it was causing birds to die. Carson's book evoked the image of a "silent spring" in which no birds would sing. She suggested that DDT accumulated in the tissues of birds, especially predatory and fish-eating birds like eagles and falcons. By causing their eggshells to thin, DDT was destroying their ability to reproduce.

The question of whether DDT does hurt the reproductive ability of bird populations is still not completely resolved. A thorough review of scientific literature revealed that while some studies show a correlation between eggshell thinning and DDT, others did not.[12] However, the evidence, plus the fact that many birds at the top of the food chain like falcons and eagles have recovered in number since DDT was banned, suggests that DDT was at least partly responsible. (It is also possible, though, that other chemicals, such as polychlorinated biphenols [PCBs], which are used in electrical transformers, contributed to eggshell thinning.)[13]

Canada began tightening restrictions on DDT in 1969, and production and import were officially discontinued in 1985. In 1972, the U.S. EPA imposed a nearly complete ban on the pesticide, due more to political pressure rather than clear scientific evidence. This ban is viewed as an important victory in the texts, a triumph of environmental activism over the evils of modern technology. But some of the consequences were unfortunate.

Pesticides that are more toxic to humans replaced DDT and they had to be applied more often. These posed (and continue to pose) serious dangers to farm workers.[14]

In at least one country, Sri Lanka, a DDT spraying program, which had virtually eliminated malaria in Sri Lanka, was stopped. When Sri Lanka stopped using DDT, the number of malaria cases rose again to 2.5 million in the years 1968–1969.[15] Today, throughout the world, malaria still kills between 1 and 2 million people per year.[16]

Apple Hysteria

One legacy of *Silent Spring* is periodic hysteria over small amounts of chemicals. In early 1989, the CBS show "60 Minutes" called *Alar*, a chemical used on apples, "the most potent cancer-causing agent in our food supply." And the elegant actress Meryl Streep appeared on the Phil Donahue Show to alert parents to its dangers.

The U.S. EPA had been considering a ban on Alar because of animal tests suggesting that it might be carcinogenic. But an environmental group, the Natural Resources Defense Council, didn't want to wait for EPA to decide. It orchestrated a public relations campaign against *Alar* that scared nearly everyone. Parents inundated pediatricians with phone calls and schools stopped serving apples.

As the furor mounted, the EPA, the U.S. Food and Drug Administration, and the U.S. Department of Agriculture issued a statement assuring parents that eating apples did not pose "an imminent hazard" to children.[17]

Alar is a growth regulator, not a pesticide—it keeps apples on trees so that they can stay crisp and attain a deep red color. It is regulated by the Pesticide Management Regulatory Agency in Canada, and by the EPA in the United States.

While a few tests on animals had shown that it could cause tumors in animals, the doses were so massive that some animals died simply because the dose overwhelmed their systems, not because of cancer.[18] According to one source, a human being would have to eat 28,000 pounds (12,727 kilograms) of apples daily for seventy years to produce tumors like the ones the mice developed.[19] Yet the *Alar* hysteria was so intense and the political pressures so great that the manufacturer halted production.

Facts, Not Fears

What are the facts about pesticide residues? British researchers Richard Doll and Richard Peto are highly respected for their studies of the causes of cancer.[20] In 1986, they concluded that all environmental pollution, taken together, may have contributed to 2 percent of all recent cancer deaths. As for pesticide residues, they are "unimportant" as an explanation for any cancer today, these experts said.[21]

Lifestyle, family history, and diet appear to have a lot more to do with whether people develop cancer. When cancer rates in the United States are adjusted to take into account the changing age of the population and to exclude the contribution of smoking, the risk of cancer is either the same or decreasing.[22] The Canadian Cancer Society estimates that 35% of all cancers are related to unhealthy diet (low in fruits and vegetables).[23]

It is ironic that people are so concerned about synthetic pesticides and yet ignore natural ones. Plants produce natural toxins to protect themselves against insects and other predators. When natural chemicals are tested on animals, some turn out to be carcinogenic, just as do some synthetic chemicals. (About the same percentage of the natural pesticides—about 50 percent—cause malignant tumors in animals as do synthetic pesticides.)[24] Based on animal tests, coffee and cocoa, spices such as cinnamon and mustard, and fruits such as pineapples and plums all have natural carcinogens.[25]

Plants that are naturally pest-resistant have higher concentrations of natural pesticides.[26] In fact, the U.S. 1996 National Research Council report quoted earlier, which said we shouldn't worry much about chemicals in our foods, also stated that natural components may be of "greater concern" than synthetic ones.[27] An Environment Canada publication claims that the risk caused by drinking a daily glass of apple juice produced from Alar-treated fruit would be 58 times less risky than consuming the natural carcinogens in one mushroom.[28]

In creating and using synthetic pesticides, human beings can control the amounts and kinds of pesticides that are used. When toxins are made naturally by the plants themselves, humans cannot control them very well.

Bruce Ames, a prominent biochemist at the University of California at Berkeley, and his colleague Lois Swirsky Gold point out that people ingest about ten thousand times more of these natural pesticides than synthetic ones![29] The reason that these don't harm us, they explain, is that "the many layers of general defenses in humans and other animals protect against toxins, without distinguishing whether they are synthetic or natural." These natural defenses can't tell whether toxins are plant-made or laboratory-made. They protect humans against both.

Bans on pesticides may actually have serious health consequences. An impressive array of studies indicates that fruits and vegetables reduce the risk of a number of cancers, and synthetic pesticides have made a major contribution to health by reducing the cost of producing fruits and vegetables.[30] Prohibiting the use of many chemicals is likely to decrease the supply and raise the price of fruits and vegetables. This will reduce the consumption of these healthful foods, especially by poor people.

Talking to Your Children

Agricultural chemicals can benefit society as well as have bad consequences. That simple fact is often ignored in the textbooks. Here are some questions that you can answer.

❧ Do pesticides on our food cause cancer in humans?

This is very unlikely. While some scientists speculate that pesticide residues can increase our risk of cancer, Canadian cancer experts maintain that the public's fear of chemicals is "out of proportion to the risks."[31] Some pesticides have caused cancerous tumors in *animals*, but it is difficult to know if humans would react in similar ways. Also, those animals have usually been fed enormous quantities of the pesticides.

❧ What was wrong with DDT?

The buildup of DDT in the environment may have contributed to the serious decline in the numbers of birds such as falcons and eagles. However, the claim that DDT is a human carcinogen is not supported by the evidence.

Produce Prices: Grocery Stores versus Organic Food Stores (price in $CDN/lb)

	Grocery Stores		Organic Food Stores	
	Safeway	**IGA**	**Capers**	**On Broadway Specialty Foods***
Red Cabbage	.49	.59	.99	.59
Bananas	.69	.69	1.49	1.19
Russett Potatoes	.59	.49	.99	.79
Yellow Onions	.39	.49	1.79	.79
Golden Apples	1.29	1.19	1.99	1.39
MacIntosh Apples	.79	.59	.99	1.19
Romaine Lettuce	.79	.69	1.39	.99

Source: September 25, 1997; Vancouver, British Columbia)
* produce organic except lettuce

❦ Should we buy only organic food?

No. There is *no* reason to believe that organic food is safer than food grown and processed under the usual conditions. Naturally pest-resistant crops have their own powerful toxins. Health experts emphasize the importance of eating fruits and vegetables, and pesticides and herbicides help keep the costs of these foods low and the supply high. Organic foods are often more expensive than other foods, and this discourages people from eating them.

Activities for Parents and Children

Here are some activities that will help put agricultural chemicals into perspective for your children.

At the Organic Food Store
Take your children to an organic food store. Have them look at the fruits and vegetables, and record some of the prices. Then take them to a regular grocery store and have them look at the appearance of the same fruits and vegetables and record their prices. Discuss the differences in price and quality. They might find something like those in the table on page 238.

Explain to them that when farmers do not use pesticides, insects destroy more of the crop. This lowers the supply and causes prices to be higher. Also, since the quality is lower, demand for organic products is lower, and "organic" farmers cannot obtain the cost savings that come from producing large quantities.

If all fruits and vegetables were as expensive as those in the organic food stores, families, especially poor families, would be less able to afford them. Thus, these people would have poorer diets, which would contribute to many health problems. You could call the Canadian Cancer Society's Cancer Information Service (1-888-939-3333) and ask for its booklet "Healthy Eating: Reducing Your Risk of Cancer."

At a Nursery or Garden Centre

Take your children to a nursery or garden centre. Show them the various pesticides and herbicides. Ask them to read (or read to them) the safety instructions on the containers. These instructions are there to ensure that the products are used safely to protect both the person handling the chemicals and the environment. Explain to your children that many products are dangerous if used improperly, but, if used according to the instructions, the products are safe.

Agricultural Progress

The table on page 241 compares several characteristics of various countries. They show the extent to which these countries use modern farming methods, including tractors and fertilizers. Looking at the data, your children will see that there seems to be a connection between modern farming methods and longer life expectancy and higher incomes. Explain to your children that many factors influence income levels and life expectancy, but one important factor is the abundance of inexpensive food provided by modern agriculture.

Notes

1 Catherine Dee, ed., *Kid Heroes of the Environment* (Berkeley, CA: EarthWorks, 1991), 15–16.

2 Anne Pedersen, *The Kids' Environment Book: What's Awry and Why* (Santa Fe: John Muir, 1991), 80, 82.

3 Mary Metzger and Cinthya P. Whittaker, *This Planet is Mine: Teaching Environmental Awareness and Appreciation to Children* (New York: Fireside, 1991), 146.

4 Namowitz, Samuel N., and Nancy E Spaulding, *Heath Earth Science* (Toronto: D.C. Heath Canada, Canadian ed., 1987), 494.

5 Siebert, Myrtle, and Evelyn Kerr, *Food for Life*, (Toronto: McGraw-Hill Ryerson, 1994), 299.

6 Pedersen, 84, 86.

Life Expectancy and Farming Methods

Country	Life Expectancy 1994	Tractors per Million Population	Million Tons of Fertilizer per Million Population	Annual per Capita Income 1991 (GNP in US$)
Canada	78.5	30,819	82.0	21,260
Switzerland	78.5	17,703	26.2	33,510
Austria	76.5	46,518	39.7	20,380
United States	76.0	19,095	74.1	22,560
Denmark	76.0	31,724	123.7	23,660
Portugal	75.5	13,932	28.3	5,620
Chile	75.0	3,155	26.1	2,160
Bulgaria	73.5	5,934	80.2	1,840
Mexico	73.0	2,095	33.5	2,870
Argentina	71.5	7,264	5.9	2,780
Thailand	68.5	2,897	19.1	1,580
China	68.0	713	23.3	370
Iran	66.0	2,326	23.5	2,320
Peru	65.5	941	7.3	1,020
Philippines	65.5	176	9.7	740
Guatemala	64.5	694	21.8	930
Brazil	62.0	5,943	25.9	2,920
India	58.5	1,171	14.9	330
Bangladesh	55.0	60	10.7	220
Somalia	54.5	299	0.4	150
Kenya	53.0	463	5.4	340
Ethiopia	52.5	92	2.6	120
Haiti	45.0	43	0.2	370
Zimbabwe	42.0	2,703	22.7	620
Chad	41.0	51	1.8	220
Rwanda	40.0	19	0.6	260

Sources: Marlita Reddy, ed. *Statistical Abstract of the World* (New York: Gale Research, 1994), table 57 (tractors), 449; tables 58, 59, 60 (fertilizers), 457, 464, 471; and *Encyclopedic World Atlas* (New York: Oxford University Press, 1994), Per Capita Income in U.S. Dollars, V1, Life Expectancy, V3.

7 Environment Canada, *Understanding Pesticides,* 6.

8 National Research Council Committee on Comparative Toxicity of Naturally Occurring Carcinogens, *Carcinogens and Anticarcinogens in the Human Diet* (Washington, DC: National Academy Press, 1996), Executive Summary, 5.

9 Environment Canada, *Understanding Pesticides,* 1.

10 Thomas R. Dunlap, *DDT: Scientists, Citizens, and Public Policy* (Princeton, NJ: Princeton University Press, 1981), 59.

11 Harland Austin, Julian E. Keil, and Philip Cole, "A Prospective Follow-Up Study of Cancer Mortality in Relation to Serum DDT," *American Journal of Public Health*, Vol. 79, No. 1 (January 1989), 43.

12 Holly Lippke, *DDT: An Overview*, PERC Working Paper 93–3, Political Economy Research Center, Bozeman, MT, 1993.

13 J. Gordon Edwards, "DDT Effects on Bird Abundance and Reproduction," in *Rational Readings on Environmental Concerns*, ed. by Jay H. Lehr (New York: Van Norstrand Reinhold, 1992), 195–216, at 205.

14 Kenneth Mellanby, "With Safeguards, DDT Should Still Be Used," *Wall Street Journal*, September 12, 1989, A30.

15 M. B. Green, *Pesticides—Boon or Bane?* (Boulder, CO: Westview, 1976), 101.

16 Lippke, 11.

17 Michael Fumento, *Science Under Siege: Balancing Technology and the Environment* (New York: William Morrow and Company, Inc., 1993), 21–47.

18 Joseph D. Rosen, "The Death of Daminozide," in *Pesticides and Alternatives,* ed. by J. E. Casida (New York: Elsevier, 1990), 59.

19 Thomas Gale Moore, *Environmental Fundamentalism* (Stanford, CA: Hoover Institution, 1992), 6.

20 Richard Doll and Richard Peto, *The Causes of Cancer* (Oxford: Oxford University Press, 1986), 1245–1265.

21 Doll and Peto, 1250.

22 Bruce N. Ames and Lois Swirsky Gold, "Environmental Pollution and Cancer: Some Misconceptions," in *Rational Readings on Environmental Concerns*, ed. by Jay H. Lehr (New York: Van Nostrand Reinhold, 1992), 151–67.

23 Cancer Information Service, *Canadian Cancer Encyclopedia*, (Regina: Canadian Cancer Society, 1997), Site 907, pp. 1.

24 Bruce N. Ames and Lois Swirsky Gold, "Pesticides, Risk, and Applesauce," *Science*, May 19, 1989, 755–757.

25 Lois Swirsky Gold, et al., "Rodent Carcinogens: Setting Priorities," in *Science,* Vol. 258, October 9, 1992, 261-265, and Lois Swirsky Gold, Thomas H. Slone, and Bruce N. Ames, "Prioritization of Possible Carcinogenic Hazards in Food," in *Food Chemical Risk Analysis*, ed. by David Tennant (London: Chapman and Hall, 1997).

26 Ames and Gold, 756.

27 National Research Council Committee on Comparative Toxicity of Naturally Occurring Carcinogens, Executive Summary, 5–6.

28 *Understanding Pesticides*, 2.

29 Ames and Gold, 755.

30 Bruce N. Ames, Mark K. Shigenaga, and Tory M. Hagen, "Oxidants, Antioxidants, and the Degenerative Diseases of Aging," Proceedings of the National Academy of Sciences U.S.A., Vol. 90, September 1993, 7915–22.

31 Canadian Cancer Society, *Healthy Eating* (Toronto: Canadian Cancer Society, 1996), 3.

Chapter 18

A Garbage Crisis?

Tanja Vogt, a student at West Milford High School in New Jersey, read a newspaper article about the local school board. The board had decided to continue using food trays made of Styrofoam (a trade name for foamed polystyrene plastic) in the school cafeteria. The cafeteria served food on polystyrene trays because they cost a nickel less than paper ones.

Tanja had learned in her science class that polystyrene was not biodegradable. It would stay in a landfill forever. "I asked myself, why would we use these things if they're harmful to the environment?" Tanja said. She and her friends campaigned to get rid of the plastic trays and even persuaded students to pay an extra nickel. The school board changed its mind.[1]

Most parents and teachers would be proud of Tanja and her classmates, and they should be. The students perceived an environmental hazard and took action. The only problem is that their action was based on inaccurate information about solid waste disposal since plastic trays are not necessarily more harmful than pressed paper trays. By some measures, they are more environmentally sound.

Too Much Garbage

Our children are taught that North America faces a garbage crisis. They learn that our wasteful life-styles produce too much garbage, that each Canadian produces more garbage than anyone else in the world, more even than Americans, and that there is no place to bury it.

* ✤ "On average, about one-third of the garbage you produce is packaging. If every North American family could avoid packaging completely, there would be nearly 10 million fewer garbage cans full of garbage each year in dumps." This suggested by the children's book, *Earthcycles and Ecosystems.*[2]

* ✤ Several textbooks tell the story of the Mobro garbage barge that left New York City in 1988 looking for a place to dump its cargo of three thousand tons of garbage. Rejected by states all along the East Coast, the barge cruised to Mexico, Belize, and the Bahamas seeking a place for its garbage. The wandering barge appeared night after night on the news and became a focus for the garbage debate in the United States. But, in the end, it returned to New York and was allowed to deposit its cargo, which was incinerated in Brooklyn.[3] As it is generally told, however, the story conveys the idea that space for garbage is scarce and getting scarcer.

* ✤ The text *Science Directions 9* points to "the steadily increasing volume of solid waste that must be disposed of. Landfill sites quickly become filled. It is increasingly difficult for local governments to find new sites for solid waste disposal because many people do not want these sites near their community."[4]

Students are also taught that products that "biodegrade" or decompose are environmentally preferable to those that don't.

❋ Biodegradable wastes "can be broken down and changed," says the text *Journeys in Science*. It goes on to say: "Plastic does not break down in the Earth. Therefore, plastic objects add to the problem of land pollution."[5]

❋ Environment BC's *Green Team* told a grade seven class in Vancouver, British Columbia: "To make plastic, they take oil, from deep down in the ground, they mix it with six to ten of the deadliest chemicals known to human beings, they mix it to make plastic."[6]

❋ *Science Directions 8* discusses the choice between "disposable diapers," which "may take 300 years to decompose," and cloth diapers, which "can be reused after washing, and decompose relatively easily."[7]

Where Does It Go?

The truth is that there is no garbage crisis. And plastic isn't really Public Enemy Number 1.

Municipal solid waste is the term used for waste produced by households. Modern societies like our own produce more waste than traditional societies, but throughout history all societies have had to deal with garbage. Some amount of waste is a natural by-product of living. The best we can do is figure out how to manage it with minimal harm to ourselves and the environment.

There are four principal approaches to disposing of solid waste: reducing the amount of waste, recycling or composting, incinerating, and putting it in landfills. Although textbooks discuss all of these, most children's textbooks emphasize landfills, the major repositories of solid waste.

A landfill is a place where garbage is deposited and then covered up. There are two kinds of landfills for municipal garbage.

✸ Older landfills are essentially holes in the ground where garbage is placed and then covered with dirt. (Some are located in clay soils, because clay reduces leakage.)

✸ Newer landfills are also holes in the ground, but the hole is lined with plastic to prevent chemicals from leaking into groundwater, methane gas is vented, fluids are caught and purified, and garbage is covered daily with dirt.[8] Modern landfills are a big improvement over most earlier models.

Most people don't really know much about landfills. But Dr. William Rathje does. He's an archaeologist at the University of Arizona who studies modern civilization the same way that archaeologists study ancient ones—by digging up waste sites. (He cheerily calls himself a "garbologist.") Rathje has learned a lot of things. Some of these are surprises. For example, in his "digs" in the 1980s he learned that:

✸ Fast-food packaging of all kinds makes up less than 1 percent of the materials in landfills, whether measured by weight or volume.[9]

✸ Expanded polystyrene foam (Styrofoam) represents no more than 1 percent of the volume of garbage.[10]

✸ Disposable diapers represent only 1.4 percent of the volume.[11]

✸ All plastic products account for less than 16 percent of landfill space, and this percentage hasn't gone up over the past 20 years.[12]

✸ Paper takes up well over 40 percent of landfill space. Newspapers alone average about 13 percent.[13]

✸ Rathje has found in his digging more than two thousand readable newspapers, some of them from as far back as 1952.[14]

A Landfill Crisis?

While there is no "garbage crisis," in some places there is a shortage of landfills. New ones must be continually developed since most only last for about ten years. (Newer landfills tend to be much larger than older ones.)

The problem isn't space. Clark Wiseman of Gonzaga University points out that all the garbage produced by the United States for the next one thousand years could fit in a landfill forty-four miles (70.81 kilometres) square by 120 feet (36.57 metres) deep. That's right. One thousand years![15] This is only one-tenth of 1 percent of all the land area of the continental United States. And since Canada has one-tenth of the population of the United States, and a larger land mass, the problem of space is even less of an issue.

Rather, the problem is simply that people are not eager to have a landfill next door. The reason has more to do with the possible effect on property values than on risk to health. Landfills are no longer built in areas where the water table is shallow or the soil is permeable and thus the chemicals can leak out.

Even the old landfills rarely pose much risk. Once they have been shut down, they needn't remain wastelands. Consider Everett Crowley Park. It is a park in South Vancouver built on an old landfill near the Fraser River. Citizens who were concerned about their neighbourhood reclaimed the old dump, closed in 1967. The turned it into a scenic area where people go to picnic, walk, and enjoy the wildlife. The nature lovers who enjoy watching the coyotes hunt rabbits in the underbrush see no evidence of the park's former use.[16]

And some citizens and towns are willing to put up with having a landfill nearby—for a price. Private landfill operators can produce a package of incentives that benefit cities and individuals.

In 1991, the provincial government refused to allow the City of Toronto to sell its garbage to the community of Kirkland Lake, where it would have been safely dumped in an open-pit mine.[17] But the government of Charles City County, Virginia, allowed a regional landfill to be built in return for $1.1 million per year. This fee allowed property taxes to be cut by 20 percent. Local residents were willing to allow a landfill in the area in exchange for lower property taxes.[18]

In fact, in 1995 the *Wall Street Journal* concluded that the supposed landfill crisis is a myth. "New capacity, it turns out, hasn't been hard to come by because expanding old dumps isn't terribly difficult," wrote reporter Jeff Bailey. Siting new ones isn't impossible, either. Conclusions such as this, however, have not deterred the Canadian Council of Ministers of the Environment from their 1988 goal of reducing the disposal of solid wastes in this country by 50 percent by the year 2000.[19]

Public Enemy No. 1?

As William Rathje discovered, *neither* plastic *nor* paper is likely to "biodegrade", that is, break apart into its original "natural" components—in a typical landfill. The inertness of plastic is actually an advantage, since it won't produce chemicals that can leak out. And when environmental impacts other than landfill space are considered, plastic may have some other advantages.

* A study published in *Science* magazine compared the manufacture of paper and polystyrene cups. Martin Hocking concluded that producing paper cups required more chemicals, more steam, more electricity, and more cooling water, and produced more air pollution and wastewater.

* Another study, this one by Franklin Associates, found that plastic bags can be produced for 20 to 40 percent less energy than paper bags, and produce less air and water pollution than do paper bags.[20]

Although textbooks criticize polystyrene because it does not "biodegrade," it gained its status as a "public enemy" because some foamed polystyrene products were formerly produced using CFCs (chlorofluorocarbons). These chemicals may be depleting the ozone layer, as discussed in Chapter 14, but polystyrene is no longer made with CFCs,[21] although some substitutes (HCFCs) still may have a depleting effect. Rather than praise this development, many activists shifted to criticizing polystyrene because it fills up landfills.

Mountains of Waste

A major theme of environmental texts is that Canadians are wasteful. Discussions of solid waste elaborate on this theme.

* Textbooks typically state that Canadians produce about 400 kilograms of household garbage per person per year.[22]

* The *Green Team* told a grade seven class that "the average Canadian produces about eighty cans of garbage a year ... someone from the States, about sixty, someone from Africa, about five. So there's some big differences there."[23]

* *Save the Earth: An Action Handbook for Kids* urges children to emulate students at Dartmouth College. They carried around a garbage bag for one week to put all the garbage they produced so they could see how much they personally created.[24]

Figures on waste seem to be mostly guesswork. William Rathje says he has seen estimates ranging from 2.9 to 8 pounds per person per day (1.3 to 3.6 kilograms). His own studies suggest that in some parts of the United States households produce less than three pounds of garbage per day.[25]

Statistics Canada estimates that individual Canadians produce less than 1 kilogram of garbage per day. Comparisons between countries can prove difficult, however, as waste is defined and measured differently between countries, and even between measuring agencies. Lynn Scarlett, a researcher for the Reason Foundation, estimates that American households produce 3.2 pounds of garbage per day (1.45 kilos). One reason American figures may be higher than Japanese or European figures is that recycled products such as aluminum cans, newspapers, and glass are included in American solid waste figures, while Japanese and European statistics include only items that actually go to the dump.[26]

William Rathje actually measured garbage thrown out by households in the United States and Mexico (he wasn't digging into landfills in this experiment; he and his associates examined household garbage cans). He found that American households produce one-third less garbage than Mexican households.[27]

Why? Modern packaging actually reduces waste, he explains. When vegetables are bought frozen in cardboard boxes, very little is wasted. In contrast, in Mexican households, vegetables are more often bought raw, so rinds, husks, leaves, stems, and other material must be removed and discarded.[28] (In North America, food processing companies often make animal feed and other products from these materials.)

Talking to Your Children

Thanks to the pioneering work of Rathje and others, we know more about the composition of solid waste than we used to. Our texts should teach that each product has its environmental benefits and its environmental costs. While glass bottles, for example, can be reused, juice boxes take up far less space, especially when they are crushed. Furthermore, our texts should teach the lesson that good solid waste management can minimize the environmental harm caused by any product. Now you can answer your children's questions.

❀ Are we running out of landfill space?

No. While there may be a shortage of space in some places, it is likely to be temporary. The much-talked-about landfill shortage of the late 1980s has disappeared. Even though people don't want landfills "in their backyards," they may welcome them if the owners provide benefits such as lower property taxes.

❀ Does plastic hurt a landfill?

No. Since it is inert, plastic isn't going to produce chemicals in a landfill that could leak out. And while it does not "biodegrade" or decompose, the fact is that hardly anything decomposes in a landfill because there is not enough oxygen and water to cause biodegradation.

❀ Are Canadians too wasteful?

This is a question that each family should probably answer for itself. But claims that Canadians throw out far more than others are exaggerated.

Activities for Parents and Children

The following activities may help your children think more carefully about solid waste.

Orange Juice: Fresh or Frozen?

Packaging may not be as wasteful as your children think. With your children along, buy a can of frozen orange juice concentrate and some fresh oranges. Make the frozen orange juice according to the package instructions. Save all of the packaging from the frozen orange juice.

Now make the same amount of juice from fresh oranges. Save all the orange rinds as you make the juice.

Weigh the squeezed orange peels and compare them with the weight of the empty orange juice container (or just look at the space they take up). Ask your children which form of packaging produces more waste that will go into the landfill.

Eight-year-old Devin made twenty-four ounces of fresh orange juice, and had twenty-eight ounces of empty orange rinds when he was through. When he made the same amount of juice from concentrate, the only waste was the empty can, which weighed one ounce.

Once the juice has been fresh-squeezed, ask your children what happens to the skin and pulp. Of course, unless you have a compost pile, it is thrown away. Tell your children how commercial juice producers use the pulp and skin for animal feed, orange extracts, and flavoring oils. In light of that re-use, which method of delivering orange juice is less wasteful?

Make Your Own Landfill

Some books for children have an experiment that is supposed to show that some things, like food scraps, will decompose in a landfill and other things, like plastic, will not. These experiments are flawed because very little actually decomposes in a landfill. The essential elements for decomposition—air, high moisture levels, and microbes—are missing from most landfills. The following experiment more accurately reflects what happens in a landfill.

❀   Get a small plastic food container or glass jar with an airtight lid. Select small quantities of the following: newspaper, foam plastic cup, food scraps (orange or potato peel), and a plastic bag. Make a list of these items and their condition. Pack these items into the container as tightly as possible and pack it as full as possible. The objective is to leave as little air in the container as you can. Then wrap the container in aluminum foil so that no light can get in. Leave the container tightly sealed for four to six weeks. After that time, open the container and examine each item. Can your children read the newspaper? Even items that are considered "biodegradable" rarely degrade under landfill conditions.

A Short History of the Soda Can

Most children do not understand or appreciate how competitive market forces often cause producers to reduce the amount of material they use in their packages. For example, plastic grocery bags were 70 percent thinner in 1989 than they were in 1976.[29] Here is another example, beverage cans.

In the 1960s, producers used steel to make beverage cans. They switched to lighter aluminum in the late 1960s and 1970s and since then have gradually reduced the amount of aluminum per can. Today, pop cans are extremely light. Show your children the graph below and discuss its implications.

Reduction in Weight of Beverage Cans, 1970s–1990s

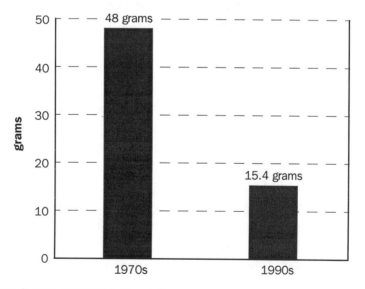

Source: Canadian Soft Drink Association

Notes

1 Catherine Dee, ed., *Kid Heroes of the Environment* (Berkeley, CA: EarthWorks, 1991), 73–75.

2 Beth Savan, *Earthcycles and Ecosystems* (Toronto: Kids Can, 1991), 82.

3 Savan, 83.

4 Douglas A. Roberts, *Science Directions 9* (Edmonton: Arnold, 1991), 300.

5 Peter Beugger and Larry Yore, *Journeys in Science 5* (Toronto: Collier Macmillan, 1990), 57, 100.

6 Observation of the *Green Team* at Sir William Van Horne Elementary in Vancouver, BC, June 18, 1997.

7 Roberts, 148–149.

8 William Rathje and Cullen Murphy, *Rubbish! The Archaeology of Garbage* (New York: HarperCollins, 1992), 16.

9 Rathje and Murphy, 97.

10 Rathje and Murphy, 98.

11 Rathje and Murphy, 162.

12 Rathje and Murphy, 101.

13 Rathje and Murphy, 103, 104, 106.

14 Personal conversation with William Rathje, July 1996.

15 Lynn Scarlett, "A Consumer's Guide to Environmental Myths and Realities," Policy Report #99, National Center for Policy Analysis, Dallas, TX, September 1991, 3, quoting Clark Wiseman.

16 Judy Quan, *Everett Crowley Park: Paradise Reclaimed* (Vancouver: The Evergreen Foundation, 1997).

17 Patrick Luciani, *Economic Myths: Making Sense of Canadian Policy Issues* (Don Mills, ON: Addison-Wesley Publishers, 1996), 156.

18 Scarlett, 37.

19 National Roundtable on the Environment and the Economy, *The National Waste Reduction Handbook* (Ottawa: 1991), 6.

20 Scarlett, 14.

21 Letter from David Jolly, Environmental Affairs Representative, Dart Container Corporation, September 11, 1992.

22 Roberts, Vol. 9, 296.

23 Observation of the "Green Team" at William Van Horne Elementary School, Vancouver, BC, June 1997.

24 Betty Miles, *Save the Earth: An Action Handbook for Kids* (New York: Alfred A. Knopf, 1991), 13.

25 William L. Rathje, "Rubbish!" *Atlantic Monthly*, December 1989, 101.

26 Scarlett, 8.

27 Rathje and Murphy, 217.

28 Rathje and Murphy, 217.

29 Scarlett, 32.

Chapter 19

The Recycling Myth

In the 1970s, citizens throughout North America, concerned about the state of the environment, started aggressively pushing the government to provide them with an efficient and accessible system of recycling. By the 1980s, the Blue Box had been introduced in Ontario, its first test market. Residents conscientiously sorted their recyclable glass, paper, and metal waste, and left their filled Blue Boxes on the curb where the materials would be picked up and transported to become new products. The programs were the envy of environmentalists everywhere, and by 1997, over 9,000 similar programs had sprung up across the continent.[1]

But Bruce Van Voorst, a writer for *Time* magazine, noticed a problem a few years ago.[2] In apartments and in homes around the United States, he observed, Americans were washing glass bottles and separating them into piles of green, clear, and amber. They were bundling up newspapers in one container, putting mixed white paper in another, and placing computer paper in a third. They were hauling the whole collection out to the curb or over to the local recycling centre.

Van Voorst had discovered a "dirty secret." A lot of the carefully separated materials were never actually recycled. "More than 10,000

257

tons of old newspapers have piled up in waterfront warehouses in New Jersey," he wrote, and for the entire United States the figure could exceed 100 million tons. In Seattle, a recycler pondered what to do with six thousand tons of bottles that couldn't be reused.

Guy Crittendon, a writer for *The Next City*, found similar situations this side of the border. He found mountains of glass left sitting where they had been collected in Northern Ontario. No one had an economic incentives to buy them or haul them away. And bottle depots in Alberta and Saskatchewan consistently lose money.[3]

Swamped by waste, the recycling centres couldn't handle all the debris that dutiful citizens were saving from the landfill. A lot ended up in incinerators, landfills, or storage areas.

The Pressure Is On

Children are taught that the Earth faces disaster. The chief hope for preventing catastrophe is recycling. The pressure on children to recycle, and to persuade their parents to recycle, is enormous.

* "You can help your family to reduce rubbish, save trees and stop land from being used for garbage dumps by setting up your own fine paper recycling program," says *Earthcycles and Ecosystems.*[4]

* "The disposal of waste paper results in more pollution, whether your local garbage is buried or burned," argues *Science Directions*. "As an alternative, you can buy recycled paper whenever possible, and save your used paper for recycling."[5]

* The answer to mineral shortages "lies mainly in conservation. It involves eliminating waste, recycling used materials, and developing substitutes from more plentiful materials,"[6] says *Heath Earth Science.*

* "Using less of the Earth's resources, using them wisely, and re-cycling them are some ways to conserve the Earth's natural re-sources," says the text *Journeys in Science* "What can you do to conserve the Earth's natural resources?"[7]

* The same text asks students: "Does your province require a de-posit on all beverage containers? How might this help conserve resources?"[8]

A Major Misunderstanding

Our children learn that recycling consists of separating aluminum cans, glass, newspaper, and some plastics and taking them to the curb or to a neighbourhood recycling centre. Of course, that is only half the story. Nothing is truly recycled until a new product made of recycled materials is purchased by a willing customer.

Yet not everything can be turned into new products. Consider paper, which accounts for 40 percent or more of landfill volume. Wil-liam Rathje of the University of Arizona points out that there is nei-ther a market for this amount of recycled newspaper, nor enough mills to process all the paper that could be collected.

In 1987 New Jersey passed legislation that required every com-munity in the state to recycle, and the recycling rate for newspapers jumped from 50 percent to 62 percent. This created such a glut that the price of newsprint fell from $45 per ton to minus $25 per ton. That's right. Recyclers had to pay $25 per ton for someone to haul the newspapers away![9]

In Europe, the recycling craze has gone further, and the results have not been good. In 1991, the German government enacted a re-cycling law. It requires businesses to take back from customers and recycle all forms of packaging, including bottles, cans, containers, cartons, and sacks. By 1994, the nonprofit company that collects and sorts the items was $412 million in debt,[10] and in 1993 the government admitted that some of the returned packaging would be incinerated or put in landfills.[11]

Even More Laws

Weak demand for recycled products has led several provincial and state governments to pass laws requiring that certain products, such as newspapers and other paper goods, contain a minimum percentage of recycled material, or that a certain proportion of soft drink containers be reusable. The U.S. Congress has also considered such legislation and the White House has issued executive orders to encourage the use of recycled products.

The goal is understandable—no one wants piles of yellowing newspapers or mountains of unsanitary glass bottles stuck in warehouses with nowhere to go. But forcing people to buy all the recycled material that is piling up creates its own problems.

Often, recycled material is already more expensive than virgin material because of the cost of collecting all the dispersed material and because recycling requires different processing equipment. To require every item to contain a specific amount of recycled material raises prices even more since manufacturers must make costly investments in plants and equipment that would not otherwise be necessary.

These laws also discourage innovative ways of dealing with waste. Manufacturers and packagers must be more concerned with whether the material can be recycled than with other characteristics. For example:

❋ Lynn Scarlett of the Reason Foundation points out that recycling laws could eliminate the one-pound coffee "brick packs" you now find in retail stores. These packages hold the same amount of coffee as metal cans, but weigh less than one-third of traditional metal cans, and they take up little space. Recycled-content laws would force the use of the cans instead.[12]

* Christopher Boerner and Kenneth Chilton of the Center for the Study of American Business point out that single-layered packaging for food is easier to recycle than packages that have several layers of plastic and paper, but the multilayered packaging extends the shelf life of food, and eliminating it will increase food waste.[13]

The Point of It All

So, we have people forced to separate their trash, and now we have people forced to use recycled products. We should at least stop and ask what we are getting for all this mandatory effort. As we saw in Chapter 18, the answer is: Not very much. Recycling may reduce somewhat the amount of paper and other materials that go into landfills, but as we saw, space for landfills is not a very pressing problem.

And there are other real concerns.

* Most texts declare that recycling newspapers and other paper saves trees. "Every tonne of paper you recycle saves 17 trees from the chainsaw," says the children's book *Earthcycles and Ecosystems*. "It also saves fuel (for chainsaws, pulp mills and other forestry operations) and reduces air and water pollution from the mill."[14]

* But the trees that will be "saved" are usually those planted specifically to make pulpwood for paper. More recycling would reduce the incentive to maintain and plant such trees. Economist

Clark Wiseman estimates that if paper recycling reaches 40 percent (it is about 30 percent now), demand for paper from trees would fall by about 7 percent.[15] The industry would be disinclined to maintain their husbandry of the forests.

There are some environmental problems with recycling, too.

✸ Transporting recyclables to processing plants requires separate collection trucks, and producing the finished goods consumes energy and causes pollution just as production of paper from wood does.[16]

✸ De-inking of waste paper produces sludge that may contain chlorinated organic chemicals, which are often considered toxic. Toxic or not, the sludge must end up somewhere, probably in a landfill.

So, although it is technically possible to recycle almost all trash, doing so would itself use resources—labour, energy, and materials. And it would pose its own environmental stresses.

On a Brighter Note

In 1995, 62 percent of all aluminum cans were recycled.[17] The reason for this high figure is economics. Producing aluminum from raw ore requires enormous amounts of energy.[18] Producing new cans from old ones uses much less energy. Making new cans from old ones saves money. Although the price varies from time to time, returned aluminum cans fetch between $400 and $600 per ton.[19]

Recycling aluminum cans started in 1968 when the Reynolds Metals Company started a pilot recycling centre. The company was responding to public concerns about litter and wanted to forestall expensive bottle deposit bills. The rapid rise in energy prices during the 1970s plus fears of energy cutoffs soon made recycling permanent.[20]

About ten years ago, members of a Veterans of Foreign Wars chapter outside St. Paul, Minnesota, learned that the small push-pull tabs that are used to open aluminum cans are of a higher quality than the rest of the aluminum can. Per kilogram, they are worth more than returned aluminum cans, and collecting them is less cumbersome. The veterans began to raise funds for a local charity. The Minneapolis house now raises $80,000 a year from tabs, and the program has spread to other parts of the country, and to other charities.[21]

No one is being forced to recycle or buy aluminum cans or aluminum tabs. Recycling happens because the used products (the cans and tabs) have value, and people can earn money if they go to the trouble of collecting them.

Other materials are recycled voluntarily, too. In 1992, about 33 percent of all paper and cardboard in Canada, for example, was recycled.[22] One reason is that collection costs are low, since places such as grocery stores and shopping malls always have lots of boxes.

Junkyards recycle cars, metals, glass, paper, and plastic. Members of the Institute of Scrap Recycling Industries, a trade association in the United States, recycled 9 million cars in 1990, nearly the same as the number of new cars sold that year. These businesses also recycled 60 million tons of ferrous metals, 7 million tons of nonferrous metals, and 30 million tons of paper, glass, and plastic.[23]

In sum, when it is economically feasible, recycling can be an excellent alternative to hauling discards to the landfill. However, recycling does not always represent the best use of resources. Our children's textbooks should reflect the complexity of the recycling issue.

Talking to Your Children

Your children are taught that recycling is the closest thing we have to a solution to our environmental problems. You can now respond to their questions with a more realistic view of recycling.

❈ How much should we recycle?

We should recycle when it makes sense to do so. For one thing, we want to be sure that recycling actually takes place. Separating materials and putting them in a recycling box does not mean that materials are being recycled or that landfill space is being saved. If real recycling is to occur, the collected materials must be turned into new products that people want to buy.

❈ When does recycling make sense?

Recycling makes sense if people are using it to make products that others want, and if all the costs associated with recycling are not higher than the price people are willing to pay for the recycled product. Clearly, recycling aluminum cans is working. So is recycling cardboard and scrap steel. Businesses exist to recycle these products, and no one is being forced to save them or take them.

❈ Will recycling save trees?

Unfortunately, no. Much of our paper comes from trees that are planted specifically to grow pulpwood for paper. If the demand for paper declines, the industry will divert its resources from forest maintenance.

❈ Why not force people to buy recycled materials?

Such laws will make products more expensive and discourage innovative ways of dealing with waste (like reducing the amount of packaging). Parents should also consider whether such interference in normal activities is what we want from our governments.

Activities for Parents and Children

The following activities will also help your children put recycling into perspective.

A Visit to the Recycling Centre

Take your children to the local recycling centre and have them talk to the manager. Recycling may help conserve resources and alleviate disposal problems but it also has its drawbacks. What happens to the glass, newspaper or other recyclables that are sorted and collected? Where do they go? What are they used for? How much does it cost?

Your Garbage Bill

Show your children the two utility bills that include fees for garbage collection below. Ask them to examine the numbers carefully.

Utility Bill #1			Utility Bill #2		
Reading Date 1/22/99		Reading 465462	3/31/99	4/30/99	
Water Rate/ 625 Gal.	Sewer Rate/ 625 Gal.	Consumption	Trash Rate/ Can	Number of Cans	Trash Charge
$0.011	$0.008	1912	$1.50	6	$9.00
	Charges			**Charges**	
	Water	$21.38		Water	$15.00
	Sewer	$15.30		Sewer	$10.00
	Trash	$15.00		Trash	$9.00
Date Due 3/15/99	Amount Due	$51.68	Date Due 5/30/99	Amount Due	$34.00

Point out that with Bill #1 the family pays the same amount each month for garbage collection no matter how much trash the family leaves at the curb. In this case, recycling does not change the price the family pays for trash. A family that produces just a little trash pays as much as the family that produces large bundles.

Now have your children look at Bill #2. This city charges a fee ($1.50) for each trash can it picks up. A family that produces a lot of trash pays more than a family that produces a little. The family's cost can change every week, depending on how many cans of trash the family uses. Which bill is likely to encourage recycling?

Now compare your family's bill to these two bills. (Of course, you may not have any bill for trash other than your property tax bill.)

If you are charged by the trash can, you can discuss with your children what you as a family might do to cut down on trash and thus save money. If you are not charged this way, point out how little incentive your family has to reduce the amount of trash you throw out. Some cities have reduced landfill usage by this "pay-as-you-throw" method.

Costs of Recycled Products

Take your children to a stationery store and compare the costs of recycled versus nonrecycled paper. Sometimes recycled paper is more expensive (but not always). Discuss with your children whether you will purchase recycled paper if it is more expensive. If so, how much more are they willing to pay?

Discuss with your children why recycled products may be more expensive than normal products. For example, collecting paper from many different sources is often more difficult than cutting down trees and making pulp at a mill near the trees. Higher prices suggest that the recycled product uses more resources—more labour, more materials, or more energy (or perhaps more of all three). Is this really what we want?

If markets for recycled paper increase, the prices of recycled paper should go down as companies benefit from economies of scale. Some paper companies have already designed plants that do a better job of manufacturing paper from recycled paper. But is all that effort and expense really helping the environment? This is a difficult question to answer.

Notes

1 Guy Crittendon, "The Blue Box Conspiracy," *The Next City*, Fall 1997, 34–40.

2 Bruce Van Voorst, "The Recycling Bottleneck," *Time*, September 14, 1992, 52–54.

3 Crittendon, 34–40.

4 Beth Savan, *Earthcycles and Ecosystems* (Toronto: Kids Can Press, 1991), 86.

5 Douglas A. Roberts, *Science Directions 8* (Edmonton: Arnold Publishing, 1991), 321.

6 Samuel N. Namowitz and Nancy E. Spaulding, *Earth Science* (Toronto: DC Heath Canada, Canadian ed., 1987), 85.

7 Peter Beugger and Larry D. Yore, *et al.*, *Journeys in Science 5* (Toronto: Collier Macmillian Canada, 1990), 105, 103.

8 Beugger and Yore, *et al.*, 105.

9 William Rathje and Cullen Murphy, *Rubbish! The Archaeology of Garbage* (New York: HarperCollins, 1992), 206.

10 James V. DeLong, *Wasting Away: Mismanaging Municipal Solid Waste*, Competitive Enterprise Institute, Washington, DC, May 1994, 30.

11 Boerner and Chilton, *Recycling's Demand Side: Lessons from Germany's "Green Dot,"* St. Louis, Washington University Center for the Study of American Business, August 1993.

12 Lynn Scarlett, "Recycling's Invisible Costs," *Wall Street Journal*, March 3, 1992.

13 Boerner and Chilton, 10.

14 Savan, 87.

15 Quoted in Jane S. Shaw, "Recycling," *The Fortune Encyclopedia of Economics*, ed. by David R. Henderson (New York: Warner, 1993), 459.

16 Scarlett, 20.

17 Figure from the Aluminum Association, Washington, D.C., May 1996.

18 Rathje and Murphy, 204.

19 Rathje and Murphy, 200.

20 Shaw, 458.

21 For more information about the pull tab recycling program, you may contact NorthGreen Communications, Inc., 641 East Lake Street, Wayzata, Minnesota.

22 Organisation for Economic Co-operation and Development, *OECD Environmental Data Compendium 1997*, 163.

23 Rathje and Murphy, 202.

Chapter 20

What We Can Do

Most of the textbook materials discussed in this book have one major flaw: lack of balance. Although we have found factual errors, the key problem is usually that environmental books tell only one side of an often complicated story. They are remarkably consistent in presenting material that supports doomsday scenarios, political action, and pessimistic forecasts.

In this concluding chapter, we would like to help you evaluate what is taught in your children's schools and suggest some steps to offset the myths and half-truths that pass for environmental education. Let's begin with what we see as the proper goals of environmental education.

The Purpose of Environmental Education

Environmental education should help students understand the complex living world and the natural laws or principles that govern it—that is, it should be grounded in science. In addition, it should be taught with an understanding of economics, which is simply the study of why people make the choices they do. Environmental study offers an opportunity to help children develop the critical thinking and decision-making skills that will help them make wise choices.

Understanding Science

Too often, the science conveyed in our texts gives a false impression of certainty. This is especially misleading with environmental issues, because the science surrounding them is often ambiguous and in a state of flux. The impression of certainty stunts children's curiosity and denies them the unfolding of scientific discovery.

Children should be encouraged to view current debates over environmental issues as part of the search for truth, not as a morality play. These debates can make science interesting and can introduce children to the way knowledge is obtained, how its validity is established, and the tentative nature of many of our conclusions.

Scientists use rigorous methods to collect and analyze information, but they do not always draw the same conclusions from these data. For example, some scientists think that higher CO_2 levels will make the world hotter, warmer, wetter, and greener. Others point to factors that could make the planet cooler.

By exploring these controversies, teachers (and parents) have an opportunity to meld the classroom with the real world and introduce children to the puzzles that have yet to be solved. This, we believe, is much better preparation for becoming responsible adults than the crisis-based approach prevalent in our schools.

Understanding Economics

Unlike science, economics is rarely taught in schools, and when it is, the classes are usually at the high school level. Yet an understanding of economic principles is essential to an understanding of environmental problems.

People have to make choices about how to use our land, air, and water. In making these choices, people respond to incentives. Sometimes incentives help the environment and sometimes they hurt it.

Many of our environmental problems stem from the fact that no one owns the water or the air or the fish or the wildlife. They are a "common pool" resource. Common pools create some harmful incentives.

❋ People may choose to use a lake or river as a waste dump. There is no owner of the water who can insist that the pollution be stopped.

❋ People may capture too many animals and fish, sometimes leading to extinction. Because wildlife isn't commonly owned, no one can be sure that an antelope or deer that isn't captured will be there in the future. Anyone has a right to take it.

Over time, societies have figured out ways to provide incentives for protecting the environment. In some cases, we have laws that limit emissions of waste or prohibit excessive hunting of animals. But sometimes laws designed to protect the environment create harmful incentives. We saw in Chapter 5 that the U.S. Endangered Species Act can actually discourage people from protecting wildlife. And the ban on CFCs to protect the ozone layer has caused a black market in illegally imported CFCs.

Economics helps us to understand the unintended consequences of well-meaning legislation. It also helps us understand why the industrialized countries often have more attractive environments than poor Third World countries. The textbooks generally ignore the fact, but economic growth actually leads to increases in environmental protection.

Why? People want an attractive natural environment. When they are poor, other demands take precedence. But when basics such as food and shelter have been satisfied, people often seek to improve their environment. With economic growth, societies have the wherewithal and the ability to protect the environment and restore it where it has been damaged.

Evaluating Your School's Curriculum

You are now ready to consider your children's environmental curriculum. Your first objective should be to find out whether your child's environmental education is balanced. One-sided presentations, such as the ones identified in the book, are easy to detect. Just ask some general questions.

* In general, are theories presented as theories or as scientifically established "facts"?

* Is there a pervasive bias against economic growth and modern technology?

* Are human beings presented as being "against" nature rather than part of it?

* Is there an effort to make children feel guilty about the material advantages Canadians enjoy?

* Is the overall presentation of environmental problems gloomy and pessimistic?

* Are children being frightened into becoming environmental activists?

On any specific environmental issue, compare the curriculum with the information in this book. For example:

* Does the curriculum on acid rain mention the findings of the NAPAP study?

* Do the global warming materials discuss both the critics and the proponents of the idea that the world will get much warmer?

If the information contained in this book is not covered, the curriculum is ignoring legitimate debates and presenting only one side to your children.

Be alert for recommendations of political action. It's not uncommon for texts to recommend that students write their city, provincial, and federal representatives about environmental laws. While such letters have some merit, these activities cross the line between education and political activism. When they are based on one-sided information, they are not appropriate for schools.

Reviewing Materials

A comprehensive review of your children's curriculum starts with textbooks, but does not stop there. Supplemental materials, outside speakers brought into classes, and library offerings are also important.

Textbooks generally fall into three categories: those that contain very little environmental information, those that cover environmental information outside the main subject of the text (usually as extra features or specific chapters), and those with environmental education as a main focus. (See Appendix A for the texts we reviewed, which are typical of the texts produced by the major publishers for children at the 5–10 grade levels.)

Texts provide only a general guideline for teachers, who are usually free to cover material in the text or to ignore it. They are also free to bring in additional materials. With help from parents, a good teacher can use an inadequate text and still provide good education. (This book could be a good source of balance.)

However, supplemental materials often come from environmental organizations. While some of the materials fall into the "learning about nature" category and are useful, others are emotion-laden tracts. Sometimes corporations also unwittingly sponsor environmental education materials and activities that are inaccurate and misleading.

Schools often bring in outside speakers. These may range from a local Forest Service employee to the local president of a radical group like Earth First! Many advocate the same environmental messages presented in the texts.

Many schools also include field trips, outdoor work projects, and even overnight camps in their environmental curriculum. Some of these programs teach children about nature, but others promote the views of activist environmental groups.

What Parents Should Do

If, after evaluating the curriculum in your children's school, you find more indoctrination than education, you may wish to remedy the situation. This section will recommend some measures you can take.

Talk with Your Children's Teachers

Most teachers are conscientious and desire good information. Many are unaware that there are major scientific debates on environmental issues. If you share your concerns about the teaching materials in a friendly, non-confrontational way, many teachers will respond helpfully. Once they learn there is another side to some of the issues, many teachers will be willing to present it.

If, on the other hand, teachers at your children's school are committed to an agenda rather than dispassionate education, you face a more difficult task. You may be in a school district that is committed to indoctrinate students in the environmental views favoured by activist groups. Unfortunately, these individuals and groups are not generally receptive to providing both sides of issues.

Recommend Speakers (or Be One)

Parents can suggest speakers who offer more complete information. Many private organizations, not as well known as the activist organizations that lobby the government, are accomplishing general environmental improvement. These may include organizations such as Ducks Unlimited, a local arboretum or land trust, an organization that protects injured wildlife, or even a local electric utility that is using some of its land to protect an endangered species. Their representatives could tell children about their work. If you are knowledgeable about an environmental topic, offer yourself as a speaker.

Seek Out New Library Books

When it comes to books in the library, the best idea is to urge the school librarian or the school board to buy additional books that provide balance. (See Appendix C for a list of these books.) Don't try to have books removed—the goal should be to enlarge information, not to censor books already on the shelves. Perhaps you can offer to donate, or persuade a local business to donate, more balanced books.

Organize Parents

If the problem seems insurmountable, you may want to join with other parents and bring your concerns to the school board or even the provincial government.

All this involves political organization, which is not easy and takes considerable time and effort. You may face a long-term battle with highly organized environmental groups. While winning is difficult, it is not impossible.

Start with small steps. For example, parents could urge the local school board to require that all parents be notified in advance in writing whenever supplementary environmental materials are used, or when outsiders are asked to lecture. You could also request that the school use only texts that cite their sources. While citation of sources is a normal standard of scholarship, our children's textbooks rarely cite any sources. By asking for such citations, you would be making an important point.

Educate Your Children

Ultimately, you may have to take on the responsibility of reeducating your children. To do this, you should start by educating yourself. This book provides the basics, but other informative, balanced books are found in Appendix C.

You should be alert to the non-school sources of information your children receive. Environmental information is everywhere—from the McDonald's bag that contains your child's hamburger to G.I. Joe toys and Saturday morning television shows. Much of it is exaggerated.

Finally, we hope that you will explore environmental issues with your children. If you emphasize the spirit of inquiry, you can offset the tone of certainty and the gloom and doom typical of their texts. You will also convey an important message about education. Your children will learn that studying the environment can be an adventure that takes them to frontiers that await investigation and understanding. With your help, that adventure is within their grasp.

Textbooks Reviewed

The authors reviewed these textbooks for their coverage of environmental issues only. The authors did not review the subject matter content of the nonenvironmentally related information in these texts. Criticisms of the environmental content does not imply criticism of the nonenvironmental content of these texts. Canadian textbooks were reviewed by Liv Fredricksen.

The textbooks reviewed for this book were published by many of the top-selling publishing companies in the country. Textbook publishers do not release sales figures on individual textbooks so it is impossible to determine the exact proliferation specific textbooks. By selecting the top publishing firms, we believe that these texts are among the most commonly used texts.

Addison-Wesley

Chiras, Daniel D. *Environmental Science: A Framework for Decision-making*. 2d ed. Menlo Park, CA: Addison-Wesley, 1989.

Davis, James E., and Phyllis Maxey Fernlund. *Civics: Participating in Our Democracy*. Menlo Park, CA: Addison-Wesley Publishing Co., 1993.

Dispezio, Linner, and Lisowski Lube. *Science Insights: Exploring Earth and Space*. Reading, MA: Addison-Wesley, 1995.

Essnfeld, Bernice, Carol Gontag, Randy Moore et al. *Biology*. Reading, MA: Addison-Wesley Publishing Co., 1994.

Fariel, Robert E. et al. *Earth Science*. Menlo Park, CA: Addison-Wesley Publishing Co., 1984.

King, David C., Norman McRae, and Jaye Zola. *The United States and Its People*. Menlo Park, CA: Addison-Wesley Publishing Co., 1993.

D. C. Heath (A Raytheon Company)

Bailey, Thomas A., and David M. Kennedy. *The American Pageant*. Lexington, MA: D. C. Heath and Co., 1991.

Carle, Mark A. et al. *Physical Science: Challenge of Discovery*. Lexington, MA: D. C. Heath and Co., 1991.

Gritzner, Charles. *World Geography*. Lexington, MA: D. C. Heath and Co., 1989.

Snyder, Robert E. et al. *Earth Science: The Challenge of Discovery*. Annotated Teacher's Edition. Lexington, MA: D. C. Heath and Co., 1991.

Spaulding, Nancy, and Samuel Namowitz. *Heath Earth Science*. Indianapolis, IN: D. C. Heath, 1994.

Ver Steeg, Clarence L. and Carol Ann Skinner. *Exploring Regions Near and Far*. Lexington, MA: D. C. Heath and Co., 1991.

Warner, Linda A. et al. *Life Science: The Challenge of Discovery*. Lexington MA: D. C. Heath and Co., 1991.

Glencoe (Macmillan/McGraw-Hill)

Boehm, Richard G., and James L. Swanson. *Glencoe World Geography*. Mission Hills, CA: Glencoe Publishing Co., 1989.

Boehm, Richard G., and James L. Swanson. *World Geography: A Physical and Cultural Approach*. 3d ed. Lake Forest, IL: Glencoe Publishing Co., 1992.

Daniel, Lucy et al. *Merrill Life Science*. Columbus, OH: Glencoe Publishing Co., 1994.

Farah, Mounir, and Andrea Berens Karls. *World History: The Human Experience*. 3d ed. Lake Forest, IL: Glencoe Publishing Co., 1992.

Jackson, Carlton L., and Vito Perrone. *Two Centuries Of Progress*. Mission Hills, CA: Glencoe Publishing Co., 1991.

Jones, Henke L., Ted Tsumura, and T. Bonekemper et al. *Health and Safety for You*. Columbus, OH: Glencoe Publishing Co., 1987.

LaRaus, Roger, Harry P. Morris, and Robert Sobel. *Challenge of Freedom*. Mission Hills, CA: Glencoe Publishing Co., 1990.

Merki, Mary Bronson, and Don Merki. *Health: A Guide To Wellness*. 3d ed. Mission Hills, CA: Glencoe Publishing Co., 1993.

Merki, Mary Bronson. *Teen Health, Decisions for Healthy Living, Annotated Teacher's Edition*. Mission Hills, CA: Glencoe, 1990.

Nash, Gary B. *American Odyssey: The United States in the Twentieth Century*. Lake Forest, IL: Glencoe Publishing Co., 1991.

Remy, Richard C. *U. S. Government: Democracy in Action*. New York: Glencoe Publishing Co., 1994.

Thompson, McLaughlin, and Smith. *Merrill Physical Science*. Columbus, OH: Glencoe Publishing Co., 1993.

Welty, Paul Thomas, and Miriam Greenblatt. *The Human Expression: World Religions and Cultures*. 4th ed. Lake Forest, IL: Glencoe Publishing Co., 1992.

Globe (Simon & Schuster, A Paramount Communications Company)

Bernstein, Leonard et al. *Concepts and Challenges in Earth Science.* 3d ed. Annotated Teacher's Edition. Englewood Cliffs, NJ: Globe Book Co., 1991.

Bernstein, Leonard et al. *Concepts and Challenges in Life Science.* 3d ed. Annotated Teacher's Edition. Englewood Cliffs, NJ: Globe Book Co., 1991.

Bernstein, Leonard. *Biology.* Annotated Teacher's Edition. Englewood Cliffs, NJ: Globe Book Co., 1990.

O'Conner, John R., and Robert M. Goldberg. *Exploring American Citizenship.* Englewood Cliffs, NJ: Globe Book Co., 1992.

Schwartz, Melvin, and John O'Conner. *Exploring a Changing World.* Englewood Cliffs, NJ: Globe Book Co., 1993.

Harcourt Brace Jovanovich (Holt, Rinehart and Winston)

Bacon, Phillip. *World Geography: The Earth and its People.* Orlando, FL: Harcourt Brace Jovanovich, 1989.

Emiliani, Cesare, Linda B. Knight, and Mark Handwerker. *Earth Science.* Orlando: Harcourt Brace Jovanovich, 1989.

Goodman, Graham, Emmel et al. *Biology.* Orlando, FL: Harcourt Brace Jovanovich, 1989.

Cuevas, Lamb, and Lehrman. *Physical Science.* Orlando, FL: Harcourt Brace Jovanovich, 1989.

Olsen, Larry K., Richard W. St. Pierre, and Jan M. Ozlas. *Being Healthy.* Annotated Teacher's Edition. Orlando: Harcourt Brace Jovanovich, 1990.

Poehler, David et al. *Health.* Orlando, FL: Harcourt Brace Jovanovich, 1987.

Swanson, John Colby et al. *Essentials of Health*. Orlando: Harcourt Brace Jovanovich, 1986.

Watkins, Patricia et al. *Life Science*. Orlando, FL: Harcourt Brace Jovanovich, 1989.

Holt, Rinehart and Winston (Harcourt Brace Jovanovich)

Arms, Karen, and Pamela Camp. *Biology*. Austin, TX: Holt, Rinehart and Winston, Inc., 1995.

Bacon, Phillip. *States and Regions*. Orlando, FL: Holt, Rinehart and Winston, Inc., 1991.

Boyer, Paul. *The American Nation*. Austin, TX: Holt, Rinehart and Winston, Inc., 1995.

Budziszewski, J., and Lawrence J. Pauline. *We the People*. Austin, TX: Holt, Rinehart and Winston, Inc., 1989.

Cuevas, Lamb et al. *Holt Physical Science*. Austin, TX: Holt, Rinehart and Winston, Inc., 1994.

Garraty, John A. *The Story of America*. Austin, TX: Holt, Rinehart and Winston, Inc., 1991.

Garraty, John A. *The Story of America: Beginnings to 1877*. Annotated Teacher's Edition. Austin, TX: Holt, Rinehart and Winston, Inc., 1992.

Garraty, John A. *The Story of America: 1865 to the Present*. Volume 2. Austin, TX: Holt, Rinehart and Winston, Inc., 1992.

Goodman, Harvey D. et al. *Biology Today*. Annotated Teacher's Edition. Austin, TX: Holt, Rinehart and Winston, Inc., 1991.

Greenberg, Jerrold, and Robert Gold. *Holt Health*. Orlando, FL: Holt, Rinehart and Winston, Inc., 1994.

Hartley, William H., and William S. Vincent. *American Civics*. Freedom Edition. Austin, TX: Holt, Rinehart and Winston, Inc., 1992.

Israel, Saul; Douglas Johnson, and Dennis Wood. *World Geography Today*. Holt, Rinehart and Winston, Inc., 1980.

McFadden, Charles, and Robert Yager. *Science Plus: Technology and Society*. Blue Edition, Austin, TX: Holt, Rinehart and Winston, Inc., 1993.

McFadden, Charles and Robert Yager. *Science Plus: Technology and Society*. Green Edition, Austin, TX: Holt, Rinehart and Winston, Inc., 1993.

McFadden, Charles and Robert Yager. *Science Plus: Technology and Society*. Red Edition, Austin, TX: Holt, Rinehart and Winston, Inc., 1993.

Ramsey et al. *General Science*. New York: Holt, Rinehart and Winston, Inc., 1988.

Ramsey et al. *Modern Earth Science*. Orlando, FL: Holt, Rinehart and Winston, Inc., 1989.

Sager, Robert J., David M. Helgren, and Saul Israel. *World Geography Today*. Revised Edition. Austin, TX: Holt, Rinehart and Winston, Inc., 1992.

Towle, Albert. *Modern Biology*. Annotated Teacher's Edition. Austin, TX: Holt, Rinehart and Winston, Inc., 1993.

Houghton Mifflin Company

Armento, Beverly J. et al. *From Sea to Shining Sea*. Boston, MA: Houghton Mifflin Co., 1991.

DiBacco, Thomas V., Lorna C. Mason, and Christian G. Appy. *History of the United States*. Boston, MA: Houghton Mifflin Co., 1993.

Getchell, Bud, Rusty Pippin, Jill Varnes et al. *Health*. Boston, MA: Houghton Mifflin Co., 1987.

Getchell, Bud, Rusty Pippin, Jill Varnes et al. *Perspectives on Health*. Boston, MA: Houghton Mifflin Co., 1987.

Macmillan/McGraw-Hill (Harcourt Brace Jovanovich)

Audesirk, Gerald, and Teresa Audesirk. *Biology: Life on Earth.* New York: Macmillan, 1993.

Banks, James A. et al. *United States and its Neighbors.* New York: Macmillan/McGraw Hill, 1993.

Banks, James A. et al. *The World Around Us: Regions Near and Far.* New York: Macmillan/McGraw Hill, 1993.

Banks, James A. et al. *World Regions.* Riverside, NJ: Macmillan/McGraw-Hill, 1993.

Ely and Norton. *Physical Science.* Riverside, NJ: Macmillan/McGraw-Hill, 1986.

Jantzen, Michel et al. *Life Science.* New York: Macmillan, 1986.

Merrill (Macmillan/McGraw-Hill)

Biggs, Alton et al. *Biology: The Dynamics of Life.* Columbus, OH: Merrill Publishing Co., 1991.

Feather, Ralph M. et al. *Earth Science.* Lake Forest, IL: Merrill/Glencoe, 1993.

Feather, Ralph M. et al. *Science Connections.* Blue ed. Columbus, OH: Merrill Publishing Co., 1990.

Feather, Ralph M. et al. *Science Connections.* Red Ed. Columbus, OH: Merrill Publishing Co., 1990.

Hantula, James Neil et al. *Global Insights.* Columbus, OH: Merrill Publishing Co., 1988.

Heimler, Charles H. *Focus on Life Science.* Columbus, OH: Merrill Publishing Co., 1989.

Heimler, Charles H., and Charles D. Neal. *Principles of Science: Book 2.* Columbus, OH: Merrill Publishing Co., 1986.

Hunkins, Francis P. and David G. Armstrong. *World Geography: People and Places.* Columbus, OH: Merrill Publishing Co., 1984.

Kaskel, Albert, Paul J. Hummer, Jr., and Lucy Daniel. *Biology: An Everyday Experience.* Lake Forest, IL: Merrill/Glencoe, 1992.

Meeks, Linda, and Philip Heit. *Health: A Wellness Approach.* Columbus, OH: Merrill Publishing Co., 1991.

Meeks, Linda, and Philip Heit. *Health: Focus on You.* Columbus, OH: Merrill Publishing Co., 1990.

Oram, Raymond F. *Biology: Living Systems.* Annotated Teacher Edition. Columbus, OH: Merrill Publishing Co., 1989.

Turner, Mary Jane et al. *American Government: Principles and Practices.* Columbus, OH: Merrill Publishing Co., 1991.

Prentice Hall (Simon & Schuster, A Paramount Communications Company)

Baerwald, Thomas J., and Celeste Fraser. *World Geography.* Needham, MA: Prentice Hall, 1993.

Beers, Burton F. *World History: Patterns of Civilization.* Englewood Cliffs, NJ: Prentice Hall, 1993.

Cobel, Charles R. et al. *Earth Science.* Englewood Cliffs, NJ: Prentice Hall, 1991.

Cormler, Robert J. et al. *Magruder's American Government.* Englewood Cliffs, NJ: Prentice Hall, 1992.

Davidson, James West, and John E. Batchelor. *The American Nation.* 3d ed. Englewood Cliffs, NJ: Prentice Hall, 1991.

Davidson, James West, and Mark H. Lytle. *The United States: A History of the Republic.* 5th ed. Englewood Cliffs, NJ: Prentice Hall, 1990.

Donatelle, Rebecca J., Lorraine G. Davis, and Carolyn F. Hoover. *Access to Health.* Englewood Cliffs, NJ: Prentice Hall, 1988.

Gray, Pamela Lee et al. *America: Pathways to the Present.* Englewood Cliffs, NJ: Prentice Hall, 1995.

Haber-Shaim, Yuri. *Introduction to Physical Science.* Englewood Cliffs, NJ: Prentice Hall, 1987.

Hurd, Dean et al. *General Science: A Voyage of Adventure.* 3d ed. Englewood Cliffs, NJ: Prentice Hall, 1992.

Hurd, Dean et al. *General Science: A Voyage of Exploration.* Englewood Cliffs, NJ: Prentice Hall, 1992.

Hurd, Dean et al. *General Science: A Voyage of Discovery.* Englewood Cliffs, NJ: Prentice Hall, 1992.

Hurd, Dean et al. *Prentice Hall Physical Science.* Englewood Cliffs, NJ: Prentice Hall, 1991.

Leinwand, Gerald. *The Pageant of World History.* Needham, MA: Prentice Hall, 1990.

Luckmann, Joan. *Your Health!* Englewood Cliffs, NJ: Prentice Hall, 1990.

Maton, Anthea. *Ecology: Earth's Natural Resources.* 2d ed. Englewood Cliffs, NJ: Prentice Hall, 1994.

Maton, Anthea. *Human Biology and Health.* 2d ed. Englewood Cliffs, NJ: Prentice Hall, 1994.

Maton, Anthea. *Matter: Building Block of the Universe.* 2d ed. Englewood Cliffs, NJ: Prentice Hall, 1994.

Miller, Kenneth R. and Joseph Levine. *Biology.* Englewood Cliffs, NJ: Prentice Hall, 1991.

Pruitt, Crumpler et al. *Health: Skills for Wellness.* Englewood Cliffs, NJ: Prentice Hall, 1994.

Schraer, William D., and Herbert J. Stoltze. *Biology: The Study of Life.* 4th ed. Needham, MA: Prentice Hall, 1991.

Seehafer, Roger Wayne, Carol Bershad, and Deborah S. Haber, Program Consultants. *Health: Choosing Wellness.* Needham, MA: Prentice Hall, 1989.

Seehafer, Roger Wayne, Carol Bershad, and Deborah S. Haber, Program Consultants. *Health: Choosing Wellness.* 2d ed. Needham, MA: Prentice Hall, 1992.

Wright, Jill et al. *Life Science.* Englewood Cliffs, NJ: Prentice Hall, 1991.

Wright, Nebel J., and Richard T. Wright. *Environmental Science: The Way the World Works.* 4th ed. Englewood Cliffs, NJ: Prentice Hall, 1991.

Scott Foresman (A Division of Harper Collins Publishers)

Alexander, Gretchen M. *Life Science.* Teacher's Edition. Palo Alto, CA: Scott Foresman and Co., 1983.

Barber, Kissamis et al. *Earth Science.* Glenview, IL: Scott Foresman and Co., 1990.

de Blij, Harm J. et al. *World Geography: A Physical and Cultural Study.* Glenview, IL: Scott Foresman and Co., 1989.

Divine, Robert A. et al. *America: The People and the Dream.* Vol. II: The Later Years. Glenview, IL: Scott Foresman and Co., 1991.

Patrick, John J., and Richard C. Remy. *Civics for Americans.* 2d ed. Glenview, IL: Scott Foresman and Co., 1991.

Richmond, Julius B., Elenore T. Pounds, and Charles B. Corbin. *Health for Life.* Glenview, IL: Scott Foresman and Co., 1990.

Wallace, King, Sanders et al. *Biosphere: The Realm of Life.* Glenview, IL: Scott Foresman and Co., 1988.

Wallbark, T. Walter et al. *History and Life.* Updated Edition. Glenview, IL: Scott Foresman and Co., 1993.

Silver Burdett & Ginn (Simon & Schuster, A Paramount Communications Company)

Ainsley Jr., W. Frank et al. *Comparing Regions.* From the series: People in Time and Place. Morristown, NJ: Silver Burdett & Ginn, 1993.

Alexander, Fiegel et al. *Silver Burdett Earth Science*. Morristown, NJ: Silver Burdett & Ginn, 1990.

Alexander, Fiegel et al. *Silver Burdett Physical Science*. Morristown, NJ: Silver Burdett & Ginn, 1990.

Alexander, Peter et al. *General Science, Book One*. Needham, MA: Silver Burdett & Ginn, 1989.

Alexander, Peter et al. *General Science, Book Two*. Needham, MA: Silver Burdett & Ginn, 1989.

Bass, John C. *Our Country*. Morristown, NJ: Silver Burdett & Ginn, 1993.

Cooper, Kenneth S. *The Eastern Hemisphere*. Morristown, NJ: Silver Burdett & Ginn, 1991.

Greenlow, Linda L, W. Frank Ainsley, Jr., and Gary S. Elbow. *World Geography: People in Time and Place*. Morristown, NJ: Silver Burdett & Ginn, 1992.

Hatfield, Claudette Butler et al. *World Geography*. Teacher's Edition. Morristown, NJ: Silver Burdett & Ginn, 1992.

Helmus, Timothy M. et al. *The United States Yesterday and Today*. Morristown, NJ: Silver Burdett & Ginn, 1990.

Miscellaneous Publishers

Brockway, Carolyn Sheets, Robert Gardner, and Samuel F. Howe. *Allyn and Bacon General Science*. Newton, MA: Allyn and Bacon, 1985.

BSCS, Green Version. *Biological Science: An Ecological Approach*. Dubuque, IA: Kendall/Hunt Publishing Co., 1992.

Camp, Daugherty, and Kirts. *Managing Our Natural Resources*. Albany, NY: Delmar Publishers, Inc., 1991.

Camp, William, and Roy Donahue. *Environmental Science: For Agriculture and the Life Sciences*. Albany, NY: Delmar Publishers, 1994.

Campbell, Neil A. *Biology*. Redwood City, CA: The Benjamin/Cummings Publishers Co. Inc., 1993.

Chiras, Daniel D. *Environmental Science: A Framework for Decision-making*. 2d ed. Menlo Park, CA: The Benjamin/Cummings Publishing Co., Inc., 1988.

Christensen, John W. *Global Science*. 3rd ed. Dubuque, IA: Kendall/Hunt Publishing Co., 1991.

Curtis, Helena and Sue N. Barnes. *Biology*. New York: Worth Publishing Company, 1989.

Daley, Robert B., W. John Higham, and George F. Matthias. *Earth Science: A Study of a Changing Planet*. Newton, MA: Cebco, A Division of Allyn and Bacon, Inc., 1986.

Jordan, Winthrop D., Miriam Greenblatt, and John S. Bowes. *The Americans: A History*. Evanston, IL: McDougal/Littell, 1994.

Kane, William M., Senior Consultant. *Understanding Health*. 2d ed. New York: Random House School Division, 1987.

Lineberry, Robert, George C. Edwards III, and Martin P. Wattenberg. *Government In America: People, Politics, and Policy*. 5th ed. New York: HarperCollins Publishers, 1991.

May, Ernest R. *A Proud Nation*. Evanston, IL: McDougal, Littell & Company, 1989.

Milani, Jean P. Revision Coordinator. *Biological Science: An Ecological Approach*. 6th ed. Dubuque, IA: Kendall/Hunt Publishing Co., 1987.

Person, Jane L. *Environmental Science, How the World Works and Your Place in It*. New York: J. M. LeBel Enterprises Inc., 1989.

Turk, Jonathan. *Introduction to Environmental Studies*. 3d ed. Philadelphia: Saunders College Publishing, 1989.

Turk, Jonathan, Amos Turk, and Karen Arms. *Environmental Science*. 3d ed. Philadelphia, Saunders College Publishing, 1988.

Wallace, Robert A., Gerald P. Sanders, and Robert J. Ferl. *Biology: The Science of Life*. New York: HarperCollings Publishers, 1991.

West's American Government. St. Paul, MN: West Publishing, 1993.

Canadian Pulbishers

Andrews, William A., and Sandra J. McEwan. *Investigating Aquatic Ecosystems*. Scarborough, ON: Prentice-Hall Canada Inc., 1987.

Andrews, William A., and Donna K. Moore. *Investigating Terrestrial Ecosystems*. Scarborough, ON: Prentice-Hall Canada Inc., 1986.

Baumann, Frank, et al. *Science Probe 8, Second Edition* (The Wiley Science Program). Toronto, ON: John Wiley & Sons Canada Ltd., 1993.

Beckett, Peter, et al. *Science Probe 9* (Nelson Edition). Scarborough, ON: Thomson Canada Ltd., 1995.

Beers, Burton F. *Patterns of Civilization*, Vol 2. 1985.

Beugger, Peter, Larry D. Yore, et al. *Journeys in Science* (Volume 5, Canadian Edition). Toronto, ON: Collier Macmillan Canada, 1990.

Beugger, Peter, Larry D. Yore, et al. *Journeys in Science* (Volume 6, Canadian Edition). Toronto, ON: Collier Macmillan Canada, Inc., 1990.

Bosak, Susan V. *Science Is...* 2nd ed. co-edited. Richmond Hill, ON: Scholastic Canada Ltd. and Markham ON: The Communication Project, 1991.

Dunlop, Stewart. *Towards Tomorrow: Canada in a Changing World —Geography*. Toronto, ON: Harcourt Brace Jovanovich Canada Inc., 1987.

Fagan, Margaret. *Challenge for Change*, 2nd ed. Toronto: McGraw-Hill Ryerson Ltd., 1991.

Flanagan, Frank. *Focus on Science: Exploring the Physical World*. Toronto, ON: D.C. Heath Canada, Ltd., 1979.

Gough, Douglas, and Frank J. Flanagan. *Focus on Science: Exploring the Natural World*. Toronto, ON: D.C. Heath Canada, Ltd., 1980.

Krueger, Ralph and Ray Corder. *Canada: A New Geography*. Toronto: Holt, Rinehart & Winston of Canada Ltd., 1982.

Mitchner, E. Alyn and Tuffs, R. Joanne. *Global Forces of the Twentieth Century*. Edmonton: Reidmore Books, 1991.

Namowitz, Samuel N., and Nancy E. Spaulding. *Earth Science, Canadian Edition*. Toronto, ON: D.C. Heath Canada, Ltd., 1987.

Peturson, Rod and Neil McAllister. *Innovations in Science* (Teacher Resource Package). Toronto, ON: Holt, Rinehart and Winston of Canada, Ltd., 1991.

Roberts, Douglas A. *Science Directions 8*. Edmonton, AB: Arnold Publishing, 1991.

Roberts, Douglas A. *Science Directions 9*. Edmonton, AB: Arnold Publishing, 1991.

Scully, Angus L., Smith, Carl F., and McDevitt, Daniel J. *Canada Today*, 2nd ed. Scarborough, ON: Prentice-Hall Canada Inc., 1988.

Swatridge, Leonard A. and Ian A. Wright. *Canada: Exploring New Directions*. Markham, ON: Fitzhenry & Whiteside Ltd., 1990.

Yore, Larry D., Peter Beugger, et al. *Journeys in Science* (Volume 7, Canadian Edition). Toronto, ON: Collier Macmillan Canada, Inc., 1990.

Environmental Books for Children

These books were reviewed by the authors; Canadian books were reviewed by Liv Fredricksen. They vary in the quality of their coverage of environmental issues. See Appendix C for recommended books.

Aaseng, Nathan. *Ending World Hunger*. New York: Franklin Watts, 1991.

Anderson, Madelyn K. *Oil Spills*. New York: Franklin Watts, 1990.

Baines, John. *Acid Rain* (Conserving Our World Series). Austin, TX: Steck-Vaughn Library, 1989.

Baker, Jeannie. *Where the Forest Meets the Sea*. New York: Scholastic, Inc., 1987.

Banks, Martin. *Conserving Rain Forests*. Austin, TX: Steck-Vaughn Library, 1990.

Becklake, John, and Sue Becklake. *The Population Explosion*. London: Gloucester Press, 1990.

Becklake, John. *The Climate Crisis: Greenhouse Effect and Ozone Layer*. New York: Franklin Watts, 1989.

Bloyd, Sunni. *Endangered Species* (Our Endangered Planet). San Diego: Lucent Books, Inc., 1989.

Bosak, Susan V. *Science Is...* . Markham, ON: The Communication Project, 1991.

Bright, Michael. *Pollution and Wildlife*. New York: Gloucester Press, 1987.

Bruchac, Joseph. *Native American Stories*. Golden, CO: Fulcrum Publishing, 1991.

Caduto, M. J., and J. Bruchac. *Keepers of the Earth: Native American Stories & Environmental Activities for Children*. Golden, CO: Fulcrum, Inc, 1988.

Carr, Terry. *Spill! The Story of Exxon Valdez*. New York: Franklin Watts, 1991.

Cherry, Lynne. *The Great Kapok Tree: A Tale of the Amazon Rain Forest*. San Diego: Harcourt Brace Jovanovich Publishers, 1990.

Condon, Judith. *Recycling Paper*. New York: Franklin Watts, 1990.

Cowcher, Helen. *Antarctica*. New York: Scholastic, Inc., 1990.

Cowcher, Helen. *Rain Forest*. New York: Farrar, Straus and Giroux, 1988.

Crutchins, Judy, and Ginny Johnston. *The Crocodile and the Crane: Surviving in a Crowded World*. New York: William Morrow and Company, Inc., 1986.

Cullis-Suzuki, Severn. *Tell the World: A Young Environmentalist Speaks Out*. Toronto: Doubleday Canada, 1993.

Dee, Catherine, ed. *Kid Heroes of the Environment*. Berkeley, CA: Earth Works Press, 1991.

Degler, Teri, and Pollution Probe. *The Canadian Junior Green Guide*. Toronto: McClelland & Stewart, 1990.

Dehr, Roma, and Ronald M. Bazar. *Good Planets Are Hard to Find: An Environmental Information Guide, Dictionary and Action*

Book for Kids (and Adults). Vancouver, BC: Earth Beat Press, 1989.

Dehr, Roma, and Ronald M. Bazar. *Kid's Ecology Book: Good Planets Are Very Hard to Find!* Vancouver, BC: Earth Beat Press, 1991.

Dolan, Edward F. *Drought: The Past, Present and Future Enemy.* New York: Franklin Watts, 1990.

Dolan, Edward. *Our Poisoned Sky.* New York: Dutton Children's Books, 1991.

Dorros, Arthur. *Rain Forest Secrets.* New York: Scholastic, 1990.

Drutman, A. D. *Protecting Our Planet: Activities to Motivate Young Students to a Better Understanding of Our Environmental Problems* (for primary grades). Carthage, IL: Good Apple Publishers, 1991.

Duden, Jane. *The Ozone Layer.* New York: Crestwood House, 1990.

Duggleby, John. *Pesticides* New York: Crestwood House, 1990.

Elkington, John et al. *Going Green: A Kid's Handbook to Saving the Planet.* New York: Puffin Books, 1990.

Facklam, Howard, and Margery Facklam. *Plants: Extinction or Survival?* Hillside, NJ: Enslow Publishers, Inc., 1990.

Facklam, Margery, and Howard Facklam. *Changes in the Wind: Earth's Shifting Climate.* San Diego: Harcourt Brace Jovanovich Publishers, 1986.

Facklam, Margery. *And Then There Was One: The Mysteries of Extinction.* San Francisco: Sierra Club Books, 1990.

Farris, Katherine, Editor. *The New Kids' Question & Answer Book* (From the Editors of OWL Magazine). Toronto: Greey de Pencier Books, 1993.

Fine, Charles Christopher. *The Hunger Road.* New York: Atheneum, 1988.

Foreman, Michael. *One World.* New York: M&S, 1990.

Fradin, Dennis B. *Disaster! Famines.* Chicago: Children's Press, 1986.

Freeman, Don. *The Seal and the Slick*. New York: Viking Press, 1974.

Gallant, Ray A. *The Peopling of Planet Earth: Human Population Growth Through the Ages* New York: Macmillan Publishing Company, 1990.

Galle, Janet and Patricia Warren. *Ecology Discovery Activities List: A Complete Teaching Unit for Grades 4-8*. West Nyack, New York: Center for Applied Research in Education, 1989.

Gang, Paul, *Our Planet, Our Home: Teacher's Guide*. Tucson, AZ: Zephyr Press, 1992.

Gay, Kathlyn. *Garbage and Recycling* (Issues in Focus). Hillside, NJ: Enslow Publishers, Inc., 1991.

Gay, Kathlyn. *Water Pollution*. New York: Franklin Watts, 1990.

Gay, Kathlyn. *The Greenhouse Effect*. (A Science Impact Book) New York: Franklin Watts), 1986.

Gertson, Rich. *Just Open the Door: A Complete Guide to Experiencing Environmental Education*. Danville, IL: Industake Printers and Publishers, Inc., 1983.

Gold, Susan Dudley. *Toxic Waste*. New York: Crestwood House, 1990.

Goodman, Billy. *A Kid's Guide to How to Save the Planet*. New York: Avon Books, 1990.

Greene, Carole. *Caring for Our Water* (Caring for Our Earth). Hillside, NJ: Enslow Publishers, Inc., 1991.

Gutnik, Martin J. *Ecology*. New York: Franklin Watts, 1984.

Hadingham, Evan, and Janet Hadingham. *Garbage! Where it Comes From, Where it Goes*. New York: Simon & Schuster, 1990 (A NOVA Book).

Hare, Tony. *Acid Rain* (Save Our Earth Series). London: Gloucester Press, 1990.

Hare, Tony. *Polluting the Sea* (Save Our Earth). London: Glouchester Press, 1991.

Hare, Tony. *Rainforest Destruction*. London: Gloucester Press, 1990.

Hare, Tony. *The Ozone Layer* (Save Our Earth Series). London: Gloucester Press, 1990.

Harris, Jack C. *The Greenhouse Effect*. New York: Crestwood House, 1990.

Herman, Maring Lachecki et al. *Teaching Kids to Love the Earth* Duluth, MN: Pfiefer-Hamilton Publishing, 1991.

Hirschi, Ron. *Where Are My Prairie Dogs and Black-footed Ferrets?* New York: Bantam Books, 1992 (National Audubon Society).

Hocking C., C. Sneider, J. Erickson, and R. Golden. *Global Warming and the Greenhouse Effect* (Great Explorations in Math and Science GEMS). Berkeley, CA: Lawrence Hall of Science, 1990 (A Teacher's Guide).

Hocking, C., J. Barber, and J. Coonrod. *Acid Rain: A Teacher's Guide.* Berkeley, CA: Lawrence Hall of Science UC, Berkeley, 1990 (LHS GEMS Series).

Hoff, Mary King, and Mary M. Rodgers. *Our Endangered Planet: Groundwater*. Minneapolis, MN: Lerner Publications, 1991.

Hoff, Mary King, and Mary M. Rodgers. *Our Endangered Planet: Oceans*. Minneapolis, MN: Lerner Publications Company, 1991.

Hoff, Mary King, and Mary M. Rodgers. *Our Endangered Planet: Rivers and Lakes*. Minneapolis, MN: Lerner Publications Company, 1991.

Hoose, Phillip. *It's Our World, Too! Stories of Young People Who are Making A Difference*. Boston, MA: Little, Brown and Co., 1993.

Javna, John. *50 Simple Things Kids Can Do to Save the Earth*. Kansas City: Andrews and McMeel, 1990.

Johnson, Rebecca. *The Greenhouse Effect: Life on a Warmer Planet*. Minneapolis, MN: Lerner Publications Company, 1990.

Kalbacken, Joan, and Emilie U. Lepthien. *Recycling* (A New True Book). Chicago: Childrens Press, Inc., 1991.

Kalman, Bobbie, and Janine Schaub. *Wonderful Water* (Primary Ecology Series). Niagara Falls, ON: Crabtree Publishing Company, 1992.

Knapp, Brian. *World Disasters: Drought*. Austin, TX: Steck-Vaughn Library, 1990.

Koral, April. *Our Global Greenhouse*. New York: Franklin Watts, 1989.

Kronewetter, Michael. *Managing Toxic Wastes* (Issues for the 90s). Englewood Cliffs, NJ: Julian Messner, 1989.

Lambert, David. *Pollution and Conservation*. New York: Bookwright Press, 1986.

Landau, Elaine. *Tropical Rain Forests Around the World*. New York: Franklin Watts, 1990.

Lee, Sally. *Throwaway Society*. New York: Franklin Watts, 1990.

Lefkowitz, R. J. *Save It! Keep It! Use It Again! A Book about Conservation and Recycling*. New York: Parents Magazine Press, 1977.

Leger-Haskell, Diane. *Maxine's Tree*. Victoria, BC: Orca Book Publishers, 1990.

Leinwand, Gerald. *The Environment* (American Issues Series). New York: Facts on File, 1990.

Levine, Shar and Allison Grafton. *Projects for a Healthy Planet: Simple Environmental Experiments for Kids*. Toronto: John Wiley & Sons, 1992.

Lewis, Barbara A. *Kid's Guide to Environmental Action: How to Solve the Social Problems You Choose—and Turn Creative Thinking into Positive Action*. Minneapolis, MN: Free Spirit Publishing, 1991.

Love, Ann, and Jane Drake. *Take Action*. Toronto: Kids Can Press, 1992.

Lucas, Eileen. *Water: A Resource in Crisis*. Chicago: Childrens Press, 1991.

Luoma, Jon R. *Troubles Skies, Troubled Waters: The Story of Acid Rain*. New York: Penguin Books, 1984.

MacEachern, Diane. *Save Our Planet: 750 Everyday Ways You Can Help Clean Up the Earth* New York: A Dell Trade Paperback, 1990.

MacRae-Campbell, Linda, and Micki McKisson. *Our Only Earth: A Curriculum for Global Problem Solving*. Tucson, AZ: Zephyr Press, 1992.

McCoy, J. J. *How Safe is Our Food Supply?* (An Impact Book). New York: Franklin Watts, 1990.

McGrath, Susan. *Saving Our Animal Friends*. Washington, DC: National Geographic, 1986.

McGraw, Eric. *Population Growth*. Vero Beach, FL: Rourke Enterprises, Inc., 1987.

Mason, Adrienne. *The Green Classroom*. Markham, ON: Pembroke Publishers Ltd., 1991.

Metzger, Mary, and Cinthya P. Whittaker. *This Planet Is Mine: Teaching Environmental Awareness and Appreciation to Children*. New York: A Fireside Book, 1991.

Miles, Betty. *Save the Earth: An Ecology Handbook for Kids*. New York: Alfred A. Knopf, 1991.

Miller, Christina G., and Louise A. Berry. *Jungle Rescue: Saving One New World Tropical Rain Forest*. New York: Atheneum, 1991.

Miller, Christina G., and Louise A. Perry. *Acid Rain: A Source Book for Young People*. New York: Julian Messner, 1986.

Miller, Christina G., and Louise A. Perry. *Coastal Rescue: Preserving our Seashores*. New York: Atheneum, 1989.

Miller, Christina G., and Louise A. Perry. *Wastes* (A First Book). New York: Franklin Watts, 1986.

Mutel, Cornelia Fleischer, and Mary M. Rodgers. *Our Endangered Planet: Tropical Rain Forests* Minneapolis, MN: Lerner Publications Co., 1991.

O'Connor, Karen. *Garbage* (Our Endangered Planet). San Diego: Lucent Books, 1989.

Parkin, Tom. *Green Giants: Rainforests of the Pacific Northwest*. Vancouver, BC: Douglas & McIntyre, 1992.

Pearce, Fred. *The Big Green Book*. New York: Grosset & Dunlap, 1991.

Peckham, Alexander. *Global Warming*. New York: Gloucester Press, 1991.

Pederson, Anne. *The Kid's Environment Book: What's Awry and Why*. Santa Fe: John Muir Publications, 1991.

Pringle, Laurence. *Ecology: Science of Survival*. New York: Macmillan Publishers, 1971.

Pringle, Laurence. *Global Warming: Assessing the Greenhouse Threat*. New York: Arcade Publishing, 1990.

Pringle, Laurence. *Living in a Risky World*. New York: Morrow Junior Books, 1989.

Pringle, Laurence. *Living Treasure: Saving Earth's Threatened Biodiversity*. New York: Morrow Junior Books, 1991.

Pringle, Laurence. *Rain of Troubles: The Science and Politics of Acid Rain*. New York: Macmillan Publishing Company, 1988.

Pringle, Laurence. *Restoring Our Earth*. Hillsdale, NJ: Enslow Publishers, Inc., 1987.

Pringle. Laurence. *Saving Our Wildlife*. Hillside, NJ: Enslow Publishers, Inc., 1990.

Pringle, Laurence. *Throwing Things Away: From Middens to Resource Recovery*. New York: Thomas Y. Crowell, 1986.

Pringle, Laurence. *Water: The Next Great Resource Battle*. New York: Macmillan Publishers, 1982.

Pringle, Laurence. *What Shall We Do With the Land? Choices for America*. New York: Thomas Y. Crowell, 1981.

Rinard, Judith E. *Wildlife Making a Comeback: How Humans are Helping*. Washington, DC: National Geographic Society, 1987.

Ross, Bonnie. *Waste Away: Information and Activities for Investigating Trash Problems and Solutions*. Woodstock, VT: Vermont Institute of Natural Science, 1989.

Savage, Candace. *Trash Attack! Garbage and What We Can Do About It*. Vancouver, BC: Douglas & McIntyre, 1990.

Savan, Beth. *Earthcycles and Ecosystems*. Toronto: Kids Can, 1991.

Schwartz, Linda. *Earth Book for Kids: Activities to Help Heal the Environment*. Santa Barbara, CA: Learning Works, Inc., 1990.

Simon, Noel. *Vanishing Habitats*. New York: Gloucester Press, 1987.

Simons, Robin. *Recyclopedia: Games, Science Equipment, and Crafts from Recycled Materials*. New York: Houghton Mifflin, 1976.

Sobel, David, ed. *The Ocean Book: Aquarium and Seaside Activities and Ideas for All Ages*. (Center for Marine Conservation) New York: John Wiley & Sons, Inc., 1989.

Stille, Darlene R. *The Greenhouse Effect* (A New True Book). Chicago: Childrens Press, Inc., 1990.

Stille, Darlene R. *Water Pollution* (A New True Book). Chicago: Childrens Press, Inc., 1990.

Stone, Lynn M. *Endangered Animals* (A New True Book). Chicago: Childrens Press, 1984.

Student Environmental Action Coalition. *The Student Environmental Action Guide*. Berkeley, CA: EarthWorks Press, 1991.

Suzuki, David, and Barbara Hehner. *Looking at the Environment*. Toronto: Stoddart Publishing Co. Ltd., 1989.

Szumski, Bonnie, and JoAnne Buggey. *Toxic Wastes: Examining Cause and Effect Relationships* (Juniors Opposing Viewpoints Series). San Diego: Greenhaven Press, Inc., 1989.

Tanaka, Shelley. *A Great Round Wonder: My Book of the World*. Toronto: Douglas & McIntyre Ltd., 1993.

Tesar, Jenny E. *Global Warming* (Our Fragile Planet Series). New York: Facts on File, 1991.

Tesar, Jenny E. *Shrinking Forests* (Our Fragile Planet Series). New York: Facts on File, 1991. Tesar, Jenny E. *Threatened Oceans* (Our Fragile Planet Series). New York: Facts on File, 1991.

Tesar, Jenny E. *The Waste Crisis*. New York: Facts on File, 1991.

Thom, Valerie. *RE...Think! Activities on Solid Waste Management, Recycling, and Litter for Elementary Students*. White Rock, BC: Pitch-In Canada, 1991.

Tilsworth, Debbie J. *Raising an Earth Friendly Child: The Keys to Your Child's Happy, Healthy Future* (Level I). Fairbanks, AK: Raven Press, 1991.

Timberlake, Lloyd. *Famine in Africa.* New York: Gloucester Press, 1986.

Turck, Mary. *Acid Rain.* Don Mills, ON: Collier Macmillan Canada, 1990.

Versfield, Ruth. *Why Are People Hungry?* New York: Gloucester Press, 1988.

Wilcox, Charlotte. *Trash!* Minneapolis: Carol Rhoda Books, Inc, 1988.

Winckler, Suzanne, and Mary M. Rodgers. *Our Endangered Planet: Population Growth.* Minneapolis, MN: Lerner Publications Co., 1991.

Zipko, Stephen J. *Toxic Threat: How Hazardous Substances Poison Our Lives.* Englewood Cliffs, NJ: Julian Messner, 1990.

Books for a Well-Stocked Environmental Library

The books in this appendix should be in your child's junior high school or high school library. Some offer a more balanced view of environmental issues; others offer insights that are often ignored in environmental teaching today. Generally written in nontechnical language, they will broaden your children's understanding of environmental issues.

Avery, Dennis. *Global Food Progress 1991*. Indianapolis: Hudson Institute, 1991.

Bailey, Ronald, ed. *The True State of the Planet*. New York: The Free Press, 1995.

Balling, Robert C., Jr. *The Heated Debate: Greenhouse Predictions Versus Climate Reality*. San Francisco: Pacific Research Institute, 1992.

Bast, Joseph L., Peter J. Hill, and Richard Rue. *Eco-Sanity: A Common Sense Guide to Environmentalism*. Lanham, MD: Madison Books, 1994.

Bernstam, Mikhail S. *The Wealth of Nations and the Environment*. London: Institute for Economic Affairs, 1991.

Brubaker, Elizabeth. *Property Rights in the Defence of Nature*. Toronto: Earthscan Publications, 1995.

Budiansky, Stephen. *Nature's Keepers: The New Science of Nature Management*. New York: The Free Press, 1995.

Burroughs, William James. *Does the weather really matter?: The social implications of climate change*. Cambridge: Cambridge University Press, 1997.

Clawson, Marion. *Forests: For Whom and For What?* Baltimore: Johns Hopkins University Press, 1975.

Field, Barry. *Environmental Economics: An Introduction*. New York: McGraw-Hill, 1994.

Frederick, Kenneth D., and Roger A. Sedjo, eds. *America's Renewable Resources: Historical Trends and Current Challenges*. Washington, DC: Resources for the Future, 1991.

Fumento, Michael. *Science Under Siege: Balancing Technology and the Environment*. New York: William Morrow, 1993.

Glickman, Theodore S. and Michael Gough, eds. *Readings in Risk*. Washington, DC: Resources for he Future, 1990.

Goudie, Andrew. *The Human Impact on the Natural Environment*. 4th ed. Cambridge: The MIT Press, 1994.

Luciani, Patrick. *Economic Myths: Making Sense of Canadian Policy Issues*. Don Mills, ON: Addison-Wesley Publishers Ltd, 1996.

Mann, Charles C., and Mark L. Plummer. *Noah's Choice: The Future of Endangered Species*. New York: Alfred A. Knopf, 1995.

Rathje, William, and Cullen Murphy. *Rubbish! The Archaeology of Garbage: What Our Garbage Tells Us About Ourselves*. New York: Harper Collins Publishers, 1992.

Simon, Julian L., ed. *The State of Humanity*. Cambridge, MA: Blackwell, 1996.

Simon, Julian L., and Herman Kahn. *The Resourceful Earth: A Response to Global 2000*. New York: Basil Blackwell, 1984.

Wildavsky, Aaron. *But Is It True? A Citizen's Guide to Environmental Health and Safety Issues*. Cambridge: Harvard University Press, 1995.

Academic and Scientific Advisory Panel

The following experts have reviewed the issue-specific chapters indicated below (chapters 6–19). They agree that the content of the specific chapter they reviewed accurately reflects scientific understanding of the issues discussed and the surrounding debate. Organizations are listed for purposes of identification only and their appearance in the list does not imply in any way that they endorse or approve of this book. The authors, and not these experts, are solely responsible for any errors or omissions in this book.

Chapter 6: Will Billions Starve?

NICHOLAS EBERSTADT, Visiting Scholar, American Enterprise Institute, Washington, DC; Visiting Scholar, Harvard Center for Population and Development Studies.

THOMAS POLEMAN, Professor of International Food Economics, Cornell University.

Chapter 7: Natural Resources—On the Way Out?

JAMES GWARTNEY, Professor of Economics, Florida State University.

MURRAY WEIDENBAUM, Chairman, Center for the Study of American Business; Professor of Economics, Washington University, St. Louis, Missouri.

Chapter 8: Are Our Forests Dying?

RONALD N. JOHNSON, Professor of Economics, Montana State University.

GARY LIBECAP, Professor of Economics and Law and Director, Karl Eller Center, University of Arizona.

DOUGLAS W. MACCLEERY, Assistant Director, Timber Management, United States Forest Service, Washington, DC.

Chapter 9: The Rain Forest—One Hundred Acres a Minute?

SANDRA BROWN, Professor of Forest Ecology, University of Illinois—Champaign/Urbana.

ARIEL E. LUGO, Director, International Institute of Tropical Forestry, United States Forest Service, Puerto Rico.

ROGER SEDJO, Senior Fellow, Resources for the Future, Washington, DC.

Chapter 10: American Wildlife–On the Edge?

DEAN LUECK, Assistant Professor of Economics of Agriculture and Resource Economics, North Carolina State University.

JACK T. WENDERS, Professor of Economics, University of Idaho.

Chapter 11: Where Have All the Species Gone?

DAVID G. CAMERON, Former Professor of Biology and Genetics,
Montana State University.

MATTHEW CRONIN, Senior Research Biologist, LGL Alaska Research
Associates, Inc.; Former Research Geneticist, United States
Fish and Wildlife Service.

Chapter 12: The Air We Breathe

MIKHAIL S. BERNSTAM, Senior Research Fellow, Hoover Institution,
Stanford University.

ROBERT W. CRANDALL, Senior Fellow in Economic Studies,
The Brookings Institution, Washington, DC.

D. H. STEDMAN, Phillipson-Brainerd Professor of Chemistry,
University of Denver.

Chapter 13: A Hotter Planet?

ROBERT BALLING, Director, Office of Climatology; Associate Professor
of Geography, Arizona State University.

ROY W. SPENCER, Engineer, National Aeronautics and Space
Administration, Huntsville, Alabama.

Chapter 14: Sorting Out Ozone

SALLIE BALIUNAS, Senior Scientist, George C. Marshall Institute,
Washington, DC.

FRED SEITZ, President Emeritus, Rockefeller University, Past
President, National Academy of Sciences.

D. H. STEDMAN, Phillipson-Brainerd Professor of Chemistry, University of Denver.

Chapter 15: Acid Rain

PATRICIA IRVING, Manager, Environmental Science Department, Pacific Northwest Laboratory, Richland, Washington; Former Director, National Acid Precipitation Assessment Program (NAPAP).

J. LAURENCE KULP, Affiliate Professor of Civil Engineering, University of Washington; Former Director of Research, National Acid Precipitation Assessment Program (NAPAP); Former Professor of Geochemistry, Columbia University.

Chapter 16: Not a Drop to Drink?

INDUR M. GOKLANY, Manager, Science and Engineering, Office of Policy Analysis, Department of the Interior, Washington, DC.

ROGER E. MEINERS, Professor of Economics and Law, University of Texas—Arlington.

BRUCE YANDLE, Alumni Distinguished Professor of Economics and Legal Studies, Clemson University.

Chapter 17: Don't Eat That Apple!

GORDON W. GRIBBLE, Professor of Chemistry, Dartmouth University.

JOSEPH D. ROSEN, Professor of Food Chemistry and Director of the Graduate Program, Cook College, Rutgers University.

STEVEN SAFE, Distinguished Professor of Veterinary Physiology and Pharmacology, Texas A&M University.

Chapter 18: A Garbage Crisis?

M. B. HOCKING, Professor of Chemistry, University of Victoria.

WILLIAM RATHJE, Professor of Anthropology and Director,
The Garbage Project, University of Arizona.

CLARK WISEMAN, Professor Economics, Gonzaga University.

Chapter 19: The Recycling Myth

M. B. HOCKING, Professor of Chemistry, University of Victoria.

WILLIAM RATHJE, Professor of Anthropology and Director,
The Garbage Project, University of Arizona.

CLARK WISEMAN, Professor Economics, Gonzaga University.